The LONG
SHADOW of
DARKNESS

The LONG SHADOW of DARKNESS

A Season of REMEMBERING and HEALING

JODY AND VICKI DALIA

A true story of sex-trafficking of the younger child

credo
house publishers

Published in the United States by Credo House Publishers,
a division of Credo Communications LLC, Grand Rapids, Michigan
credohousepublishers.com

ISBN: 978-1-625861-34-4

Cover and interior design by Frank Gutbrod
Editing by Mike Vander Klipp

Printed in the United States of America

First edition

Dedicated to all our children, but especially the older ones who lived through this period of time with us. They've heard parts of this story, but now they can learn the whole truth.

Dedicated also to the many young victims who have survived trafficking . . . and to the ones who didn't.

CONTENTS

". . . that we should waste and wear out our lives in bringing to light all the hidden things of darkness, wherein we know them . . . . These should then be attended to with great earnestness." Joe Smith, 1839

Inevitable question: "How could you have not remembered this?"
Vicki: "Who would want to remember a childhood like this?"

INTRODUCTION

This is a story about remembering...remembering after three decades of not remembering . . . of remembering, first, the complicated shame of incest, then the horrific rituals and orgies of Satanism and finally the most heinous form of child sexual abuse—one perpetrated by one's own family for profit. In my wife's case, this grooming had already started by age three, and by age five she was a plaything to a brutal cult in Hawaii. At age nine, there was the utter degradation of the child brothel outside the White Sands missile base. And when serious abuse begins at such an early age, before the brain is fully developed, there is profound psychological damage—such as multiple personality.[1]

In the late 1980s and early 1990s when this story takes place, words like "traumatic amnesia" and "repressed memories" were just coming into vogue. Even with a degree in psychology, I had never heard these words before. There were no guidebooks or published stories of what it was like to remember an incredibly abusive childhood—one that had hibernated below consciousness for decades. Once Vicki started therapy and she began remembering the horror of her past abuse, our lives suddenly turned turbulent and chaotic. We were in unexplored territory with no idea of what was happening to us. And that was one of the most frightening parts: there were times we thought we'd stepped off the edge of sanity—that the chemical soup in her brain had gone rancid.

---

1   Now referred to as Dissociative Identity Disorder, but I will use the old name in this story because all my notes use it.

This is a story that needs to be told, both to portray the shocking and disruptive nature of that season of remembering (common with severe buried trauma) and for the scandalous content of those memories. It is relevant for victims of similar abuse, for their families and for those in the helping professions as well as those who want to investigate the darkest crevices of the human experience.

Since the story is two and a half decades old and authenticity is a major criterion for me, I have quoted extensively from contemporary journal entries that are noted as such. They are printed verbatim with modifications only for clarity—and in a few instances changing some of the indecent slang into more formal language. There are also recorded a few extended conversations (phone and otherwise) that are not noted as journal entries but were likewise extracted from our journals. They were originally chronicled immediately after they occurred. Another source was a manuscript that I wrote in 1992 when the events of this season were still very fresh in my mind. I can assure you that this is a true story. I have avoided any kind of embellishment—not that it needs it. This story is incredible in its own right.

One of the unexpected things that I discovered while writing was how malleable human memory is. There is an almost inevitable tendency to polish the events in our past into a story line that we find agreeable with our self-conception. Consequently, I have included scenes that neither Vicki nor I are particularly proud of, but I wanted to provide the flavor of the dysfunction that is part and parcel of the ignorance of buried trauma and forgotten abuse. I also wanted to assure the reader that productive, rewarding lives—even among individuals with this unthinkable kind of background—are still possible. Yes, it is more difficult but very possible. And likely even more rewarding because of the overcoming that such hard work brings with it.

Parts of this story come from my therapy journal and I probably exaggerated some; I always wrote in a highly emotional state. Some of the memories were too disgusting or embarrassing and, thankfully, Jody did not use them; some I would not allow to be printed as is and he—as he likes to say—"disinfected the language."

I also want to make it plain that these breakdown periods in our family were only about ten percent of the time, but it was a high-intensity ten percent.

The rest of the time I was functioning quite normally: waking the kids and getting them off to school or homeschooling them or changing diapers or going for a walk with Jody and the current babies. It was making business calls and trying to line up jobs and nursing the littlest one and planning the meals and doing the laundry and cleaning up. It was taking weekly trips to the biggest town an hour away and taking the kids to their church meetings on Wednesdays and buying fruit by the bushel at the produce market and whatever else needed to be done. It was making love to my friend and confidant and going on Friday night dates. It was birthday parties that always happened no matter if I was having a PTSD attack at the time. These parties included a cake and the child's favorite meal and often a hike at the nearby park. We must have hiked every trail there until we found the one that was our favorite. During our last family reunion in 2016 with seventeen of our eighteen kids, the married spouses and thirty-two grandkids, by popular demand, we again hiked that favorite trail. Jody and I marveled at how rewarding it was to see not seven or eight kids wading in the pool of water underneath the falls, but over twenty-five, with the rest in their parents' laps impatiently waiting until they were old enough to join their siblings and cousins. I remember feeling in that moment that all of our experiences as a family were suddenly all worthwhile, and everything that we went through made sense.

Yes, we had fun times along with the hard times and the fun times were the majority. But it was what it was. I didn't abuse myself; all I did was recover from my childhood for the sake of my family and the life I wanted to have.

It will be obvious but the regular script is my (Jody's) voice. The script in italics is Vicki's voice. This will be consistent through journal entries, contemporary or reflective musings and any other writing. Most of the journal entries are set off from the narrative text and noted as such, but for shorter citings a single quote ('. . .') indicates verbatim script copied from journal entries whether in regular script or italics.

We both apologize for some of the explicit scenes that are in the journal entries, but we could not figure out how to talk about this horrific type of sexual abuse any other way. You will notice as the story unfolds and the abuse deepens that Vicki's voice fades. That was the case some twenty-five plus years ago when she quit writing in her journal as her past overwhelmed her, and then again as I was putting this story together and asking for her input. Just reading what I wrote brought on nightmares for her—over five decades after the abuse was perpetrated. Composition was impossible for her; it brought up too much muck. But such is the effect of this kind of carefully calculated early childhood abuse.

Again, I want the reader to feel comfortable that this is the truth that we experienced.

A word of warning: if sexual abuse is in your background—whether you remember it or not—this book may upset you in a way that you are not prepared to deal with. If that is the case, I urge you to find competent professional help.

THE JOURNAL
October, 2005

We had been waiting almost ten years for a second chance to search for that journal. A criminal investigator had told us that Tom's (Vicki's father) type almost always kept a record of their doings—and that's what we wanted. The opportunity came abruptly, amid an unanticipated crescendo of emotions. After living for over forty years in their suburban Raleigh, North Carolina, home, Vicki's parents were forced to break up housekeeping. Tom had fallen and was in the hospital with a serious hip problem. He could no longer walk, not to mention take care of Virginia, his wife of almost sixty years. Amid talk of hip-replacement surgery for Tom, Vicki's mother—eighty-seven years old and suffering from dementia after a suspicious series of strokes—couldn't be left alone. Vicki's sister, promptly taking charge, pressed us into service after she'd been down in Raleigh for one very exhausting week. It was our turn now. And that wasn't a problem for me, even though it was inconvenient. Virginia had been more of a mother to me than had been my own mother. But Vicki's relationship with her mother was much more complicated and conflicted, setting off a cascade of emotions that had long been roiling just below the surface.

So Virginia came four hours west to our house, despite the fact that we still had eight kids at home and didn't even have a bedroom for her. It was to be only for a week or two while Vicki's sister set up a long-term nursing situation. But Virginia died unexpectedly after nine days with us—just after our daughter's wedding shower—compounding that conflicted torrent of emotion for my wife.

Then there was the funeral. Virginia's sister brought Tom up to the mountains and he artfully plied for sympathy from his wheelchair. If Virginia's death hadn't been such a tragedy, I would have laughed. Tom could work a crowd with the best of them; he was eating up the attention. You'd think it was a debut rather than a funeral. But Vicki and I kept our mouths shut and our suspicions to ourselves. We wanted to get back inside their house.

We wanted to search for that journal. In particular, we were hoping against hope to snatch the entire chest—Tom's old military footlocker that had been up in the attic. I knew it had been there because I'd seen it some ten years earlier. I'd opened the chest and I knew it was what we'd been looking for. That was where we had been told we would find his journal. But something uncanny happened back then: something beyond mere coincidence, and I couldn't examine the contents of the chest. That opportunity vanished and we had been waiting for a second chance ever since.

Yes, the paraphernalia of Tom's Darkness would have been nice, but we no longer needed confirmation. For years on our seemingly benign trips to visit, Vicki had been scouring the house for evidence. That's how we'd found the chest. She'd also found serious pornography next to the TV, and hidden in his dresser drawer she'd even discovered a book entitled *How to Molest Little Girls*. But the idea of getting a journal in his own handwriting, of learning the extent of his depravity—to learn what we didn't know . . . . That's what we wanted most of all.

And one of those things that we wanted to find out more about was that mystery house. In one of her lucid moments just two years earlier, Vicki's mother Virginia had blurted out of the blue, "You know your father has a house where he keeps girls?"

We didn't know. But we certainly were intrigued. It made perfect sense. We searched the tax records and hadn't found anything. Where was this house? Did that house explain all those twenty-dollar bills, decades of twenty-dollar bills, a seemingly endless supply of twenty-dollar bills?

Jody searched diligently through the attic and the rest of the house. But that trunk wasn't there. So our hopes of finding that journal vanished. It would be a question that I would save for my father until later. I would pick my time, because if he didn't know at that point that we knew of his sordid history, such a question would certainly give it away.

Despite going through Daddy's desk and any paperwork we could find looking for the journal or clues about the house where he kept girls, again, we found nothing. My father was a very careful man. He had to be to do all the things he'd done and not get caught.

What we did find was an old journal of my mother's from 1946. It was an introduction to the other half of the enigma that was my parents. While Mother was not malevolent like my father, she was at least as baffling. She entitled it "My Great Adventure." Jody later read through the sporadic entries full of excitement and hope. It began in the spring with her decision to join the civil service and go to post-WWII Germany. My grandfather was in favor of the adventure, my grandmother against it. My mother was 29 years old and if she wanted children—and she certainly did—she needed to take some risks. Since graduating from Meredith College she had been working as a secretary for Duke Power and living at home. She'd had, at the most, only one serious relationship in the last decade, and her two brothers and sister were already married. I think she decided her chances to find a husband were better in postwar Europe than in the States where all the troops were returning.

My father's name first pops up after my mother had been in Germany for just a few weeks. Then it comes up again and again, and the journal abruptly ends. Oh, how I wish she'd kept it up. I mean, kept it up without those the rose-colored glasses that she constantly wore.

I also found a photo from my parents' wedding. It was taken on August 6, 1948. They were still in post-war Germany. My burly father was in his army dress uniform with a "cat-who-ate-the-canary grin," gazing up at his commanding officer with a son-like adoration, looking for approval. My mother is beside him with a corsage in her hands, stooped slightly because with her heels on she was taller than my father. She is nervously smiling and her buck teeth, which she considered so embarrassing, are obvious. I was born almost eight months later, the oldest of what would be their four children, at seven-and-a-half pounds.

I have questions to go along with that old photo. Lots of questions. Questions that I wish I'd had it together to ask my mother when she was alive, before the dementia set in—not that I would have gotten an honest answer. But

I'll ask them now anyway; I'll ask them here as Jody and I start this narrative: Mother, was my father a depraved monster when you married him? If so, why did you do it? You were an educated woman from an educated and prestigious family. Was his depravity not obvious or were you oblivious to it for some reason? Did you naively think all men were like your sweet and gentle father? Was your desperation to get married and have a family blinding? And if he wasn't a monster then, what happened to him that turned him into one? When did it happen? What made him that way? Was it his highly dysfunctional family background? Or was it just a series of wrong choices that brought him to such a confluence with evil? And why didn't you leave him along the way? Do you remember me begging you to leave him? Do you? I earnestly prayed for that almost every night when I was growing up. Did you ever, just once, take those rose-tinted glasses off? Certainly you knew, you had some inkling of what was going on . . . ?

INCEST IN THE FAMILY TREE

1949—1975

My mother was the third of four children in an old-fashioned family that valued family. Her father graduated from Wake Forest at 19 years old. He was something of an egghead and read seven languages. He started out as a teacher, then became a principal, and finally was the assistant superintendent of public education for North Carolina, which is how his family settled in Raleigh. He was a deacon in the largest Baptist church in the city and well-respected in the community—as the huge outpouring at his funeral attested. His wife, my Grandmother Florence, had a four-year music degree from Meredith College as did all of her sisters. Her brothers all went to Wake Forest. My mother grew up with extended family living with them. Grandmother's brothers and sisters used it as home base when going to college, and both of my great-grandmothers and my great Aunt Dell used it as hospice.

But mine was also the kind of family where there were skeletons in the closet, as my uncle found when he researched the genealogy of our family tree. I was astounded at the amount of sexual abuse it revealed and how it seemed to show up in each generation. My great-grandfather, Alfred, had been very successful in business owning a general store and hundreds of acres of farm land in Camden County—enough to lose a million dollars in the 1929 crash. The local Baptist church was named after him. But he was known in the community as a really mean man. He married Florence, the oldest daughter of the town tramp. I suspect this precipitated the search for respectability and hence all nine of his children went to college—which was very rare for that day.

Several years into his marriage Alfred took his wife's younger sister in. It wasn't as a good deed: rather, it was a well-kept family scandal. Great-Aunt Dell was seven years old at the time and through the years Alfred was seen by family members sneaking into her bedroom at night. Aunt Dell never got an education and later became a traveling companion for Alfred. She was billed as his secretary but everyone knew differently. I met her during her last years at my grandmother's home. She was a solitary figure and used to sit in the chair to the left of the fireplace but rarely spoke. She was stodgy and wore glasses. Looking back, I wonder if she was mentally stunted. There was a catatonic look in her eyes as if the light had long ago gone out.

The whole family was forced to keep this secret, and I think it fostered the tradition of keeping those kinds of family secrets—including keeping them from ourselves. I think it was the origin of that peculiar squinting that allows you to not to see what's going on right in front of you that my mother became adept at. That kind of secrecy is destructive enough in itself, but it has much broader consequences. Based on current knowledge of sexual perpetrators I suspect all the girls in the family—at least—were abused by Alfred. I know that my grandmother was diagnosed with hysteria which is now commonly associated with PTSD.

My mother and her siblings used to spend part of their childhood summers back at the family farm. They worked harvesting sweet and Irish potatoes and other vegetables to earn money that went toward things like a family piano. I can't help but think that she and her sister were abused during those summers. They both married abusers. Jody and I have noticed the uncanny pattern of victims marrying victims, and unfortunately some victims are or will become abusers. We have hypothesized that there is some kind of psychic attraction between victims of sexual abuse. And since a common reaction among victims is simply not to remember their abuse, they are an easy mark in the future for predators who somehow sense this. And as parents, when you've blocked out the horror of your own abuse and are unable to see what going on right in front of you, how can you protect your children?

Of course, I didn't know any of this growing up. For me, my grandparents' house in Raleigh was a place of refuge. I felt safe there. Staying at my grandparents' brought feelings of peace and quiet that seemed embedded in the walls. They'd lived in that house for fifty years. My grandfather was the most gentle man I'd ever known; I never heard him even raise his voice. His affectionate name of "Flossie" for my grandmother Florence and the kindness he showed her were the reasons I named a daughter after her and a son after him. Grandmother never raised her voice but had a more feisty personality. But there was a lot of love and respect that flowed between them that kept me going during my childhood and though my not-so-perfect marriages.

Every year, after my father got his new orders from the Army and before we moved to the new location, we spent a month with my grandparents. This included a week in the mountains with an uncle and aunt that I loved and another week was at Nag's Head at my Great-Aunt Ruth's cottage. At my grandparents' house there were always family meals; the dining room was the most used room in the house. There were no raised voices, no cuss words, and everyone under their roof acted respectfully—it was so unlike my own home.

I remember that after lunch everyone was required to take a nap because Grandmother's doctor ordered her to take a two-hour nap for her hysteria. After that we had ice-cream pie on the back porch where we talked and rode the porch swing. The women then went to the kitchen to prepare dinner and the kids played in the back yard. After dinner my grandfather always did the dishes, then he would retire down to his huge library in the basement.

I think I inherited my spirituality from that house. It was quiet—a good kind of quiet. We always said grace at meals, and I remember vacation Bible school as being one of the highlights of my summer. Granddaddy read the Scriptures daily to Grandmother and to us when we were there. He would tell us inspirational stories. He always gave us a copy of Ideals *magazine for our perusal. It was so different from my house and it gave me a bedrock of hope that helped me survive.*

On the surface, my father's family couldn't have been more different from my mother's. Much of what I know about his family came from him late in his life when he was at the assisted living center—after my mother died. Jody and I would go the nursing home specifically to pick his brain. I wanted to find out more about my childhood and his. And I was always hoping—although by then I knew better—for an apology; but mostly we both wanted to understand what made Daddy tick. They weren't regular visits by any means because they upset me so much even though I was sixty years old and he was in his eighties and in declining health and strength.

I had a primal fear of him that never went away—until he died. That was on Christmas day—the best present I ever got. My sister called with the news, and I dragged Jody almost two hours through a very dangerous ice storm to kiss his now-lifeless body on the forehead and wish him well on his journey to hell, which is where I was sure he was going. Mostly, though, I wanted to see his body and know for certain that he was dead. He had been bigger than life and I needed that assurance.

But I'm getting ahead of myself.

He had grown up in Mobile, Alabama, in a working-class neighborhood in a small rental house not far from the Catholic church. His father, Geter Jack, had been moderately successful, opening several auto-parts outlets for all the new cars that were hitting the roads in the 1930s. Then, as my father tells it, his father's penchant for drinks with the Padre of the local Catholic church took his business and then his life.

At age 14, my father became the family breadwinner. The family must have been getting help from the church because his employment consisted of a paper route and other odd jobs. My father also mentioned the Padre occasionally slipping him five-dollar bills and I can't help but wonder . . . because my father did the same thing with twenty-dollar bills, and Jody was always suspicious. Two years later my father bailed on the family, lying about his age, and joined the Merchant Marine. He was fond of talking about being a carefree teenager, cruising the Gulf coast in his fire-engine red T-bird looking for girls.

He got married in his late teens and soon had a son. He switched to working the docks at the shipyard in Mobile. That continued until the draft cornered him in the early 1940s. With another child due he joined the army and went to war.

He ended up in Antwerp, Belgium, after D-Day, unloading material for the Allied invasion of Europe. More than once he told of joking with Werner von Braun, who he later knew personally and idolized, about dodging his V-2 missiles, and Von Braun replying in his thick German accent that my father tried to mimic, "Ef I ad a few more months, I vouldn't have messed."

Through the years I have found myself reading "true crime" books on serial killers trying to understand my father. I knew from an early age that his family was somehow different. For one thing, we never saw them—so unlike my mother's family. Every once in a while there would be a phone call and an emergency, and *my mother would urge him to take responsibility. Then he would be gone for a few days. At first, I thought my mother's motivation was just "family." Later, I suspected her relationship with him may have precipitated his divorce and she felt guilty. His first wife, with child support mandated by the military, raised those two boys alone. My first contact with his family came at age thirteen, when his mother was picked up in Mobile. She was homeless and wandering the streets with, I am told, $20,000 in cash in her pocketbook. The police called my dad's sister, my Aunt Jean. Her husband had just been killed in a plane crash and she couldn't handle anything else. She momentarily left her grieving to pick up Grandma Lillian and bring her to us.*

But with Grandma Lillian there was no coming home from school and finding a kind-hearted grandma who reached out to hug you and say hello. She just sat in her chair in the living room of our small house and stared. I don't remember her saying a word. She was so different from my mother's mother. There was something wrong with her that I didn't understand as a young teenager, but now I suspect severe childhood abuse.

Grandma Lillian went back to live with Aunt Jean and I never saw her again. My father never mentioned her name without spewing hatred towards her. He was never specific but always intense.

I only met my two step brothers late in life, when my father was in the nursing home and having near-brushes with death. They were polite and concerned, relatively well-adjusted, and I liked both of them. They, of course, had no idea of the advantage they got from only receiving his genetics and child support and not that day-to-day fatherly "touch."

I was born in Bremerhaven, Germany, on March 30, 1949.

There was a photo in the Raleigh paper of our happy young family upon our return some three months after my birth. My father is in full dress uniform and my mother is cradling me in her arms, looking down with a victory smile on her face. She had come home with a husband, a baby and three years' worth of adventure stories living in post-war Germany and traveling throughout the Continent.

My father was stationed at an army base near Atlanta and, with my mother's prodding, earned a GED and then a college degree from the University of Georgia. My mother was busy at home with three children while my father took classes at night. Those three years would be our longest stay in one place until I was a teenager. In between I grew up as an Army brat, changing locations every year or two.

Looking back, I see myself as a silent child who rarely spoke and did everything I was supposed to do, including earning good grades in school and not causing any waves at home. Every once in a while a more assertive person would come out of me, but most of the time I was a shadow child staying in the background and hoping people would not notice that I existed. Most of the time I was scared to death. My sister, who was a year younger than me, became the spokesperson and took on the role of the oldest child. I, on the other hand, was the family scapegoat.

Mother was a full-time mom and loved her job. We belonged to the symphony and went to theatrical productions. We went swimming almost every day during the summer at the base swimming pool. She helped us with homework during the school year. Every night we had sit-down dinners after my father came home, and my mother took the time to fix meals we'd all like. On cross-country trips, which were almost yearly, we stopped to see every possible educational site. I remember being burned out at the Grand Canyon and not getting out of the car despite my mother's coaxing. There were new Easter clothes every year and wonderful surprises at Christmas. I know it sounds like an ideal childhood . . . .

Yes, life would have been idyllic if Dad hadn't been around. He would go on public rants denigrating Mother that embarrassed all of us. He had an explosive, unpredictable temper and with his beefy right arm he could give us a terrible swat in the back seat of the car. For that reason, I always wanted to sit in the very back of our station wagon. But worst of all, he was obsessed with pointing out the anatomy of virtually every woman we passed and grading her for us. He would start with "Now, that's a good-looking woman . . . ." and my ears would perk up even though I hated it. I would look to my mom who seemed oblivious to him. Beginning with the bleached blonde hair, my father would work his way down these women's bodies, scoring in graphic detail what he liked and didn't like. I would just go numb—which in retrospect I suspect my mother was doing also.

Ironically enough, even though he wasn't respectful of my mother, he made sure we were. I can still hear his words: "She's the best friend you'll ever have." I guess he was comparing her to his mother.

My father was not a one-dimensional figure and he did not stand out like Frankenstein; to be fair, most people liked him. He worked the crowds like a politician, and he could be charming, kissing the ladies' hands at church, which made me want to puke. Even though I was terrified of him, he always told me I could do anything I wanted and he, along with my mother, encouraged ambition. He was a great salesman, very manipulative, and I picked up on that. He had a very successful booth at the flea market for years, that Jody pointed out was likely for laundering money. He helped my younger brother start his own business, which became a meteoric success; when it just as spectacularly collapsed, he worked with Jack bailing him out of jail and other painful and embarrassing situations. Later in life, when I started my own business that became very successful, he was proud of me. He was not a chauvinist when it came to his kids. I'm sure I picked up many business skills from him. I just needed to get out of the house, away from him and get lots of therapy: I mean lots of therapy.

When I was fourteen, my father got orders to deploy for a tour in Vietnam and he decided to retire. He was needed at home because my brother Stephen was already starting to do some serious acting out. My parents bought a house midway between my grandparents in the city and my aunt, who was then a school principal, out in the suburbs of Raleigh.

I entered high school at Broughton and made mostly A's but was a nervous wreck. I had to hurry off the bus each morning to have a colitis attack, which a doctor diagnosed as stress, and then I also had disabling migraines that seemed to come out of nowhere. Back then no one made the connection that something might be seriously wrong with me psychologically.

What I remember most about high school was looking wistfully out the window from my math classroom to the orphanage across the street where I did volunteering through my church youth group. It was a two-story brick building that housed about a hundred kids. I thought the kids who got to live there were so lucky: they lived in a place where they could lay their heads down at night and feel secure. I had an obsessive daydream of living there. It seemed like such a nice, safe place. I was probably the only kid of the two thousand at my school who felt like that. But if you'd asked me then, I couldn't have told you the truth behind those profound longings. I just didn't remember; it was not part of my conscious life.

Unlike my sister who always had a serious boyfriend and dates every weekend, I was a strange teenager. I preferred babysitting to dating even though my mother nagged continually. I'm sure Mother was thinking of her own youth and possible spinsterhood. Babysitting was enough for me; it got me out of the house, which was the most important thing, and I loved playing with the babies and making a little money. To ease the pressure I was getting from my mother, I finally saw a cute boy in the neighborhood who didn't seem frightening. Jim was shy and passive and that suited me. With enough trips around the block to get his attention, I lured him into dating early in my junior year. Even though our relationship had been disintegrating at the end of my senior year, by the time I crossed the stage to get my diploma I knew that I was six weeks pregnant under that graduation gown.

Jim's boss, who also dated his mother, urged Jim to have me get an abortion; he knew where to get the only kind available back then—an illegal one. Jim and I were at a stalemate because I wasn't having any part of it. Finally, his mother, Ida, intervened. With her connections in the legislature where she worked, she arranged for a marriage that predated the conception.

Jim and I moved to Charlotte that summer so he could repair his flagging grades at a community college and so I could avoid the embarrassment of my situation. Some people might have thought I would have been depressed moving to a new town, living in a low-rent area and having no friends, but I loved being on my own. I was free. I had Tripp just six weeks before my nineteenth birthday and that just sweetened the pot for me. I loved my baby!

We moved back to Raleigh in late spring and my mother immediately enrolled me in classes at State. To make up for that lost year she pushed me to graduate in three years by going year-round with a heavy course load. But I couldn't wait to get back from classes each day and pick up my baby. I studied during his naps and after he went to bed. During the summer I spent our time taking stroller rides, going to the pool, doing a little shoplifting and getting kudos for my beautiful baby. I instituted sit-down dinners for our young family and forced Jim to play with Tripp for an hour before he went out, which he inevitably did, with the boys. When I was sick of studying, I would sew at night. I remember hanging out clothes and feeling content as a mother, housewife and student. But in the background was a vague thought: There must be something more . . . .

When I graduated with a sociology degree and couldn't find a job, my father pulled a few strings and found a position for me in the probation department. He had a lot of connections that I didn't understand at the time. That job introduced me to that "something more" that was missing from my life and was the undoing of my marriage. Jim had only two courses left and seemed to be majoring in sunbathing while I was making the money and doing all the housework and childcare. He refused to pick up Tripp from the babysitter's after his classes and watch him until I got home, and that was the final straw. Meanwhile, in my job downtown I was swamped with male attention from all the lawyers and that only served to accent that deficit at home.

Finally, I gave Jim an ultimatum and, to be fair, he tried. We started double-dating; once a week we went out to eat and went dancing with friends, but it was too little too late. I was suddenly the hot young thing at the courthouse. I was educated, pretty and I dressed attractively with all the latest fashions that I sewed myself. I was coming out of my shell and I loved it. It was the free-love 1970s and that kind of attitude was rampant downtown.

TWILIGHT

JODY'S DREAM

1974

I was running down out of a mountain. The terrain behind me was rough and war-torn, and I was exhausted both physically and psychologically. Although I didn't remember anything specific, I was desperate to get away. I stumbled over boulders on my way downhill, recklessly colliding with whatever was in front of me. I just wanted to escape and get to flat ground and get the past behind me.

Having reached the bottom, I staggered forward and then began to collect myself. I had survived.

"Oh, yeah," I remembered, "I'm supposed to meet someone."

But I wondered how in the world that was supposed to happen. The conflict had been devastating and had lasted for years—maybe a lifetime. If I barely remembered this rendezvous, would that special someone also remember? Had that someone even survived the war? And if they had, did they remember? And was it still important to them?

And where were we supposed to meet? I didn't remember that; did they? I was wandering through an arid, desolate area where there didn't appear to be any roads. It was perpetually dusk and difficult to see. There were no markers to define the landscape, just desert scrub. How were we supposed to get together? It seemed to be an impossibility. It was depressing to try to calculate the impossible odds of this person surviving the battle, and then remembering that we had an appointment, and then with our world in such disarray, to remember where we were supposed to meet. I didn't even remember.

Then in the distance I thought I heard a motor. It was impossible to see very far in the twilight, but I strained to hear and, yes, it was definitely a motor. And to my surprise I was standing on a dirt road. It wasn't much more than a path. It was actually the exact spot for the rendezvous and I saw the ghost of what appeared to be an old army jeep lumbering toward me. I couldn't discern any passengers, but I couldn't help feeling myself getting excited.

It would be years before I would understand the first part of that dream . . . but it accurately describes our childhoods. And now with the perspective of some forty-plus years, I can only smile at the wild ride that was in front of me.

MATCHMAKER'S MATCH

February, 1975

Vicki and I met with the help of a mutual friend who was matchmaking. "She's good looking, intelligent and currently available," he promised me.

My first date with Ms. Currently Available was at Raleigh's brand new health food's restaurant called the "Irregardless." Replacing a former organic food coop, the restaurant had some of my paintings as part of its cheap and Spartan decor. Vicki was waiting outside when I arrived and I remember the flattering, yellow Indian-print dress with a long string of buttons down the front that she was wearing. As we stood in line she said hello to one suit after another as they walked past us, explaining to me that they were attorney friends of hers. I briefly wondered what she was doing with me—a not-for-profit artist who over the last few months had just shed his shoulder-length ponytail and trimmed up his scruffy beard. We seemed to be very different people. We had finished college at nearby North Carolina State a year apart, but she had spent three years as a probation officer and was now in her first year of law school. The latter was a bit intimidating to me. On the other hand, I was tired of trying to make it through writing and painting and was now paying the bills with pickup construction work.

After the meal we continued our date at Pullen Park under a cobalt-blue, cloudless, early February sky. The trees were bare but the weather was graciously southern winter-warm. I relaxed on a wooden bench and let Vicki unwind. In a lengthy monologue she painted herself as a thoroughly liberated woman and I imagined her story as a feature article in *MS* magazine. She'd started the first women's consciousness-raising group in Raleigh. She'd fought long and hard for three frustrating years as a probation officer for "her" girls, trying to get them drug treatment and other alternatives instead of futile time behind bars. She'd even been thrown out of court a couple of times for going braless before lecherous old bachelor judges, eventually getting an in-house, week-long, paid suspension from the probation department that she spent playing tennis. Then she decided she could further "the cause" more effectively as an attorney, and it was off to law school where she was currently in her second semester as a minority student in a majority black law school in Durham. Her goal was to fight for women's and children's rights. She wound down the conversation in a more subdued tone by saying she wasn't the mothering kind, which she proved a few weeks later when Tripp, her six-year-old curled up to go to sleep around the pedestal of our nightclub table.

The first night we spent together she told me she had been molested when she was eleven. She didn't seem to remember much; I'm not sure she wanted to remember anything, or even talk even about it. I don't know why she brought it up except, perhaps, to clue me into who she was. She didn't tell me who, but I assumed it was her father. Her tone of voice was raw and intimate with a touch of shame. I thought I heard a vulnerable little girl talking through that time tunnel and that pitiful lament pulled at my heart strings. Her admission came across to me as a disclaimer, which struck me as odd and out of character for her. With almost everything else in her life she tended toward a healthy self-promotion. I didn't feel like I had permission to talk about it—not that I knew what to say—and the subject was dropped.

After spending most of our nights together I was gone for five days in mid-March on a job at my father's in Charlotte. I met her at her apartment the evening I returned. But I was bothered by something out-of-kilter. I couldn't put my finger on it, but I sensed something was wrong. She told me her son was at her parents' house for the weekend and we had the night to ourselves, but this nagging, uncomfortable feeling would not go away. The excitement of seeing her evaporated, and I was disturbed over this sudden, inharmonious feeling that didn't make any sense.

We headed down to the railroad tracks for our usual walk and by the time we returned I understood that she'd spent the intervening nights at an old boyfriend's place. I was suddenly face-to-face with the pain of betrayal. I didn't want the kind of relationship that was so widespread in the wonderland of our "free-to-be" subculture. I had just assumed that we were on the same page about this. But apparently we weren't; I abruptly left.

The last Sunday in March, some five days later, I was watering the neglected plants in my living room when a silhouette appeared at my screen door. I couldn't see who but it was a *she* wearing a long dress. With a mixture of thrill and trepidation I suspected it was Vicki. The height and width were about right. I was slowly coming to terms with what this might mean when her voice called out.

"Are you going to invite me in?"

I was expecting an apology. Reading my continued silence she finally said with clipped irritation, "Look, I'd rather have you."

She let herself in. The strained stillness continued. She was wearing the yellow Indian print dress that she knew I liked, and she walked around nervously, which was definitely not her style.

She broke the lingering, uncomfortable silence. "It's my birthday today. Would you like to come with me to a party at my parents' house?" Her normal confidence was not there. It was strange to feel that lack in her voice.

Before I could answer, she broke in, "You cut your beard!"

I thought I caught a thread of disappointment. "This morning."

"You look very clean cut. My parents will like that. How about coming with me to the party?" Before I could answer she noted the books I'd been reading on Zen Buddhism and near-death experiences.

"It's what left of my religion."

"Oh," she said in a very flat tone that indicated her feigned interest. "Why don't you explain it to me while we're driving?"

She noted a half-finished painting on my easel and reminded me that I'd been wanting to take her to the museum. For some reason I responded to that and within a few minutes we were getting into her car. She knew I liked driving her little green Austin America and she gladly gave up the driver's seat. We headed downtown but the art museum was closed. Before long we were driving through the quiet, sprawling city to her parents' neighborhood.

There wasn't much conversation. She broke the awkward silence by telling me that she was afraid to be alone at night. It was that same small voice that had told me that she'd been molested. But I barely heard that; instead it sounded like a flimsy excuse rather than an apology. I wasn't sympathetic and didn't respond.

Her parents' neighborhood was upper-middle class with large, two-story homes and mature pine and tulip trees shading all but the center of the streets. With a rush of excitement she grabbed my hand as we exited the car and gently tugged. We began walking around the block. With an enlivened nostalgia she took me back in time, explaining what it was like to grow up here—much like my own teenage years. The houses back then were full of kids, both very young children and teenagers like herself. She animatedly recalled the several families of kids where she was a regular on Friday or Saturday evenings. They were endearing stories that did not sound like the liberated woman that I was self-consciously holding hands with—the one that took so little care of her own son.

She told me of being a candy striper and working with handicapped kids at the hospital. As if through a time warp, I caught a glimpse of a much different person in a much different time where kids were cherished and important. Halfway around the neighborhood she pointed out Jim's house and retold the history of their relationship, and then she continued with a part I'd never heard before. With a bottle of champagne uncorked and on ice, Jim's mother had invited Vicki's parents over to break the news of her pregnancy and marriage. Virginia had been stunned and at first speechless, then she had started balling uncontrollably. Her daughter, in the first class of women admitted to UNC, had just thrown her life away. It was a disaster.

Vicki said, "Then my father replied with perfect aplomb, 'Shut up, Virginia, we're supposed to be celebrating.' And that was the end of it. There was never another word said."

As we headed up to her parents' front door, I wondered what in the world I was doing there. Our relationship didn't make any sense, and now she was bringing me to meet her parents. I was at a loss, and very anxious. I also wondered about the strange amalgamation of character that Vicki possessed: teenage babysitter extraordinaire, girl scout and candy striper growing up in an all-American neighborhood, turning into a rabid feminist who took miserable care of her own child and wanted to change the world, fighting for women's and children's rights.

Without knocking she opened the front door. Immediately, Vicki told me about the elaborate cross-stitch mounted and framed on the wall in front of us. It had been a present to her mother from her domestic years when her son was a baby. And she told me—as she would almost every time we entered that front door—the fabled story of her mother giving her and her sister gifts of "Ginny" and "Madame Alexander" dolls for Christmas with an extensive handmade wardrobe.

We entered the living room to our right and it reminded me of my parents' house. It had moderately expensive upholstered furniture and the overall tone of avocado green so common in the 1970s. Behind me were expensive photographic portraits of the four children, each in their mid-teens. There was a mahogany hutch and bureau with a matching dining-room table in the adjacent room. On the wall in front of me there were two large south-of-the-border paintings on black velvet mounted inside tacky, homemade and hand-painted frames, as well as a large framed poster of the German Alps and Hitler's Eagle's Nest. The room was jarringly eclectic.

"Let me go help my mother and tell her that I brought someone," Vicki said and left me standing in the middle of the living room.

My natural anxiety was heightened; things with Vicki were moving faster than I could ever process and again I was wondering what I was doing standing here in the living room of her parents' house. I was about to meet them and I wasn't even sure I wanted a relationship with her. I took a deep breath to calm myself. Suddenly my intuition spiked with an alien feeling I had never experienced before—and now forty years later have yet to experience again. I was trying to understand that strange, uncomfortable feeling when a masculine voice startled me from behind. I hadn't heard anyone coming.

The voice was gruff and earthy, but not hostile. "I'm Vicki's father, Tom." He was about five-foot six and stocky, not particularly attractive, but, manifestly, the man of the house. He had a neatly trimmed mustache that reminded me of pictures I'd seen of Adolf Hitler.

I turned and we shook hands; we had a few words and he was gone. Meanwhile, I tried to process the aura that came with him. I could not index it other than to say it was strong and strange. It was profound enough that I never forgot this initial encounter with Tom.

Vicki's mother, Virginia, worked the kitchen and gathered everyone to the table. Vicki's diabetic brother, Stephen, three years younger, was on one of his intermittent stints at home. Her younger brother arrived with a girl in tow. I would later learn that Virginia was the epitome of southern hospitality. She asked Tom to say a blessing on the meal and it came out as perfunctory as any I'd ever heard. It struck me as being rude, but no one seemed to pay attention to that.

The dinner conversation was polite but stilted, and I distinctly remember Stephen's uncivil mood. The anger he radiated was palpable. He was rude to the point of rebuffing his mother time and time again as she offered food and tried to coax him to eat. She was being solicitous and getting very frustrated. Virginia eventually grew flustered after Stephen spooned several large heaps of sugar into his iced tea, bypassing the artificial sweetener right in front of him.

When the meal broke up, Tom moved into the living room with Jack, Vicki's younger brother, and his girlfriend. Vicki pointed this out to me and made a derogatory comment about how lecherous her father was.

"Invite Tripp to play basketball up at the corner," Vicki whispered a few minutes later. "My mother will like that." I did, glad to get out of the house and away from my anxiety.

Later, on the drive to Vicki's place, Tripp piped up from the back seat, "Hey, let's stop for some Breyer's ice cream and ginger snaps."

"You treating?" I asked.

"Yep," Tripp responded, waving a twenty-dollar bill around.

"Where'd that come from?" I asked in surprise.

"Grandad."

I shot Vicki a questioning look.

"That's just who my father is. He was dirt poor growing up and doesn't want his kids and grandkids growing up like that. He does it all the time. It's money from his flea-market booth."

Despite Vicki's casual attitude about the money, that incident, too, unsettled me.

We headed to Vicki's apartment and neither one of us could have guessed that the honeymoon was over, even though it was just the beginning of our relationship. It was also the introduction to the two people that would do much to shape my adult life. While at the time I could not read the obvious tea leaves, someone else with the proper skills would have seen that our relationship promised to be trying and turbulent.

METAMORPHOSIS

1975-1979

Vicki and I moved to the mountains that June, leaving behind my artist friends and her attorney crowd. This move was the best thing we could have done for our relationship. Her father doled out over two-hundred dollars—in twenty-dollar bills—to pay for the U-Haul. I was astonished that he would do that for us. Vicki also said good-bye to law school after working for her brother-in-law, an attorney, for the summer and deciding that was not what she wanted to do. Meanwhile I learned valuable carpentry skills helping a friend build a new house.

Together we learned that we loved the country life and forever forward, if possible, we would choose that option. We had a large organic garden and hiking was literally at our doorstep. There were always music festivals and craft shows going on somewhere nearby and we loved it. Life was just slower and much less of a treadmill. We didn't realize how much we both needed the extra space inherent in country living until we ran into some of the psychological baggage that we didn't know we had. We quickly learned that our relationship could sometimes became volatile.

Several weeks into our sojourn in the mountains Vicki said she needed to go to Raleigh for a short visit. She was nebulous about the reasons why, but when she returned she admitted that she had spent the night with her old boyfriend. I couldn't believe it and my world rapidly became unraveled. I remember dreaming how desperately I wanted this relationship to work out and how fragile it was.

Shortly afterward this incident in Raleigh we got into a fight that Vicki doesn't remember. She was in my face about something and I pushed her away. Before I knew it she was in the kitchen and grabbed a large knife and started after me. It seemed like slap-stick comedy from my perspective because her movements were stick-like and uncoordinated, and it would have been impossible for her to catch me. I loped around the house twice thinking how ridiculous this scene looked; she was stalking me like an enraged cartoon character. And then she wasn't behind me anymore. After a short length of time, I warily entered the back door into the kitchen. I called ahead hoping she had calmed herself down. I tried apologizing, but there was no answer. Slowly I inched my way forward, not knowing what to expect.

I saw her sitting on the floor in the corner of the adjoining dining room. Her back was against the union of two walls and her legs were splayed. She held the long knife she had chased me with in both hands—it was pointed at her abdomen. I was stunned and at a loss to understand what was happening. I tentatively called her name, but she didn't seem to hear me. I wondered how I would explain this to the authorities if she pushed that knife in. And what in the world had happened to change the raving, incoherent maniac who had been chasing me into someone self-destructive?

Our jobs ran out and we moved back to Raleigh on Thanksgiving Day. We crossed paths with Vicki's parents heading to her sister's house. They took Tripp and her father gave us a twenty to eat out since they were not having a family dinner. We rented a 100-year-old, rambling country affair without heat of any kind, but it included forty acres of land, which we considered more essential. It was an hour south of Raleigh. I found carpentry work nearby and Vicki got a job waitressing at a restaurant called The Pier.

Within a few months of this move Vicki was unable to work because of severe abdominal pain. Initially, it was diagnosed as pelvic inflammatory disease; she began reading up on the disorder and discovered that it was often associated with childhood sexual abuse. This brought the incident she had told me about with her father at age eleven more to the forefront, and it became a topic of conversation. At that time, there were virtually no books on incest, so her investigation did not go far.

After six rounds of antibiotics the infection was gone, but not the pain. Vicki was then referred to Duke University hospital where they diagnosed her condition as an advanced case of endometriosis. They recommended an immediate hysterectomy. I was surprised when she balked at this option for no reason that she could explain.

To ease the pain and postpone the decision Vicki went on birth control pills, but they exacerbated her mood swings and our house became a mine field with periodic detonations. Fights over stupid things became too regular. Upon reflection now, we have noticed a pattern—the one who was acting the most idiotic in the argument often does not remember the clashes between us. One fight we both remember well occurred that summer as we were finishing up shelling a bushel of lima beans. Vicki said something that set me off and we were soon yelling at each other. At the end, in frustration, I threw a handful of lima beans at her. Incensed, she ran off to get into her car. Several moments later I raced after her. Unable to admit, not to mention face, my fear of abandonment, I jumped on the hood of her car doing what she became fond of referring to as my "Joe Gorilla" routine. What would turn into a $250 broken windshield, finally brought me into my senses. Joe Gorilla would be part of our lives for years to come. He was an ephemeral alter-ego with unknown origins.

That outlay of cash (when I was only making four dollars an hour) in our already tight budget would have been enough to keep an override on my temper for a while, but this particular fight caught the attention of our neighbor who lived a quarter of a mile away. On one of his previous visits Vicki's father Tom had stopped by our neighbor's house to tell them to let him know if we needed any help. Our neighbor thought that this incident qualified, and called Tom. We soon received a couple of phone calls: the first came from her diabetic brother, who threatened to kill me; then we received a more tactful one from Tom asking what he could do to help.

Vicki and I both had social science degrees, and in hindsight, it baffles both of us that we were so blind to the possibility that the problems we were experiencing went deeper than a lack of will power to overcome our errant behavior. At the time, that was my assessment of the difficulty I had with my temper, and Vicki had only the slightest inkling that the incest incident that she partly remembered might be having some influence on our daily lives. The idea of psychological baggage below our level of awareness impacting our daily lives seemed far-fetched because we both thought of our childhoods as being relatively normal. When life calmed down after one of our eruptions, we would inevitably pick up the pieces and then brainstorm, with a little more humility than we'd had during the fight, how we might short-circuit this problem in the future.

Vicki dropped the birth control pills that fall. Her mood swings suddenly mellowed out and our lives became more normalized, which was a real treat. It wasn't too much longer before she figured out she was pregnant. After a lecture from her grandmother and a bribe from her mother, she filed for divorce from her estranged husband and we married.

That first baby was the beginning of a subtle but profound change in our lives. Work became more important for me and Tom helped by putting a carpentry ad in the weekly supplement to the Raleigh newspaper. Suddenly, I was in business and having to scramble to keep up with it. Before long I hired a couple of helpers. Money became less of a problem, but we were soon no longer living our dream of the country life because I was either working, or driving to work, or dead tired. That took a toll our marriage.

It was during this period we embarked on our first term of marriage counseling. We attended sessions together, and then Vicki went to a few sessions on her own, related to the incest. Nothing came of the latter other than a renewed interest in investigating the matter. With the therapist negotiating the issues, we worked on what had become a thorny problem. I was in the habit of showering at the end of the day, but Vicki wanted me to clean up as soon as I got home because she was allergic to sawdust. In exchange, I wanted her to quit pestering me with questions as soon as I walked in the door. She wanted to know what I had done during the day, where I had gone and especially who I had seen—in particular any women. I kept my end of the bargain which meant creating a new habit for me, but Vicki could not keep her word. Neither one of us recognized this for what it was at that time, but her unrelenting suspicions and the questions that came with them would be a blight on our relationship for decades to come.

Using nursing as birth control produced Sarah fourteen months after our first daughter Jennifer was born. Now living in the city, Vicki, with a double stroller, no longer looked like the flaming feminist I had met three and a half years ago. And more than anything, she loved her babies and related to them in a way that I had never seen before. When an acquaintance invited her to a mothers' meeting at a local church, she accepted. This was a group that extolled mothering and housewifery and reinforced these values with educational trainings. It engendered the same support and camaraderie as her consciousness-raising group of five years earlier but focused on themes like cooking, sewing and the like. The friendship of other young mothers eventually led her to join that church. Six months later I, too, joined the Mormon Church.[2] We eventually saw it as being halfway between her Baptist and my Catholic upbringing.

It is hard to explain the radical transformation that had come over us. Much of it had to do with having children and suddenly feeling responsible. So going to church, which would have been anathema to us just a few years earlier, unexpectedly made sense to us now.

The past lost its luster as our value system metamorphosed. We never looked back, except to wonder who in the world we had been and why, and to be grateful we were no longer on that dead-end street. To a casual observer our family life might have looked like something on TV in the 1950s: *Leave It to Beaver* or *Father Knows Best*. It was a veneer but that was important. Agreeing on a common value system gave our marriage a sense of security that we both desperately needed; our church did that for us. It also instantly created new friends who reinforced these values with family-centered activities, and we needed that too.

---

2   The Church of Jesus Christ of Latter Day Saints

A LITTLE BIT CRAZY

1979-1986

Within a year of living and working in the city and being modestly successful, it became obvious with the high price of land that our dream of five acres and our own place was a long way off. Our life began to feel like a rat race and we were again dreaming of the mountains and the country life they represented. In May of 1979, we again packed up our things, this time with three children and a little savings, and moved to the mountains.

I expected the same entrepreneurial success in the mountains, but we struggled to make ends meet for many years and there were times when they didn't. Tom donated articles from his flea market booth for us to sell and occasionally he helped with cash. Several times our church paid the bills that we couldn't. Vicki was pregnant again, much to my consternation. That was a C-section and another girl, and then there was a boy and a fourth girl. Vicki wasn't worried about our finances or my embarrassment of so many kids and so little money. It finally dawned on me that she was playing by a different set of rules and didn't mind cheating at birth control. She loved her babies; she loved having them around and caring for them. Not to mention, pregnancy and nursing were the ideal cure for her endometriosis. If we made a mistake with the birth control, that was okay with her because she got another baby. Vicki was reluctant to admit this cavalier attitude; it was only much later that we understood its origins.

One of the serendipitous moments in our financial struggles came when Vicki asked a local interior decorator for sewing work. It gradually

34

blossomed into a business—and unlike the carpentry business there was no competition. For a year we had a store downtown. While Vicki had no training in interior decorating, she had an eye for color and a knack for doing sales. I worked up the estimates and became a one-man drapery workroom, gradually learning how to craft window and bed coverings of every sort. Occasionally learning from our mistakes, we steadily became skilled and in time did wholesale work for one of the most prestigious decorators on the East Coast.

Pushed by circumstances and a lust for our own land, we kept moving further and further away from civilization and ended up buying fifty acres in one of the most remote areas on the East Coast. It was a lease-purchase on property that the owner had not been able to unload for years. It was cheap, and Vicki's parents helped with the fifteen-hundred dollar lump-sum due at purchase. We bought a mountain cabin with no bathroom and, at first, no running water. If one removed the aging gray Masonite siding, this house would have looked like the weathered and derelict buildings often portrayed in country landscapes romanticizing yesteryear. But we had what we wanted: plenty of land for our gardens, even a few animals, and dreams. We didn't have a neighbor within a quarter of a mile. Most of the people who knew us, including our parents, thought we were crazy, wondering why in the world we would want to live like this—out in the middle of nowhere on the wrong side of the poverty line. And there was some truth to their assessment.

When we moved out of those several years of dire poverty, we started marriage therapy again—this time though our church. There was no question that we needed it. By this time we had begun to suspect that our problems may have their origin within our past histories. There were now books available on incest and sexual abuse, and Vicki wanted to talk about it because she was starting to remember more about the incident that happened when she was eleven. It was constantly on her mind; even as far back as the C-section with Erin's birth, there is a note in her journal telling me that if she died in surgery, I was not to allow her parents to raise the kids and that her father was not to have any unsupervised time with our girls.

Using the analogy of an onion, our therapist told us we needed to peel off the layers one at a time, and he wanted to start with the most basic. Within a few sessions he diagnosed Vicki with PMS. My wife loved the energy she got from the premenstrual tension and used it to get things done. But that relentless drive did not always work well with me. Then I remembered a dream I'd had over a decade earlier and figured out that I had serious blood sugar problems that exacerbated my moods. I also recognized what had been obvious since college: I had an intermittent problem with depression. Applying this information helped smooth out our lives—when we remembered to use it. In addition, I was a compulsive workaholic and perfectionist and would drive myself and Vicki crazy when I didn't get everything done on my infinite to-do list. I was inevitably tired and short-tempered, which was a portent for Joe Gorilla to appear.

Then from time to time, Vicki—normally the self-controlled and competent house manager who doubled as the PR person for our business—would just plain go nuts. She went from being diplomatic to a rabid prosecuting attorney. She would start ripping into me over things that an hour earlier she would have known were going to upset the fragile status quo. I couldn't reason with her when she got into one of these moods—not that I had an abundance of that kind of patience. I didn't know what to do, but I couldn't stand the fusillade of words.

During one of Vicki's verbal barrages that she doesn't remember, I escaped by going into town to get something I needed at a department store. As I drove up the hill away from our house, my intuition told me that this wasn't a good idea; on the way back it told me emphatically not to do it again. When I arrived home I found my wife a hysterical mess on the floor with passel of worried kids surrounding her. She had been crying uncontrollably for the hour and a half that I'd been gone. She crawled to where I was standing and wrapped herself around my legs and begged me not to do that again. It was so dramatic and out of character I wondered if it was an act but that didn't make any sense. Groveling was not a normal part of her repertoire.

Later, when the house had calmed down and kids had gone to bed, she went through her litany of questions. They were compulsive and familiar and she wouldn't stop until she got an answer to each one: Who had I seen? What did the *women* look like? Were they attractive to me? Did I touch the cashier's hand when I gave her the money? Did she touch mine when she gave me the change? Feeling a little guilty, I stretched my patience and dealt with her insecurities, but doing so was exhausting. And I was conflicted. My intuition told me not to leave again, but I had often heard that disengaging was exactly what we needed to do in tense circumstances. I was slightly intoxicated with the sense of power I got from the way I handled the situation, but my intuition reiterated that our marriage wouldn't hold up if I used this strategy. But if I didn't use this strategy, what in the world was I supposed to do?

I don't want to give the wrong impression about our occasional craziness. These incidents stand out because they were uncommon. And they bothered us. In general, things hummed along like they do in most moderately functional families. We had family night once a week which sometimes included a picnic and a hike, and we usually did something with the kids on Saturday afternoons. Because of our limited finances this was often a visit to the park nearby. We also had a Friday date night which often included hikes at the park or a music concert nearby. Our kids had chores to do and pets to take care of, and there were always fun things to do and explore even if they didn't have a TV. While their lives were different from most kids their age, they were certainly not deficient.

TOM AND VIRGINIA

1986-1988

B y this time I knew Vicki's parents well. When we lived in Raleigh—
about twenty minutes from their house—we occasionally ate there,
especially for birthdays and holidays. (Vicki did not like visiting her
parents' house, so these visits were not regular.) Virginia was the consummate
hostess. She always served a Jell-O salad with dinner that she knew I loved
and she always made a big deal out of her grandchildren, which I appreciated.
The latter was completely foreign to me and it was obvious where Vicki had
gotten her enthusiasm for mothering. I inevitably compared Virginia to my
mother, who rarely saw our children, and whose interaction with them was
strikingly superficial—like she was talking to her pet dogs. It dawned on me
that my mother did not know how to be a grandmother, and I'm not sure she
liked kids anyway. This realization was disappointing and gradually Virginia
became a mother figure for me. I think she recognized that deficiency in
my background and didn't mind putting me under her maternal umbrella.
She also was not moody like my mother nor did she have any submerged
expectations like my mother, who could not let go of the fact that her oldest
child—her baby boy, her favorite—had grown up, left the nest, and was now
married to another woman with a family of his own.

Tom was generous but hardly refined with his gruff style. When we
visited he was usually downstairs watching TV. He would surface for the meal,
often grumbling about something, offer one of his ill-mannered blessings on
the food, eat without saying much, and then retire downstairs again. Vicki

assured me that it was nothing personal and that he had mellowed out since she'd left home.

She told me stories of her childhood and his temper and violence that were hard to believe of the aloof, grumpy man with the twenty-dollar bills that I had become familiar with. But I had also seen him transform into a Casanova when other women were around (the age and attractiveness of the opposite sex made no difference), which struck me as humorous but incredibly rude to his wife. Tom and Virginia's relationship was certainly not close, and it was hard to fathom what they had in common except Virginia's Baptist religion, which would not allow her to divorce unless there was abuse or adultery. It was a far cry from the tender relationship that Vicki portrayed of Virginia's parents.

The only time I ever saw the ill-tempered father of Vicki's childhood was when he and Virginia came up to the mountains six months after our second move there. Virginia wanted to play the grandmother part, to see the babies and attend a harvest festival at Tripp's school. Tom was in a foul mood and unleashed an almost continuous barrage of criticism at her. I know it lasted at least an hour; it was embarrassing to walk with them through the school, which Tom seemed oblivious to. Virginia simply ignored him, exacerbating his mood. But that one scene was an anomaly.

While I was much more familiar with the man who had the twenty-dollar bills, the Tom of Vicki's childhood was never far from my wife. Her journals from our early years in the mountains show how obsessed she became about the sexual abuse she had experienced at age eleven. It was always on her mind and whenever she got a chance, she talked with professionals about it. She was getting pressure from her mother, who wanted more contact with her grandchildren: Vicki's sister let her children go to Raleigh and visit, why wouldn't Vicki do the same? My wife remembered the role her own grandmother had played in her life, and she wanted her girls to have that relationship; but she also wanted to protect her little girls. The therapists inevitably urged caution. They advised her to investigate and make sure Tom's deviancy was not still part of his life.

On one of our visits to Raleigh Vicki found porn downstairs in the TV room. When her mother next requested that the grandchildren spend a week with them, my wife confronted her mother with what she'd found. Virginia didn't deny it; rather, she passed it off as normal male behavior, but the discovery disquieted Vicki. In the mid-1980s, sexual abuse was now being openly discussed, but there was no information available on sexual predators—in fact, that term had not yet entered the lexicon.

I was unsure whether there was a direct relationship between the porn and any danger to our girls. Almost every boy I knew had had some exposure to porn growing up, and *Playboy* was common in my father's house (of his second marriage). I sometimes saw it in the bathrooms of houses where we did drapery installations. But I did agree with Vicki about erring on caution's side.

Virginia was persistent. With all the financial help she and Tom had given us over the years it was hard to keep saying no. She reminded Vicki that recently, during a dry spell in our business, Tom had financed a trade show we did to the tune of several thousand dollars.

For the most part, I accepted Vicki's memory at age eleven, but I also knew that memories by their nature were ephemeral and untrustworthy, and that jostled with my gratitude toward Tom. Vicki's caution won out; but the quandary troubled both of us, especially when dealing with Virginia's persistence.

Vicki finally decided that she needed to confront her parents— especially her mother—about the abuse, but she didn't know how to do that. She first decided to write to her aunt, whom she was named after, and ask for advice. That letter was written in her journal in June, 1986, but it never got sent. Vicki was not emotionally up to it, and I understood.

Soon afterward, Vicki's entire family came up for Thanksgiving in 1986—first to celebrate with a dinner at the local fire hall that they had rented, and then to help us move into a friend's house until we could finish the new house we were slowly building. It was a typical get together for Vicki's family and her parents' generosity forestalled the confrontation.

Through the next year and into another pregnancy, Vicki felt increased pressure to deal with her parents on the abuse issue. But she was conflicted. She was sick much of that time and her parents had unselfishly come up several times to offer help and support. She couldn't forget about wanting our kids to have a grandmother like she'd had, and the kids too wanted to be spoiled by Virginia. They didn't understand their mother's reluctance. Vicki gave up the idea of talking to her aunt and began prepping herself to talk to her mother. There are several such notations in her journal, but in August when she invited her parents up to watch the kids while we did a large, several-day drapery installation, she still hadn't done it. She had already called her mother to come pick up the kids and take them to her sister's house in Boone when she realized the omission. She slipped her father a note as they arrived and we left: She put him on notice that she remembered what had happened at age eleven and didn't want it to happen to her girls.

Not a word was said about it.

A month later they came up again. This time to help out with Bethany's birth by again taking the kids to Vicki's sister's house. This would turn out to be one of Vicki's most difficult births. Vicki wasn't admitted to the hospital after a day of contractions, but she was told not to go too far away. With his typically gruff but generous style, Tom slipped Vicki a credit card to pay for a motel. I slept that night but Vicki labored in and out of a hot bathtub.

The next morning I was admitted and labored the entire day, to the point of exhaustion. I remember walking the halls with Jody, trying to hasten the labor, and then walking some more. Something was wrong and it wasn't until late in the afternoon that my doctor discovered that the baby was sunny side-up and that its jaw bone was caught on my pelvis.

"This is going to hurt . . . ," he said in typical medical understatement. He inserted his fingers to dislodge the baby's jaw bone and turn its head. With the onset of this excruciating pain I did something that I didn't know I knew how to do: I exited my body and hovered above the scene until my doctor was finished.

Bethany was number seven—in ten years. We left the hospital when she was six hours old as was our pattern and enjoyed the next four days to ourselves getting acquainted with the new addition to our lives. Vicki's parents then brought the kids back and everyone relished the sight of the new baby. With gratitude my wife handed the credit card back to her father.

"Go buy yourself something," Tom said nonchalantly, "something that you need. Look at it as a baby present."

Resting, pillowed up on our old bed, Vicki replied, "We need a new bed badly . . . ?"

"There's a sale on at Sears I saw. Get a nice one."

And Vicki did; she spent eight hundred dollars. I felt uncomfortable with the credit card and urged her to give it back. My wife reminded me of her father's generosity through the years and wanted to put a little on every now and then. She had no trouble thinking of things that we needed. But with time the credit card began to look more like a bribe and I convinced her not to use it again.

Just after Bethany's birth in 1987, Vicki's parents agreed to lend us ten-thousand dollars to finish our new house—after my father had refused to cosign a loan. (And then, to our surprise, my stepmother gave us five-thousand dollars.) So excited were we that we neglected to consider that this might increase Virginia's leverage the next time she brought up the subject of our girls visiting.

This would be a special time for Vicki and me. We were both focused on our goal of getting in to our new home. We planned and coordinated our days. I often stayed late after sewing to put in a few hours banging nails. Vicki just as often brought the kids up to help. Sometimes they were hauling supplies; other times they were sweeping and cleaning. Vicki researched economical and healthy alternatives to conventional construction and appliances, and she also planned the decorating. It was a time of intense cooperation. We both remember it with fondness; for the two of us it was like the honeymoon we never had.

AN INTRICATE BONDING
1988

When Vicki and I met, we had no idea of the subterranean forces impelling us. We lived in a sort of twilight, thinking it was the bright light of day—that was to be expected; it was the only kind of light we'd ever known. At the time, we were unaware of our own history and certainly of any skeletons in our respective family closets. Our relationship was hardly normal, but we didn't recognize that either. At first it was complicated by the free-love lifestyle we had each just exited. Although we had both been scarred by the casual intimacy of previous relationships, those were just the rules of the game that we were used to and we thought nothing of it. Trust between us was a long time coming, and only when it didn't fully arrive did we begin suspect that these relationship issues went deeper.

With our backgrounds in the social sciences and with the help of our marriage counseling, we eventually began to look to our parents and our youth. We both knew that things growing up at home had not been ideal. Nevertheless, like most young people we both thought of our childhoods as normal. Of course, normal is what you're used to and we were mature enough to recognize there was no such thing as perfect.

Initially, we struggled to get along and also to succeed financially. Basic cooperation between us was sometimes difficult. There was an uneven and unusual distribution of talents. We had to learn to think outside the traditional roles we had grown up with—or rebelled against—without discarding them. We both had significant skills, but they were combined with serious debits. The key for us was to learn to maximize our strengths and minimize our weaknesses; this meant that we needed an unusual level of collaboration with flexible and sometimes atypical roles. We also had to remind ourselves that we were playing doubles. As partners, one of us could not win at the other's expense; either we both won or we both lost. Slowly, very slowly we had been learning to do that.

After eleven years of marriage, eight children that we both deeply cared about and a business that we shared and depended upon, we were thoroughly bonded. I don't think anyone could have planned a more intricate process of bonding than the interdependence we had developed through necessity. Even though we were both ornery and moody from time to time, we couldn't afford to take a personal hiatus and nurse our gripes at one another's flaws— the house would cease to function and the money would not come in. We'd seen enough hard times and were proud enough that we didn't want that to happen. Self-sufficiency was one of our goals in life.

And . . . we had become friends, because we had shared so much. We shared the business we had built from scratch and that had been challenging and rewarding. We shared each other's shortcomings, which were demanding from time to time. We shared the wonder of each child's birth; the intersection of time and eternity is such a holy time. We shared their childhoods, nurturing them in the values that we thought were important. We shared our faith and had been nourished by it. This intricate bonding— that had happened so slowly that we didn't know it was going on—was just what was needed to allow Vicki to start remembering. Above all else, she needed to feel safe before she could come to terms with the sense of haunting that kept the incident at age eleven habitually on her mind.

Without realizing it, we were ready for the challenge that would stretch and bend us and the entire family in ways that we could not have imagined. There was no primer on how to survive remembering a horrific childhood. Certainly, it had been leaking into our lives for years. We had been surviving that intermittent drip and it wasn't easy.

After reading the few available books on sexual abuse, Vicki couldn't help wondering about that one incident that she had remembered. She wanted to investigate further but our church therapist said that this was beyond him; we needed to find a specialist. The problem was going to be finding a therapist experienced in that area—it was a brand-new field at the time—and one who was willing to barter because we couldn't afford the cost.

INTO THE
DARKNESS

INDIAN SUMMER HONEYMOON

April, 1988

One of Vicki's strengths was networking. When she finally made up her mind to find a therapist with experience in sexual abuse, she began calling. One call led to another and after weeks of research she found Dick. He was working with sex offenders as part of a court-mandated program in Roanoke and agreed to take Vicki on as a patient. He also agreed to barter. Our only problem was that he was two and a half hours away. These appointments would require a long drive.

I made the first trip with Vicki. Issac's office was in the rear of a nondescript professional building. The office was of moderate size with desk and a couch; the walls were lined with shelves of books. I saw many that I had read over the years. There was a small plaque amid the books that read *Don't Look at Me,* which was virtually irresistible. Dick was ex-military and had short hair. He knew exactly where we lived because he was fond of camping at the nearby park. He said that he always took his gun because of the snakes. His attitude seemed to be no-nonsense. As that initial conversation continued, we learned that he was the oldest of four siblings in his family. He had grown up taking care of his younger siblings and had developed a heart for little girls because of his several younger sisters. Seeing little girls violated upset him, and he said he was tough with the offenders that he counseled individually. That was where most of his experience with sexual abuse came from; he'd only had one other female patient.

Vicki was curious about the men. "What are the men like that you treat?"

"They all have sad stories to tell."

"Do these men come voluntarily?" she asked skeptically.

"They come voluntarily because if they don't, I call their parole officer and they are immediately back in jail."

"Do they miss a lot of appointments with excuses?"

"I don't accept any excuses," Dick said. "They are not even allowed to be late. If they want to stay out of jail, they are here every week, on time. I don't fool around with them."

"And how long are they court-mandated to come?"

"Until I feel like they can handle that part of their life better."

"It's that open-ended?" Vicki, the former probation officer, asked in disbelief.

"I generally ask for a year. If the men don't work hard, it's very simple—they go back to jail. Most of them don't like jail so they work hard. A year usually does it. These men also pay for their own therapy; the court doesn't. And it's not cheap. I don't barter with them."

Dick hardly came across as sympathetic, and I wondered how he was able to connect with these men.

"What kind of therapy do you use?" my wife asked.

"My preference is hypnosis. Most of these men are victims and like you; they don't remember much. The first step is to remember; you can't begin to process the abuse unless you first remember. Based on what you've told me I am relatively certain you have more to remember."

This sounded fascinating to me. I was suddenly much more interested and leaned forward, but I felt Vicki tense up beside me.

"I don't want to do that."

"We can work around that. And we can talk about it later. It does help you remember."

"That scares me."

Dick knew better than to push, and he reassured Vicki of that.

As our meeting drew to a close, I explained what we did for a living and what we could barter.

"That's fine. I'll keep that in mind as we go along." He pulled out his appointment book.

"I'd like to come every other week because of the distance," Vicki said.

"Then how about four o'clock? That way we can run over and it won't interfere with other appointments. Any particular day? I should mention that there's a survivor's group that meets on Monday nights. That's something to keep in mind. I recommend it. It would be a long day; but you'd get more therapy time, and groups support a different kind of healing. It would be well worth your while and there's no cost."

I was hoping for a therapist with more experience with women survivors, but Dick was willing to barter. That was a huge financial relief. Like most alpha males he exuded confidence and I came to trust him. He would talk with me, not at me. He told me that he had a seven-month-old baby brother who had died of SIDS. The infant had gotten tangled up in the crib blanket. Seeing how that affected him made him very human. He was patient with me.

Those first sessions, with five or so kids sitting in the waiting room, we discussed my background: growing up and moving every year as an army brat; my inspiring and stable maternal grandparents; and the mental health issues and mostly unknowns on my father's side. He said my childhood would have been idyllic if not for the abuse. We also went through our twelve-year-old dysfunctional marriage that included my mental health issues and Jody's rage-aholism.

Dick commented on my beautiful, intelligent children: how well behaved they were. I was still breast-feeding Bethany. My visits were probably a delight for him after dealing with perpetrators the rest of the week. For once he was helping the good guys—the victims.

His favorite method of therapy was hypnosis, which scared me. I preferred support groups. To begin with we compromised with regular talk therapy in his office and then attending the women's survivor group that met at seven o'clock at night. He was hoping the group might trigger more memory. He repeated what he'd said in our first session: that there were almost certainly more memories. Based on his experience with perpetrators, he knew a lot that I didn't. He also assured me that not remembering everything was very common.

I enrolled in the survivor's groups and was expecting a women's support group, like the consciousness-raising group I had started so many years earlier; but from the beginning I didn't like this women's group. It met in a room in an old church on the other side of town. I remember it as being dark—much of that was the mood. We sat in folding chairs around a Formica table in a dimly lit room. There were about eight women. It was all about anger. The moderator, a volunteer therapist, would lead with a couple of questions and before long the women unleashed a frenzy of anger. These women hated the men who had molested them and that hatred was virulent. Several of these women were seriously emotionally disabled and couldn't function. They couldn't hold a job and they admitted their lives were a wreck. I couldn't identify with them. Nor could I identify with the general mood of anger—so much so that within a couple of sessions I never went back. I had come seeking to understand my father; my goal was Christian forgiveness. This was not the right place to lead me there.

Their rage was so toxic that they refused to have any contact with the men in the offender's group. The rule was that the women's group started half an hour earlier and got out first. If the women had children in the children's group, they would collect them, and only after the women had vacated the building would the men's group release. During the couple of hours that we were there, the women's end of the hall was off-limits to the men. If the women were to be believed, they would have scratched the eyes out of those men, even though they didn't know them. That inevitably made me curious and I broke the unwritten rule and lingered on the night I decided that this women's group was not for me. I wanted to see those men for myself. They looked remarkably human, in no way evil or intimidating. A few even wore business suits. I couldn't help but wonder.

We moved into our new house even though it was still unfinished. With the help of the older girls Vicki cooked our evening meals outside over an open campfire, and we both fondly remember those summer evenings. After long days of sewing and then several hours of working on the house, we unwound by the outdoor fire. It was easy to work late with the excitement engendered by our own house, and—as the darkness settled in and the stars winked—to relish the camaraderie and cooperation and the sense of finally living our dream of so many years. Vicki would tell me the progress she'd made running down building materials on what was becoming a very tight budget. With more time than money, over the years we'd learned how to find almost everything at wholesale. And then we'd listen to the excitement of our kids running around, playing hide-and-seek amid the flotsam of a house under construction. They typically ate dinner much earlier than us and for them it was time to play. They were in love with the new house as well. The weather cooperated with very little rain, and then a stunning Indian summer—made to order—that seemed to keep going and going.

During the summer Tom and Virginia made another trip up to see how their investment was taking shape and, I'm sure, to garner some appreciation. Vicki knew that her mother would again bring up the subject of the three older girls visiting for a week. Virginia knew that with their loan to us that this request for the girls to visit would have more weight.

There was no driveway to our house; her parents had parked several hundred yards down the dirt road near our old residence, which was now my sewing shop. After chatting for a few minutes and examining the progress on our house, I went down with Tom to get some gifts from their car.

We passed the barn where our three-hundred-pound sow happened to be in heat. Tom seemed to be paying an unusual amount of attention to her, so I explained how crazy she got when she was in heat. It was impossible to keep her locked up at night. She broke down fences or the barn door or whatever restraint I could invent and would wander down the road. It was usually on a full moon and she'd stand outside our old house and snort and bark, waking us up. In the past she had climbed onto our neighbor's porch and cleaned out his dog food. As we approached, the pig was making a lot of racket and expecting food; when I didn't go to feed her, she turned away, exposing her red and swollen rear end.

Tom got excited in a way I'd never seen before and made several sexual innuendos that jarred me. By this time Vicki had much more clearly remembered the incident at age eleven. It had been a violent anal rape where she had felt used like an animal. Suddenly, I had no trouble believing that episode. It resonated in a way I'd never experienced before. For the first time my mind expanded to allow more possibility to Tom's character, and I wondered if his comments to me weren't a lure that he was throwing out. I didn't bite and he abruptly shut up.

That night as we discussed that incident, Vicki and I were left wondering if he was still active in his perversions. And maybe it wasn't just little girls.

With a sudden regret Vicki couldn't help but remember all those weekends when she was single and had unwittingly dropped Tripp off at her parents' house. I rehearsed how uneasy I'd always felt about those twenty-dollar bills. From that point on we decided that any unaccompanied overnight stay by our girls in Raleigh was out of the question. This incident, combined with the information she was getting from her therapy visits to Roanoke, persuaded Vicki to rethink her father's sexual deviancy. She had always assumed it had been an isolated episode between her and her father. She was now entertaining the possibly that there might be more in her background that she didn't remember—as Dick had postulated--and that given the right opportunity his perversion might only be dormant and not dead. Although we had no evidence for this idea, we weren't taking any chances.

In August my sister made the long drive with my mother to visit for the day. Mother had to be reacquainted with our kids. She hadn't seen the older ones in eight years—since my brother's wedding—and there were now four new ones. I knew why we hadn't been to Florida to see her—we couldn't afford it; but I wondered why she seemed to care so little about her grandchildren. It bothered me. There were gifts at Christmas from her, but there was no sense of genuine concern or enjoyment. The kids were initially shy of this second grandma but gradually thawed based on their experience with their other grandma. It helped when my mother pulled some candy out of her pocketbook. She seemed to be trying to relate to my kids; she just didn't know how to do it.

She was also intermittently wandering off by herself and pulling a small metal flask out of her pocketbook and turning away from everyone to take a nip. I remembered the stories my stepmother told after taking over the house that my mother vacated with parent's separation and divorce: She claimed she had found bottles everywhere, hidden in the drapery hems and in boxes in the closets. Alcohol was definitely a problem for my mother and had been for years. My father once told me how embarrassed he was to take her to business parties because she often fell asleep after a couple of drinks. There was also the story that I'd heard from my brother after I'd gone to college. My departure seemed to be a turning point in her life, where the downhill slide suddenly turned precipitous. Mother had been driving into town at night and went off the road and ran into a tree. It was not a serious accident but by the time the police arrived, my mother had switched places with our dog Rita who was now in the driver's seat. Mother was obviously intoxicated. And apparently alcoholism was a family heritage. My mother's mother had died of alcohol-related issues when my mother was a teenager, and her father died of similar issues fifteen years later, when I was just one or two years old.

My mother didn't talk much about her childhood, but I knew she had been a rebellious kid. She had grown up in the upscale neighborhood of Scarsdale, New York, and told stories of smoking at age fifteen and racing in her car and outmaneuvering the police when they tried to give her a summons. She painted herself as a wild child. She had been kicked out of college after two years but refused to give any details other than to let me know it wasn't because of her grades.

As we strolled around the park, my mother bent over with a hacking cough from time to time, and my sister took Vicki aside and said she was worried. My sister had finally convinced Mother to visit a doctor and had an appointment set up when they returned to Virginia Beach.

For the first time I saw my mother in a different light. She looked old. She was almost sixty-three, but she looked much older. She had obsessed over her looks and keeping a trim figure for as long as I could remember. As a child, on our frequent trips to the beach during the summer, she often wore a two-piece bathing suit and laid out in a folding lounge chair reading a thick paperback with a sleazy cover. I was now so used to Virginia that I wondered how this woman could be my mother—or how she could be anyone's mother. She lacked a certain competence in dealing with grandchildren—one that came naturally to Virginia. But more than anything else, I saw her as a loner.

A week after her visit to the mountains, a chest X-ray showed a spot on Mother's lung. There was a sudden fearful concern that almost fifty years of smoking had caught up with her. More tests would come later, but it did not look good.

Our first meal that autumn in our new dining room was important; I had been looking forward to it for some time. It would be a time to gather together as a family and to be grateful for our new house. But there was an unanticipated problem as we sat down at our harvest table. Vicki had been working with our daughter Jennifer on this meal most of the day, and when my wife sat down at the end of the table opposite me, to save her life, she could not find the right spot for our oldest daughter. After moving Jennifer several times, it became obvious there wasn't a "right" spot. I didn't understand why Vicki was trying to move her. It didn't make any sense and it was obviously upsetting our daughter. Vicki appeared to be callous to this latter detail, which was out of character. I pointed that out. To my dismay, in our brand-new house, with this table that finally fit our entire family, dinner erupted with accusations between the two of us and then a heated argument. Our poor daughter was humiliated and ran from the table while Vicki and I slung recriminations back and forth, ruining the meal I had so long looked forward to having as a family.

I did not understand my own behavior. I am not really sure what I was feeling other than a compelling need to protect my daughter. When I would try and be logical with myself, it did not help. Rationally, I did not believe Jody would molest our daughters. I knew my behavior was bizarre, but I had a physical, overpowering need to jump between him and them any time he got physically close. And that is what I would do, especially with the oldest. I was protecting my daughter, which my mother had not done for me—I was the oldest daughter in my family.

To save my life I couldn't explain my behavior, but the compulsion was powerful. As it would turn out, my body was already remembering things that my mind was not ready to accept. Even though I remembered details from only the one incident when I was eleven, Jennifer was now eleven. She had the same dark hair, blue eyes, and much the same facial features and body shape that I had at that age. Somebody had to protect her.

It took awhile for Vicki to solve the seating problem at the dining-room table. She finally vacated the other end of the table and sat beside me to my right. She moved Jennifer to her right and then our oldest daughter was safe and virtually out of my sight.

We were both taken by surprise with this incident, but almost certainly it had been fermenting for some time. Vicki had attended about fifty percent of her therapy appointments; she'd made the commitment to healing and set things in motion even though she seemed to be waffling. We had not had sit-down family meals in many, many months while the house was under construction. As Vicki said, her body was already starting to remember. This was a concept we had never heard of, despite our social-science degrees and all of our reading as well as our conversations with therapists.

Looking back, I'm not sure when we finally recognized that memory work was not all in Vicki's head; it was part mental and part physical. There were extremely powerful, virtually uncontrollable feelings locked up in parts of her body. Dick had not prepared her for what remembering would be like; I'm not sure he understood this part of it himself. So this first hint of what was to come dampened the Indian summer honeymoon we'd been experiencing. I was hurt because we'd been getting along so well, cooperating like we never had in the past. I couldn't figure out why she couldn't think her way around her feelings. She was throwing away all the accumulated goodwill we had built and was at a loss to explain why. I was angry and perplexed; Vicki was perplexed as well, overwhelmed with deep-seated feelings that she didn't comprehend because they were still just below the level of her awareness.

Over the next few months we had fewer and fewer family meals. Since I often worked late, Vicki started feeding the kids early. That worked well for her and it became a habit so we were only dealing with family meals on Sunday.

A SECOND MEMORY

November, 1988

I t was raining with a hint of an early November snow, and it would be a dangerous drive to therapy and especially coming home after dark. The five hours of driving was just too much. Vicki was on the phone canceling yet another appointment with Dick. Her therapy had fallen through the cracks with the move into our new house. This time she had a legitimate excuse, but this time Dick was not sympathetic. Rather bluntly, he told her to recommit herself to coming on a regular basis or he was taking her off his appointment calendar. He knew what she knew on a deeper level: She was running away from therapy.

Two weeks later on a Monday afternoon Vicki was heading east to Roanoke away from the setting sun. It was a bright yellow ball in the rearview mirror not far above the horizon. It would be dusk soon. Even though it was brisk outside, the car was warm. And even thought the leaves on the trees were gone, there was a lot of green in her mind's eye—a rich tropical green. Vicki was suddenly reminded of Hawaii where she lived when she was five and six. She remembered the military housing.

'It was almost dark and I was playing outside the front door in the garden of marigolds that the last tenant had left. To this day I am fond of the strong distinctive smell of that flower—one of my few good childhood memories. A few minutes later the door slammed behind me and my Dad grabbed my hand. I resisted and he applied more pressure to let me know he was in charge. He pulled me

toward the playground. It was in the center of the geometric cluster of apartment buildings. It was a 1950s playground made of strong, galvanized tubular metal with chain swings and a slide. In the rapidly dimming light I could barely see the grass which was worn to bare dirt into traffic patterns from use as we kids went from swing to slide to round-about.'

'He was dragging me toward a gazebo. It had eight sides. The bottom half was solid wood, like a wainscot, and the top half was a heavy lattice that blackened the inside of the structure. A bench encircled the interior of the gazebo. The darkness inside was palpable; it was scary. I was five years old and fighting my father who was pulling my under panties off. I began kicking wildly and would have started screaming, but his thick strong hand covered my mouth jerking my head back . . . .'

Early one winter morning I left our bedroom—as I had since August—to rouse the kids for school. It was still dark as I felt my way along the short hall to the stairs. We still only had the one bathroom on the second floor and that's where I was headed. It was my habit to reach the top of the steps, poke my head in the girls' room and call out "upsie daisy." Then I would use the bathroom and retreat back downstairs to the kitchen for something to eat. I didn't want to turn the light on outside of our bedroom because I thought Vicki was still asleep, but when I reached to first step, a voice called out from the blackness behind.

"You don't have to do that. I'll wake the girls up."

With a sour night behind me and a long day of sewing ahead I was running on inertia. "It's not a problem," I said dully, taking another step.

"I'll do it." There was urgency in her voice and I heard a sudden stirring from the bed. This was strange. She never got out of bed early if she didn't have to.

"Vicki, it's not a problem," I repeated with a little impatience.

"I don't want you to do it. I'll do it." It was her command voice—the one that said, Don't mess with me on this point because I'll fight to the death—that inevitably irked me. But she was immediately beside me, hastily wrapped in a bathrobe.

"What's going on?" My voice was a mixture of anger and fatigue, resentment and suspicion.

Putting on the very thin veneer of a cheery voice, she said, "I'll just start waking the kids. I need to get up earlier anyway. And I'll make them breakfast."

We walked together up the steps. She went into the girls' room and I used the bathroom and then grumbled down the several steps and fixed a bowl of homemade granola. I was sitting in the living room, occasionally stoking the fire, gradually coming out of my stupor when I heard the back door open and then shut. Then I heard the patter of the three girls running along the back deck on their way to catch the bus.

Something was odd and out of sync. I couldn't put my finger on it, but I could certainly feel it.

When Vicki showed up a few minutes later, I asked her why they hadn't used the front door. I realized I had missed seeing them off to school. And they hadn't had breakfast.

"We're running late. I told them to hurry."

Later I left our house, heading down to the sewing shop. I was halfway down to the road when the bus finally picked them up. The girls hadn't been late; they had been ten minutes early on a bitter, cold morning. And they hadn't had breakfast.

On Saturday I was sitting on the couch in the living room when I heard the clamor of the kids climbing the steps and coming to the front door. They had been playing in the woods around the house and it was about time for lunch. The younger ones entered first and through the window I saw the older girls lagging behind. They were purposefully peering inside and saw me. The front door abruptly shut and thirty-seconds later the back door opened, and I heard the three older girls race up the steps to their bedroom.

They are purposely avoiding me, I thought. What in the world is going on?

LEARNING TO FLEX

January, 1989

J *an. 10,1989. Journal entry. Life has been very difficult. The therapy I'm going through has me remembering the things that happened with my father—and my mother's part. Then I will confront them both. I've remembered two incidences, one at age five and the other a brutal, violent one at age eleven. I'm terrified to remember any more. The pain from those two was and is so intense I can hardly go about my normal day. And if remembering's not hard enough, then next I have to confront my parents . . . .*

Vicki's new strategy for dealing with the older girls was gradual, happening over a period of weeks, and it did not sit well with me. As I came to understand what she was doing, we had one confrontation after another. When we took out time to peaceably discuss the matter, she had a difficult time explaining her behavior, mostly because she didn't understand it herself. Over the years she had occasionally talked about the deficit in her own life from not having a decent relationship with her dad. Why would she want to condemn her daughters to the same fate? But her inability to explain had nothing to do with her willingness to change. She claimed she couldn't—at least, not now. That, I didn't understand and liked even less.

Even though I had a degree in psychology and had read books on abnormal psychology, which fascinated me, I was at a loss with how to deal with this new situation. Much of this had to do with the fact that most of the time Vicki was normal and could out-think and therefore easily manipulate me. It was only when—seemingly out of nowhere—certain situations arose that she acted like a cornered animal, growling and snarling as if she were ferocious—and she could be. It was then that we butted heads while I intuitively tried to plumb her motivation. If I wasn't being defensive and reacting angrily in return, I would finally decide that, yes, indeed, she was protecting a weak spot, a vulnerable place. She was hurt.

So how do you deal with a person who comes on aggressively, but underneath is going to fall apart if you push back? And falling apart for Vicki would mean a spectacular flame-out that would envelop both of us and put the household in shambles. What could I do but back off and treat her like the potentially dangerous, wounded animal that she was? At the best of times, this is what happened. At these specific junctures, if somebody was going to flex in our relationship, it was going to have to be me. The inner struggle for me to get to this point had been going on for years, and it was difficult because my usual, initial reaction was to get angry—which only exacerbated the situation. Only very gradually did I see that my flexibility was a sign of strength and not weakness. When I used that knowledge, I let her win these clashes because for me to win would be for both of us to lose. But if she won, the house at least stayed calm—and that meant that I won too. I had to trust that she had incomprehensible emotional currents surging below the surface—that that was part of the nature of her disease. And that's why she was doing therapy. She often referenced Dick when I was calm enough to listen, telling me that this kind of behavior would naturally heal with time.

Because we both worked at home, church had become our major social outlet. I remember walking up to the front door one Sunday with Vicki at about the same time as one of the other sisters. While chivalry was not one of my strong suits, I was accustomed to holding the door for any woman including Vicki. On this particular occasion Vicki broke ranks with me and raced ahead to grab the door for this other sister. My wife shot me a victory smirk, but I was mostly baffled at what exactly she'd won. I had to admit this was better than being accosted with what could sometimes be vicious questions but it was slightly emasculating. When I pointed this out, she seemed unconcerned. But in the future when she saw a similar unfortunate serendipity in the making, she would grab my hand and slow down our walk or perhaps stop me and ask about something in the landscape.

Over a period of time, she trained all the women at church not to talk to me. Initially, this might have been irritating, but it was so much better than the annoying questions that sometimes set me off. Her journal notes a scenario after church where one of the sisters grabbed my attention to ask about our milk goats. I tried to be polite but distant, knowing what was going to happen as soon as Vicki arrived. Vicki came in with a withering and then malicious stare that the woman didn't catch. Finally, Vicki rudely broke into the conversation and took it over. My immediate emotions ran the gamut from relief to intense anger, but I saved the latter for the verbal abuse that I knew was coming. I think most of the women at church would have accepted Vicki's handicap better if it hadn't been that she was so loquacious with their husbands; I know I would have. But Vicki was oblivious to that.

Not long after her chest x-ray, a biopsy confirmed that the spot on my mother's lung was indeed cancer. The prognosis was not good. She was hospitalized and soon started chemotherapy. She had to take a leave of absence from her job as a drugstore clerk. She was very tired and very angry. Vicki's relationship with my mother had always been tenuous—with the fault on both sides—but now the two agreed to stay in phone contact. We agreed to wait and see how the chemo turned out before scheduling a get-together.

AN EFFECTUAL PRAYER

February, 1989

With an immediate reprieve from my mother's situation, we decided to take a few days off to ponder and pray about Vicki's therapy. Specifically, her journal notes that she wanted to ask for a release from the blockage of memories—she now believed there were more—and whether to use Dick's hypnosis. We decided to go to Washington and to pray at the Temple there. We couldn't find a babysitter and at the last minute decided to take the kids. Our budget was tight, but we found an economical bed and breakfast and decided to make it a family vacation; the first one we'd had in five years.

After a special time of prayer at the Washington Temple, we picked up the kids at a friend's house and got to the B and B at nine o'clock. The innkeepers were our parents' age and doted on our kids like they would have their own grandchildren. The next morning it was all-you-can-eat for the kids in their small kitchen with homemade waffles, scrambled eggs, juice and sausage while we slept late. Our kids loved it.

We got a late start for the metro, which was the highlight of the kids' trip. They loved their introduction to the cosmopolitan life, and several of the older ones began making plans to live in the city when they grew up. We surfaced from the metro not far from the White House and made the tour. Vicki and I were both interested in the decorating, especially the ornate draperies, because some of our clientele included wealthy families.

Then we bought some snack food from vendors as we headed toward the Washington Monument. It was a warm winter day with an overcast sky. It was too warm for coats. The younger kids chased pigeons and I was suddenly refreshed with what was, for me, that carefree feeling of having fun and being on vacation.

I didn't notice Vicki getting nervous with the crowds. She suddenly said she wanted to cut our trip short.

"We spent hundreds of dollars just to do this," I reminded her. "Come on, loosen up." I had done the tour as a teenager with friends and wanted to share it with our kids. "We've got the Washington Monument, The Museum of Art, The Smithsonian, and I don't want to miss the Vietnam Memorial."

We sat on some benches just a long stone's throw from the Rose Garden.

"I'm too tired," Vicki started, "I can't do everything. What's at the Museum of Art that you want to see?"

"It's got everything. Classical, Modern, you name it." She was eyeing me and I could suddenly read her mind.

"I don't have a lot of energy. You know what I'm talking about. Those disgusting paintings of women with no clothes on."

I remembered many years back showing her a photo of Botticelli's *Girl on the Half Shell*. "You're talking about classical art?"

"I'm talking about pornography." Her voice was curt and we were heading into an argument.

"Are you asking me whether they have the bull-fighting scenes on black velvet?" I said sarcastically, referring to her father's taste in art. It went over her head.

"I'm not worried about those. It's the disgusting paintings of naked women that I'm worried about."

"Great," I half-muttered under my breath.

The kids drifted away from our bench as the conversation heated up. The pigeons, the squirrels and the vendors were more interesting to them. After several increasingly heated exchanges it dawned on me that there wasn't going to be enough time for us to see everything.

"Look. Let's do the Vietnam Memorial. I don't think they have any nudes there. It's about dead men."

We agreed on that.

It was a long walk; in retrospect, probably too long. The kids were fanned out as we crossed the mall; I was holding eighteen-month-old Bethany.

I was unprepared for the emotional impact of 50,000 names on black marble. It was like a time machine, taking me back to the early 1970s and the Vietnam War with all the memories and emotions of that tumultuous period in my life with a draft number of eighteen.

I was choked up to the point of tears as I resurfaced to ground level and to the present time. Vicki and I each held a baby hand as we slowly headed back toward the Washington Monument. I couldn't talk and needed time to process the experience. I wanted to be left alone.

"You know, I could never live in the city," she started off casually. I didn't respond. "Don't you think it's indecent—all these people jogging around with so little on?"

Minimally engaged, I responded without thinking. "It's a good way to see the city. I used to enjoy that part of running."

Vicki was not interested in the merits of jogging as a method of sightseeing. "You're not staring at all those women, are you?" Her voice was quiet and furtive, a bit coaxing, as we walked back along the open expanse of winter grass.

"No. Will you quit it!" I was emotionally exhausted and still trapped in that time warp. After a pause, I added, "I've heard about the Vietnam Memorial but .... It's really something. It's..."

Vicki interrupted. "Did you see the blonde that just ran by here a minute ago?"

I didn't answer. Vicki began describing her outfit, her very skimpy outfit.

"No. Did I miss something? Did she have something that you don't have?"

"No. What about the girl in the green shorts—the ones up to her crotch?"

"Don't do this to me. I'm not in the mood." I responded.

"Just answer that. Please?" She was pleading. But her voice was demanding.

"And how many more?" I asked.

"Two or three. Please?" I was incognizant of the sincerity of her entreaties.

I answered three more questions and was stretched too thin, one foot in this world and one in a world twenty years gone by. I just wanted to be alone. The rest of the long walk through the winter grass was quiet.

The elevator queue for the Washington Monument was surprisingly short. "Let's go," I said, pointing all the kids in that direction.

Vicki countered, "Let's go home. I'm worn out." I didn't read the fear in her voice.

"Come on," I chided. "You'll survive and the kids will love it."

"No." Vicki became obdurate. I was very familiar with that tone of voice and was not in the mood for it.

"Let me rephrase this: I'm going up; do you want to come?"

My wife was also familiar with my tone of voice.

We soon crammed into the small elevator and took the slow, long ride up. Vicki's face was pallid as we exited at the top. The stone portholes were too high for the younger kids so I took turns lifting little bodies so they could see the view. Vicki buzzed around me and I didn't have to be psychic to know that there were more questions coming that I didn't want to deal with.

Vicki finally pinned me in a corner away from most of the other people.

"Look," I spit out, trying with only moderate success to keep my voice low, "I'm sick of questions. I don't want to deal with anything. Leave me alone."

There was frantic look of her face, but she was suddenly quiet and thinking. Her voice was low. "Let's go down the steps."

I had done it when I was fifteen. "That's a long walk. You've been complaining about walking for over an hour." I was mad.

"Please, Jody, something about the elevator is making me claustrophobic. I was choking; I could barely breathe. Please, Jody, I was terrified."

If I hadn't been so tired and emotionally drained, I might have been more sensitive to the honest desperation in her voice.

"Leave me alone," I said. I was sick of dealing with her and I knew she had a bucket load of questions. "Let's go, kids," I said in a moderately loud voice. "We're heading down."

After the elevator emptied its next load, I stepped in, again holding Bethany. The kids followed and Vicki straggled in last. There were several people between the two of us and I was glad for the distance, but not before I saw the pained expression on her face. The cubicle was tightly packed and I turned away from her.

At the base we disgorged from the elevator and I headed for a bench some distance away. I wanted to be off from the crowd for the litany of questions I knew would be coming. The kids followed, chattering amongst themselves. But something was obviously wrong with Vicki. She moved very slowly and she had that stiff-legged gait of a wind-up tin soldier. There was a blank, dazed look on her face. Latent guilt washed over me. Okay, I told myself, be nice about it and deal with a few questions.

Vicki held it together just long enough to ask me about a short, dark-haired woman with black hair—perhaps Mexican.

"I didn't see her," I said.

"She was on the elevator."

"I gathered that."

"She had dark hair."

"You already told me that."

"She may have been Mexican."

"You told me that. I didn't see her."

Vicki's voice was stiff. "She was short. And thick."

"And don't tell me: wearing a bikini with all of her stuff showing," I said sarcastically.

From that point on the discussion got raucous. The kids moved away from us. Jennifer picked up Bethany, who had been toddling around and then had suddenly wandered away from the racket. I'm sure at that point the kids wished they had a different set of parents.

Vicki's questions changed into a loud, derogatory harangue. At first she went into her familiar rage about my innate depravity. I yelled back, but I couldn't keep up with her. I was mad but she was something else. Soon she was screaming senseless epithets, but this time she didn't stop; in fact, it grew worse. She had never acted like this in public before. Something was wrong. Seriously wrong. She seemed to be demented. I expected her to begin foaming at the mouth. For ten minutes her screaming continued just below full voice. Finally, I thought, she crossed the line into lunacy.

"I've had it," I roared back suddenly.

I bolted and headed toward the Smithsonian. Stunned into silence and the present, she tried to gather the terrified kids together. They were unsure of what to do. Neither one of their parents looked like a good choice to follow at that point.

Her voice followed me, turning from animosity to beseeching.

As I stormed off, I told myself that I did not have to put up with this kind of nonsense. Normal people just did not rave about elevator rides. And other women. How did I get stuck with such a crackpot anyway? I told myself that I needed to be tough; that was the only way some people learned. She took advantage of the fact that I was willing to answer a few questions then she walked all over me. I've got to get tough and stay tough, I reminded myself over and over.

My pep talk lasted for three blocks. During that interval I purposely steered toward crowds where there were likely to be other women—such as bus stops. I tried to pretend that I was not related to the raving ding-a-ling and accompanying brood that was a block behind. Fifteen minutes later, with my anger subsiding, I concluded that I'd showed her who was boss. I parked in an isolated alcove and waited for her to catch up. Her and all of her questions. And the kids.

With that episode the trip lost its vacation flavor. The ride back on the Metro was quiet. The train was full of tired people wrapped up in their own lives. In a muted voice Vicki, somewhat apologetically, explained her extreme reaction at the Washington Monument. The closet effect of the elevator was more than she could handle. And there was something about the Mexican woman. That struck me as strange, since I had never noticed any prejudice on her part toward other women, especially the less attractive ones. She said her reaction was exacerbated by a sense of betrayal at my unwillingness to listen to her questions and acquiesce. I tried to explain that I could only take so much.

"Since I told you everything that happened to me, answer a few questions . . . ." Her voice was sincere and expectant. She used my guilt and sympathy to check out five other women who had bothered her since we boarded the train. And she reiterated her questions about the dark-skinned woman on the elevator at the Washington Monument.

We returned home late the next day; then it was Sunday and another difficult day at church. Our return into familiar territory did not diminish Vicki's apprehensive demeanor. It was only a few days later when things began to make sense. She told me that she'd had another memory. This one was of being three years old and being in her grandparents' basement. As she skipped around the cherished study of her grandfather, an unexpected hand reached out and grabbed her and pulled her into a small closet that was covered with a fabric curtain. She almost suffocated as she was forced to perform oral sex.

The last couple of entries in one of Vicki's journals are dated February 9 and 10. The first is a brief recap of the family trip we took to Washington D.C. with a Metro ticket taped in. She mentions staying at a bed and breakfast and touring the historical sites and going to the Washington Temple. She doesn't mention our brief lapse of sanity and doesn't remember any of it now. The next day she notes that her sister had twins. She then switches to another journal and gives this brief introduction:

'I don't have anywhere else to record this mess so I'm going to use this Journal. I hope people don't hate me for the horrors in it, but it needed to be recorded for my benefit so I can let it go.'

Feb. 15, 1989 Journal entry. Realized last week after listening to a tape and because of some experiences that my feelings are totally dissociated. In the mornings I always had a horrible feeling when Jody went in the girls' room to awaken them. Then he went in the bathroom and on the way out went "oopsie daisy." I remembered getting furious with him. I wanted to get up screaming. I tried to feel where it was coming from and remembered when I was 14, 15, 16 etc. Daddy coming up to awaken us while Mother was in the kitchen making breakfast. He ran his hands over my breasts and crotch and then went out in the hall saying, "Rise and Shine."

Feb. 20,1989 Journal entry. Realized how displaced my memories are. Had terrible rage for the last two days that I directed toward Jody mostly and Jennifer somewhat. Realized it must be related to the memory of my father and uncle. But I couldn't stop screaming at Jody. Last night Jennifer went to bed really sulky. It reminded me of times I cried myself to sleep when a child. I got extremely depressed and *started worrying about all kinds of things. Her committing suicide being the strong fear. Then I realized I felt extremely vulnerable and fearful about her. I discussed with Jody and he said suicide thoughts were unrealistic about her. I realized my intense feeling of fear and vulnerability were about me and the way I felt as a child. Especially at night because I never knew when my father was coming in to get me. This morning when Jody said something to Jennifer, I had the same feeling to a smaller degree. I realized I felt that vulnerability every time my father spoke to me. And now every time Jody speaks to Jennifer, I feel the same vulnerability.*

MORE MEMORIES

March, 1989

L ooking back, I can't get over how surprised I was at how physical this process of remembering was. The memories were locked in my body. Initially, I was not aware of this and would find myself falling apart without understanding what was going on. Jody would seem so incredibility irritating and then I would recognize that it wasn't Jody at all. I would become aware of certain body feelings. They were on a deep, cellular level. I would start freaking out (and with the stuff I was remembering there was good reason) and then gradually words and images would come. It was common for me to be upset for an entire day. Then I would gradually be able to focus in on the triggering episode—what was present-day action that had activated the body feelings. I would try to get Jody to change his behavior or rearrange our circumstances to avoid being triggered again.

Between March 7th and 10th Vicki's journal notes three graphic memories which included both anal and oral sex with her father.

March 13, 1989. Journal entry. Went to Roanoke. Dick for therapy and PU group (Parents United therapy group). At this point in my life I feel like they are my salvation. Had a bad, bad, bad episode at church on Sunday. Upset by a film shown in priesthood and cried and cried and cried. Afterward was A.M.'s baptism, and Erin was singing with her. I wanted to enjoy it. Got so mad at God, at Jody, at me. Dick says my growth was retarded by the incest and I was acting more like an eight -year-old.

Vicki's every-other-week sessions with Dick were occupied with her recent memories. He was impressed. He told her most people have to work hard to retrieve memories. Our prayers were certainly answered. And, as we would find out, the uproar at the Washington Monument was standard fare for doing memory work: We both suffered through the process of her remembering.

What happened over the next few months is one thing to describe on paper but something quite different to have lived through. In writing, I have had to sort everything out to make it linear and intelligible, but at the time it seemed that everything was happening at once. We were temporarily stunned with the turmoil that came with each new memory. It was that feeling of being blindsided that was so disorienting. Then, as we came to grips with and processed one event, something else in our day-to-day life would trigger a new memory from her forgotten past, and we would feel like we'd just been hit unexpectedly again from another direction. Again, this was something neither one of us was prepared for despite the numerous books we had read. (Vicki's journal notes five books on incest and sexual abuse that she had recently read.) Then, thinking it was all over, we would pick up the pieces and go back to our daily living. And then, without warning we would be blindsided again.

Memories were not just things that popped into my head. They caused tremendous physical and emotional feelings. I was overwhelmed with feelings of horrible shame, sweats, shaking, panic attacks, feeling like I was going to pass out, dizziness, feelings of being suffocated. The words "my father molested me"—the only thing that I remembered about the abuse of my childhood—was turning into something very physical. The word "molested" turned into what it really was: "rape of a child". Remembering hurt physically and emotionally and spiritually. My body relived everything and there was a certain amount of uproar around our house. And then I would review what I had learned with Dick in my next therapy session and he would push for more details.

The feeling of remembering was not unlike giving birth. When I got to the hard part of labor, I wanted to quit and forget about having a new baby and walk out of the hospital but it was too late. I had to keep going no matter how painful it was—because the process I'd already started was irreversible. Now, I was too far gone into the process of remembering to quit, but too scared to keep going. It was my love for my family and especially my oldest daughter that pushed me to recommit and to make the long drive to therapy that next Monday—and each long drive after that.

I didn't understand the dynamics at first, but these memories had lived for all these years behind a wall of fear. I wasn't allowed to tell anyone so I never did and eventually large portions of my life were placed beyond that wall. This had allowed me to survive and be "normal." But at this point in my life I finally felt safe enough to venture beyond that wall and deal with that overwhelming fear. That's what entering into therapy meant for me.

Dick never doubted the veracity of Vicki's memories. He had been guiding people through therapy for years and that gave me comfort that Vicki hadn't lost her marbles. These wild, unpredictable episodes—what we are referring to as memory work—were what we were aiming for. In the beginning, this new remembering seemed shocking and improbable. I couldn't help but question the dynamics of this new family history that she was creating. Vicki claimed her memories were clear and she often gave visual details of her surroundings, which was an important piece of validation for Dick. But being skeptical by nature, occasionally I would ask her questions later to see whether she remembered the same facts. She did.

For the most part, I came to the conclusion that she wasn't making things up—at least, not consciously—but I was reluctant to whole-heartedly believe. She was confident she was reliving her past in this process of "remembering" and from that point on she said she remembered the scene as any person would. Sometimes she would add to a new memory a day or two later by telling me what had happened hours after the close of the last remembered scene. One piece of memory would trigger other pieces—there was a cascading effect—and that probably had much to do with the memories blindsiding us the way they did.

Ever since I had met Tom—with that initial intuition—I habitually paid attention. Vicki often reminded me of his temper and violence when she was a child. Kids getting slapped around the house or in the back seat of the car was nothing. But my father had done that as well; it was common in our generation. Her mother Virginia came from a much different kind of family, and I suspected there were limits to what she would tolerate. She was respectful of Tom's role as head of the house, but she definitely was not spineless and I assumed that at some point she would have stepped in. So she either didn't know about it or Vicki's "memories" were something else.

I had only seen Tom's verbal rage the one time I mentioned earlier. I had never seen him act out physically. Over the years I had observed enough to recognize he had a seedy side; I didn't have to be clairvoyant to see that. Vicki's description of her childhood, the part where he was scoring every woman they passed on the side of the road, was easily believable. (Vicki was almost as bad with her questions.)

Once, when he was asking me about how our sewing business was doing, I showed him a full-color brochure of some popular, extra-frilly curtains that we were copying. I was surprised at the attention he was giving to the catalog until I realized it wasn't the curtains but the photo of the woman next to them that engrossed him. He scored her for me: He liked the bleached-blond hair and dolled-up look. But one of the problems for me was that I liked Tom. He had helped us time and time again. And most of the time he helped us just to help us; I rarely discerned an ulterior motive. And it wasn't just us; he helped all of his kids. He had helped with a downpayment on Vicki's sister's first house. He helped Jack get his business going. And Stephen, the diabetic son, was constantly getting help; off and on he lived in their house.

The question for me was just how real were these memories? Were they literally memories—like most people remember? Or were they embellished? Or was this a distinction without a difference? Are memories by their very nature part truth and part fiction? It bothered me that some of Vicki's memories related instances when she was sixteen years old. I could understand forgetting the ones that happened when she was younger; I didn't remember much of my early childhood. But sixteen? How do you forget something like that when you're sixteen years old? I had a hard time accepting that.

And there was another problem for me—or, as Vicki was fond of saying, "with me." My wife's memories were shocking, yes. The words were incredibly shocking, even if it was true that they were only partially factual. But there was a tendency for me to hear them on a verbal level and not imagine what they meant to the young child that had had to live them. She sometimes accused me of suffering from a serious deficit of empathy. Part of that was the verbal battering that I took with her memories, and the process of remembering itself came across as sketchy. I wanted something more tangible; I guess, I wanted proof. And part of me didn't want to believe her memories; I didn't want to believe that Tom had been like that. Perhaps I was open-minded to a fault, but I told myself that keeping an open mind was important.

But certain things were obvious and real—like the fact that we no longer had family meals together. Dick helped Vicki see that the scene was a trigger for a certain kind of attention that my wife hated as a child. Family night was another casualty; it disappeared from our weekly schedule. Vicki's projection of her childhood self on our older girls was certainly real; I saw them less and less.

For some time Vicki had been dreading her birthday at the end of March. She knew her parents would want to come up and celebrate. It was her fortieth and her mother was already making a big deal about it. But with the steady stream of memories and nightmares she had recently experienced, she did not want to face her parents.

April 4, 1989. Journal entry. A rough weekend.

My parents called Thursday and said they were coming up for my birthday to spend the night. I told them we already had plans for the weekend so I'd discuss this with Jody and call them back. We decided spending the night was too heavy-duty, so we invited them for Saturday at lunch and they could go on over to my sister's for the night. That was fine. They came. We all played "perfect family myth" and they went their way . . . . When we arose the next morning, we decided to go for a walk. I gave the older girls chores to do and told Joey to go outside. Jennifer griped. Jody jumped in and said she was right. Joey should have chores. I kept my mouth shut until we walked and then told him that had made me furious. He defended his right to do it. I told him he was favoring Jennifer and he told me "Most men would slap their wives for a statement like that." We separated and I couldn't get over it even after he semi-

apologized. I got so tense in my uterine area I could hardly stand it. At bedtime Jody adjourned to the couch—me to the bed. I was crying and crying—hysterical at times.

Finally it dawned on me there was a memory. I remembered the Christmas Eve when I was sixteen and came home a little late from delivering presents. Daddy slapped me all over the living room. I was crying hysterically and my friend Laurie called. She called Jim who I had just started dating. He came over and we talked. I went to my room. My father offered me orange juice and I was so hurt I turned him down. Later that night he came in and said he was sorry he'd slapped me and he'd make it up to me; then he raped me. I had an orgasm. The emotional betrayal was intense. I felt a large part of my spirit leave me at the time.

With that memory I cried until noon the next day. As soon as I had the memory, however, the intense cramping in my uterine area relaxed and I was able to sleep.

DIVORCE?

April, 1989

On a Sunday in early April, as we were nearing the end of our three-hour block of worship and classes, Keith, our branch president,[3] asked if he could have a word with me. My first thought was that Vicki was confessing all my faults—and probably exaggerating them as she was prone to do. More than once I'd voluntarily come to him to unload the guilt I felt at not being able to handle my wife's craziness any better. He was remarkably understanding and nonjudgmental. He told me he'd have a difficult time dealing with the situation that I was in, and he actually thanked me for using him as a confessor.

Over the years Keith had been helpful. He had worked with our oldest son during his final year at home, which had been very trying, and had interested him in serving a church mission. Also, during one of our down times in the business, as the hospital administrator, he had pushed a huge drapery job to us. And now he was counseling with my wife almost every Sunday, sometimes for several hours at a time.

I was immensely grateful for the respite. And Vicki inevitably came out in a better mood. Dick had once told Vicki that he thought that his therapy and the PU group offered more spirituality and support than church ever could. Keith was proving him wrong. I was astounded at Keith's patience in dealing with Vicki. I think he saw counseling with her as a challenge. He occasionally talked in our Sunday men's group meeting of the many seminars he attended

---

3   The equivalent of a lay pastor in a small Mormon congregation.

on management theory and communication. He was keen on learning how to handle people and Vicki was a constant test of his skills.

Keith motioned me into his office, which also doubled as a classroom for the young men, whom he also taught. I sat on one of the several chairs against the wall and he took his seat behind his desk. He had a clean-cut, successful look, much like Vicki's younger brother. But I knew from previous conversations that he had come from a broken home. I knew how much he hated divorce. Like me, he had seen its destructiveness. Like my father, his father had been a philanderer and had left his mother, and he once confided the pain of being invited to his father's second marriage. His mother had numbed out much of his childhood years on prescription drugs. We actually had a lot in common.

"I really like working with your children," he started. "They are well-behaved and seem to be very grounded." He flattered me with a few more accolades about our kids.

He suddenly changed tact. "I'd like to come out and visit." His voice was serious.

I was taken aback. Being an hour away from church, we rarely got visitors. And he was another fifteen minutes further away.

"I'd like to talk to you about your marriage," he continued.

"Well, I guess you're getting to be an expert on our marriage," I said.

He smiled at my humor.

"Actually your wife has been putting me in a very uncomfortable position."

I tried to sympathize with the fact that he was often called on to pick up the pieces at church after one of Vicki's breakdowns, which usually centered around other women. I told him how much I appreciated it.

Keith slowly shook his head. "That's not it." His face was grim. "Vicki has asked me if the Church would help support her if she moved out."

I was stunned. Then angry. As much as I was putting up with her craziness, and now she was doing this behind my back? I immediately started thinking of ways to pay her back.

"She's brought the issue up several times." As Keith talked, it was obvious that he saw himself in the position of trying to add some balance to a precarious marriage. He said my wife had been complaining about my shortcomings, but that he was well aware of my sacrifices and was perplexed. He wanted to come out for a personal visit and work on some of the issues that Vicki had brought up. He thought he could help.

In dead earnestness, he waited for a response from me. The shock and then the anger gradually dissipated as I plumbed my inner resources, trying to get a handle on this troubling news.

Slowly, I began to chuckle.

Keith cocked his head. He had no idea what was so funny.

"Do you think she'd really do it?" My chuckle broke into a light laugh. I was suddenly struck by the ludicrousness of my wife's prattling.

"She sounded serious," he responded, confused by my reaction.

"How in the world is she going to keep track of me if we separate?" I laughed at the preposterousness of the thought. "Vicki could not survive not knowing exactly where I was, and especially with *whom*."

Whenever I was fed up with her ranting and wanted to crush her, all I had to do was just mention the name of another woman. Instantly, she was so insecure that the only thing she wanted was reassurance. I could get her to beg like a trained dog if I wanted to by simply mentioning an old girlfriend of mine. Not understanding the depth of Vicki's jealousy Keith could not appreciate the humor, but my laughter relaxed him. The keen edge was taken off and he set an appointment to come out on Friday.

I mentioned this to Vicki on our long drive home.

"That's great. He's someone you can talk to." My wife was certain that all my problems (by this she meant not being able to deal with her in a way that was more to her liking) related to a lack of therapy on my part.

I rolled my eyes and then there was a sudden well of silence from her side of the car. I knew what was coming next.

"He's not bringing his wife, is he?" The fear in her voice was palpable.

I couldn't help but laugh out loud. "I don't think so. But maybe you ought to check." I knew she would.

His wife was a major focus of my wife's jealousy, part of what I derogatorily referred to as her "twenty questions"—our weekly church debriefing. And now Vicki started up again. As if she was picking out defects in an animal bloodline, she began telling me everything negative she could think of about Keith's wife. I had to at least nod, but she preferred that I verbally agree with her. Vicki was particularly concerned with the sexual parts of her body. She was definitely her father's daughter when it came to scoring women. No matter how hard I tried I could not convince her that I had no reason to be interested in anyone else. And then sometimes Vicki's questions got lewd.

"I swear," I said in mock surprise, "it sounds like you've got the hots for her."

That shut my wife up, at least for the rest of this trip home. I told myself to remember that line in the future when I got fed up with her incessant questions. Nine times out of ten she could out-think me; it was nice to win one every once in a while.

It never ceased to amaze me that a woman so confident and competent as my wife could melt into an insecure mess over something as petty as another woman. It didn't make sense; this didn't seem like the woman I'd met some thirteen years ago; the one who seemed so comfortable in the world and capable of getting out of life what she wanted. And it didn't have to be a particularly good-looking woman. Her preferences seemed to be bleached-blonde hair and that brassy dolled-up look. If there was a deficit of clothing, that of course would set her off. It didn't take a whole lot of thinking to recognize that she was a radar for her father's preference in women.

THE OFFENDERS' GROUP

1988—1990

Based on her previous experience with the women's support group that she had started in Raleigh many years earlier, she had been disappointed with the survivor's group in Roanoke. She longed for the sharing that took place among women with a common thread of interest that had created a bond that was like family. With the promise that Dick had given her of a different kind of healing that took place in groups, she decided to try to attend the men's group when she recommitted herself to therapy late that fall.

I was in pain and willing to do whatever. I was also growing spiritually and wanted to see what I would get from the principle of forgiveness. I was promised at church that as soon as I forgave my father I would be free of pain. Understanding my father was the first step toward forgiveness. By understanding these men I hoped to understand my father.

In addition, I was a social worker at heart. For as long as I could remember I wanted to see what made this sociological group of men tick. They were the pariahs of society, the untouchables. I was learning that my father was one of them. I wanted to understand him and because of his abuse I felt connected to these men.

Vicki had to petition to join the men's group. This offender's group, which had been on-going for several years, had never had a woman victim join before. There were two women who attended—a wife and a girlfriend of two of the perpetrators—but never a survivor of sexual abuse. With the hostility of the women's group down the hall, there was a legitimate concern about the attitude that Vicki might bring into the group. But my wife, during a special interview, assured the supervisor of programs that her goal was understanding and forgiveness. She wanted to comprehend what turned a man—a man that might have been hurt as a child—into a perpetrator. Her limited knowledge of her father's background hinted that there well may have been abuse and/or neglect. But all men didn't respond to such abuse that way. So why had her father? And ultimately, forgiveness was her goal: that's what our religion taught, and she wanted to put the past behind her.

The director told my wife he would ask the men themselves; they would make the decision. The men in the offender's group were wary but curious and gave my wife tentative approval to attend.

Almost all of the men in the group were court-ordered to attend. It was part of their probation after spending a certain amount of time in jail. Parents United, which was the name of the national organization, had trained the local police and judicial system, touting a much lower recidivism rate with their program. But their rules were strict. Roll call was taken at each meeting. As with Dick, if someone didn't show up, the moderator was required to call the police, and the non-attender was immediately picked up and sent to jail. And as with Dick, the men were there and they were on time. Some of the men were allowed to work during the week and spend the nights and/or weekends in jail. The system advocated flexibility with regard to the terms of probation or parole depending on the seriousness of the abuse and the individual's danger to society; the recommendations of therapists had much to do with this outcome. There was an obvious incentive for these men to invest in their own healing.

One of the group's cardinal rules was confidentiality: what was said in the group stayed in the group. (This was before the mandatory disclosure laws that swept the country several years later.) This allowed the men to talk about what could be crimes without the fear of it being held against them in court.

I remember my first time walking in to the group. There were about twenty men that attended. We were seated in a circle with an elongated tail—

like a teardrop. At the point of the tail was the therapist. There were two women therapists who seemed to alternate moderating the group. Their job was to keep the discussion on track, to keep it real and to prevent it from becoming pornographic.

The vibrational energy was certainly calmer and more humble than the women's group. These were people who were ashamed of who they were and what they had done, and did not know how to change. At least, that is how they appeared. I was surprised at how ordinary they looked. The guy across from me to the right was a John Denver look-a-like with his skinny ponytailed girlfriend. She was very plain looking and had the same deer-caught-in-the-headlight look in her eyes as he did. The other man that I remember was potbellied and Archie Bunker-ish sitting next to his wife who was very heavy-set, with cheaply dyed red hair and a belligerent look on her face. After all, she was trying to keep a marriage together in which her husband had cheated on her with their daughters.

After I'd been going for a while another man joined. He was handsome looking in a well-cut suit and had just been caught. His highly paid attorney had started him in the group so it would look better to the judge when he was tried. It was obvious that he was trying to play the system and avoid jail time, or at least extended jail time. It was also obvious that he had a long way to go before he came to terms with what brought him there, because he was reluctant to talk.

The men that I remembered could be gregarious and charming. It wasn't their normal group persona but occasionally it came out. That gave me pause. I have noticed over the years that many sex offenders have manipulative personalities. That was often how they got away with it.

All of the men said that they had been sexually abused themselves as children, but they had not remembered it until they were court-mandated into therapy. Archie Bunker once said that he'd grown up thinking that sexual abuse was normal because he had been abused by his father and uncles as a child. He thought it was like speeding: everybody did it; you just weren't supposed to get caught. And he also said he would rail at sex offenders when they were shown on TV: "They ought to cut their you-know-what off." He had been able to compartmentalize his own behavior.

With each new arrival the custom was for everyone in the group to tell their story. I learned that John Denver had lost his wife and two daughters after he had been exposed. His wife had left and wouldn't have anything to do with him, and he was grateful for his current girlfriend. Unlike any of the other men, he was there after his parole was up because he wanted to remind himself of the cost of his misconduct. Most of the other men were not as open with information. This group was part of their parole and that was why they were there, but they didn't have much to say.

The group was always courteous and friendly to me. I knew I was an oddity to them, an example of how their victims might grow up, but a different example than the women down the hall. I knew that some of those other victims had verbally accosted these men in the halls and the parking lot. These men would not have reported it because they felt so guilty. Archie's wife once told the group how horrified she was at the anger in the women's group. I was different. I was often dressed up because I had estimates to do for our business and the men probably thought I had it together. They never saw the other parts of me, the times when I came unglued. I was someone who did not condemn them but rather wanted to understand them. I'm sure they appreciated that. In some ways it probably helped the conversations in the group for me to be there. I am sure they did not want to believe that the women's group down the hall represented how every sexually abused woman turned out.

From these men I learned firsthand how hard it was to be a sex addict in our sexually saturated society. These men were all addicts; they were obsessed with sex. It was always on their minds, and they had little control over those thoughts. They often talked about how hard it was living in our contemporary society. It was like being an alcoholic and constantly having a drink thrust into your hand. Pictures of little girls in alluring adult outfits were common on TV, on billboards and in magazines. Even cartoons were sexualized. Even Disney characters. I learned that we, as women, were contributing to the problem with our increasingly immodest dress.

The men turned me on to their handbook called Out of the Shadows[4] *This book served as a Bible to some of these men. Jody and I both read it. It talked about the nature and breadth of sexual addiction and how self-destructive it was. We learned that sex was an uncontrolled addiction for some people; one that was often clustered with other addictions. That was a possible*

---

4   Out of the Shadows: Understanding Sexual Addiction by Patrick Carnes, Ph.D. Hazelden Publishing, 2001. Originally published in 1983.

clue in discerning perpetrators. They also often went to great and crazy lengths to get that rush; sometimes that was how they got caught. Jody and I both wondered if the premature initiation into sex—obviously the case in child sex abuse—didn't somehow contribute to its addictive quality in the victim.

I also learned from my reading that most perpetrators had many victims, and it made me wonder about my father. Were there other little girls? I was keeping my eyes open. I didn't know of anyone else. I hadn't seen other addictions with him either. He didn't drink at all. Although his temper had often been violent during my younger days, I would not call him reckless. On the contrary, he was quite controlled.

Mostly, the group gave me hope. "Sex offenders" stopped being a category for me, but now represented a group of men, each with their own heartrending story. These men, to varying degrees, had made the decision to change. It was not on their own volition but because they had been caught and were being forced to attend both individual therapy and this group by the legal system. But these men now wanted to change, and if they wanted to change then maybe my father . . . . Maybe he could be rehabilitated. He could be like these men, willing to admit that he had done something wrong, and be willing to change. That would help with my healing.

Looking back on the year plus that I spent in that group, I see sex offenders as the lepers of society. We want to hide them so we don't have to be faced with the debris of our sexually saturated society. They became my friends in the sense that although we did not have a relationship outside of group, I did come to respect the effort they were putting into changing. We had that in common and I hope it was mutually reinforcing.

The group was a support to me in the sense that I started to learn what the word "forgiveness" means. I began to learn that only the Lord has the right to judge and that I was not mature or smart enough to judge the other participants of the group. I couldn't decide if their shameful acts were merely an extension of what had been done to them, or if they were a manifestation of pure evil. To this day, I have no clue whether they would abuse again if the opportunity arose. At the time, I wanted to believe that therapy could heal all and that the face that these men brought to the meetings was not simply a group persona. But now, twenty-five years later, I believe less and I know better.

THE BATTLEGROUND
OF SHAME

March, 1989

My initial excitement that the exorcism of these memories was going to be a quick-fix for my wife wore off. It had been two long months and there was no sign that things were getting better. I had naively thought that a few childhood memories along with a little debriefing on Dick's part, and we would soon start living happily ever after—like that Indian-summer honeymoon. My hope from everything I had read was that there would be some sort of cognitive regeneration when Vicki got back to the original incest episode. She would relive the horror, of course, but the evidence of healing would almost immediately commence. The confirmation would be the gradual disappearance of these haunting memories and then of the related character flaws. And there was a grain of truth to my presumption. After each memory Vicki briefly felt better and there was certainly more insight into her craziness.

After each new memory we had a fleeting respite of hope that we had finally plumbed the depth—that this was "The One" we had been looking for and it would soon be all over. But the memories kept tumbling out and each one seemed to be more traumatic than the last. While this was not universally true, it did seem to be the general pattern. That was one thing that gave me hope that we were heading in the right direction, that we would ultimately get to that core incident. But it was confusing to me that her memories did not consistently regress toward a younger and younger age;

that was definitely not a pattern. The memories bounced all over the place: one at age six, then sixteen and the next at age five.

We didn't recognize it at the time, but later it became obvious: Yes, the memories were getting more traumatic. But even more importantly, as Vicki remembered more, she was gradually spending more and more time living in the past. When you added the anticipatory unease that we never seemed to notice, the sudden flashback and memory itself that always seemed to catch us off-guard, and then the gradual defusing of the anger that inevitably came with this process, each episode took several days to process. Then there would be a pause for days or weeks. If several memories were clustered together, they might swallow up most of a week. It began to color her daily reality; she began living in a hostile, treacherous world: the world of her childhood, full of both physical and emotional pain. The fact that her reaction to living so much in the past would generate friction in our family's present day-to-day life is to be expected; I just didn't know that at the time and my capacity to handle it was limited.

As much as possible we were all just trying to keep things on an even keel by carrying on with the daily routines of life. I was inevitably thinking that this was probably the last memory because it was worse than the previous one and it would be over soon. I would tell myself to keep calm and just hang in there: a little bit longer, a little bit longer. The daily grind of sewing work at my shop was a godsend—anything to get out of the house and take my mind elsewhere.

Vicki now had no problem with incentive for her trips to Roanoke on Mondays. She considered them her salvation. So much more than anyone else, Dick and the offender's group understood what she was going through—or at least allowed her to talk about it. She could talk about sex and incest and not get stares and grasps that she had broken the taboo of silence. Church was particularly difficult because everyone wanted to pretend that things like that didn't really happen to good people; and, by definition, good people are those who go to church. The women tended to shun her; the implicit assumption was that maybe she wasn't so good. Beyond Keith, few people wanted to listen to her. Then, every so often, a woman would come up to her afterward in the parking lot and secretly confess that something like that had happened to her. But those conversations were not allowed in church. It was hush-hush—an unholy subject.

With the chaos of her memories overwhelming us, Dick told Vicki that she had gotten to a crisis point and suggested that she start coming to Roanoke every week instead of every other week. But Vicki balked. The five hours of driving combined with the long days of leaving just after noon and returning after midnight were too much. They were a drain on the family, both physically and financially.

Dick compromised by having my wife write him a letter once a day. It was an extension of their therapy time. Then she would bring them every other Monday. These letters make a poignant diary, telling of the squalid condition of her life. *'I just want to pretend I'm a normal housewife/mother with a loving husband and eight beautiful children.'* But in reality her life was filled with shadows and dark compulsions. She saw sex everywhere that she looked. Unable to admit the feelings in herself, she projected them on me. I was a lewd maniac—like her father—undressing every woman that I saw. And the quandary went deeper than that. Her father had been careful to allow her to climax, often repeatedly. *'Orgasm! How could my body respond? How could it betray me? If it could do it then, it might do it again. I want to vomit all the badness out of me—all the shame for getting any pleasure out of it.'* She was mad at her own body for its God-given capacity, which her father had abused. Living so much of her time in the past, the benefit of perspective eluded my wife.

'Dick said I was abused emotionally as well as physically. He said my father took a normal little girl's emotions of love and enthusiasm for her father and twisted them into something sexual. I didn't turn frigid because I stayed turned on—at a tremendous cost to my psyche—shame.'

For Vicki, shame was not the feeling of *doing* something bad but rather of *being* something bad. The abuse had been degrading and it had clung to the inside of her making her feel dirty and worthless. The shame that would come naturally with this kind of abasement was compounded by her father's use of the term "whore." It shows up in several of her memories as an appellation. And he used the following ditty one morning after abusing her the night before: *'You were such a good little whore that I had to come back for more.'* Her adult self recognized the obvious—that it hadn't been her fault—and a much deeper part of her remembered that she wasn't a "whore" but rather a child of God. But the internal struggle of these parts of herself created a battlefield and that often oozed into our daily lives. From time to time It certainly felt like we were living in a war zone.

The desire to deflect shame and turn it into anger is understandable. With the turmoil that her shame was causing at home, one of the first assignments that Dick gave to Vicki was designed to sharpen the focus of her anger on her father. She was to take a picture of her father and pelt it with raw eggs. It took several weeks for my wife to get the courage together. She came back smug, but it was short-lived.

> *March 7, 1989. Journal entry. Knew there was another memory down there. The one when I was seven and my mother had Jack and had to go back to the hospital. She talks about how wonderful Dad was brushing our hair and shooing us off to school. I remember it with horror. Have been in a horrible mood for days. Depressed, irritable, nauseous, neck hurts. Wanted to wait until I felt better to start remembering, but decided I was physically feeling bad because my body had already started remembering. So in I jumped. Into the murky past. Daddy doing oral sex on me. Over and over again keeping my body turned on. Making me do the same to him. Swallowing the semen. Feeling like I was going to vomit . . . Squeezing my neck. Pinching it. And for the first time trying anal intercourse. The pain happening over and over again. A seven-year-old in an orgy while my mom was in the hospital.*

Vicki had grown up hearing the story from her mother about what a great father Tom had been, taking a week of leave from active duty to care for the whole house when Virginia had gone back into the hospital on an emergency basis with sudden profuse bleeding after the birth of her youngest. And similarly, Vicki had often heard her mother brag about Tom's paternal concern when he made special arrangements to take a boat to Hawaii instead of flying because five-year-old Vicki was terrified of flying. But Vicki she remembered that voyage differently.

March 20, 1989. Journal entry. More memories. On Saturday I remembered the boat nightmare. Age five. Laying in the bottom bunk in our stateroom at night. Daddy getting in bed. Lifting my gown. Sucking my little nipples, playing with my clitoris with his finger. Then pushing my head down for oral sex on him. Pinching my neck. Hurting it.

The fact that Virginia had overlaid little Vicki's reality with this rose-colored version of her father only added to the confusion, deepening the shame. '*How could my father be like that? Maybe it wasn't his fault, maybe it was mine?*' This was Saint Tom who earned the admiration of all the other stay-at-home mothers in their Richmond neighborhood where they had lived when Jack was born. He had single-handedly cared for the baby and three older kids when Virginia had to go back into the hospital. He was certainly not a child molester. Saints weren't child molesters.

To help counteract the shame, Dick carefully choose a pet name for my wife. He called her "sweetheart." And that's what this little girl wanted to be— this little girl that went to the Baptist church each Sunday, enjoyed vacation Bible school, and did volunteer work with the handicapped children—the children with Downs Syndrome and Spina Bifida—at the local hospital. She had wanted to be *good*. And that had been taken from her—very violently taken from her.

"When is this going to end?" Vicki asked toward the end of one of her sessions with Dick. "I'm tired of having such an ugly past; I'm tired of therapy; I just want to go on with my life. I just want to be a mother again. And have a decent relationship with Jody . . . ."

"Well, if you spent one month in therapy for each year of abuse and subsequent denial, that would be close to four years," Dick said with a gentle smile.

"Four years. That's way too long."

Dick counseled patience.

"The memory work is almost over. It's got to be the hardest part ..." It didn't sound like it, but Vicki meant it as a question.

"The hardest part is always the part you're doing at the time."

Vicki did not like that answer. "What's next?"

"There's still more work to do before we go to the next step." Dick was guessing there were still important memories remaining. "You've been courageous."

Vicki liked the fact that Dick called her "courageous."

"You're such a sweetheart," he said.

Vicki wasn't the only one who hoped the memory work was almost over. I certainly did, and not only for her sake but for my own. While I didn't handle her misplaced anger perfectly, I still thought I should be canonized. This was by far the hardest thing that I'd ever done in my life. It was especially difficult to pick up the pieces after I'd lost it—after she'd attacked me for being her father. But I knew how much our children needed a mother—Lord help them if they only had me as a dad. I also figured I owed her because of my early violence; she had put up with a lot from me.

But upon years of reflection I now see something else, something much more basic and pervasive: I hated the way my father did not deal with my mother's issues and I didn't want to be like my father. At the time, he may not have recognized them as anything more than a problem with alcohol, but my father didn't care enough to step in—didn't care enough about his wife and didn't care enough about his kids. What my father would have found if he'd taken the time was that alcohol was not the problem; rather, it was my mother's way—as self-destructive as it was—of self-medicating a much deeper problem.

So there were good days and bad days around our house. Things ran relatively smoothly on good days. Vicki handled the children and her part of the business. She had less energy for scouting out work, but she did have the idea that Roanoke had more business potential because it was so much larger than any of the small towns that surrounded our home.

After meeting with Dick one afternoon that spring, she stopped at some townhouses under construction. She got a phone number and eventually met with the interior designer who did not handle window treatments and worked out an arrangement. For the next year my wife had a steady flow of clients, and her trips to Roanoke usually included some sort of business. For Vicki that meant leaving a couple of hours earlier and being able to write off dinner out as a business expense. There was a noticeable uptick in our income which I interpreted as a blessing for living through this difficult time. And it was comforting to know my wife had not lost her professional acumen.

A DEAD CAT

March, 1989

I relished Monday evenings and the time off that they gave me. Listening to my wife's memories and her sessions with Dick and her group were fine; actually, it was fascinating. But there was a certain unreality to it; it was like going to a medium or visiting an oracle as she recreated her past. I didn't want to live in the world she was creating where grown men molested their little girls—a world where these men engendered sympathy because they were victims themselves, acting out what they had learned as children or acting under dark compulsions initiated with their own abuse. For me it was too complicated emotionally and I didn't want to get too close to it. I was afraid of what might happen to me if I did.

But there was one profound complication: We both knew the next step in her healing was to confront her parents. That would definitely be real, with concrete implications. It promised to be difficult; more than difficult. While the expanding mass of her memories was consistent and created a certain amount of psychological evidence and Dick certainly believed it, even Vicki wanted something that we considered *proof*. I didn't think she could take the next step based on her memory work alone.

March 20, 1989. Journal entry. Saw a film where a little girl's goat was sacrificed to keep her quiet. Did he ever do that to me? Was my cat accidentally killed when I was three or intentionally? Did he use that threat to guarantee my silence?

Vicki decided that this film (that she initially saw in her Roanoke men's group) would be useful for our church to see, to help them understand what she was going through. Perhaps it might engender some sympathy. To our surprise, Keith agreed to show it. Then, at the last minute, Keith decided that he ought to preview it and a few of us watched it after our regular block of meetings. While Vicki and I lived in a world inundated with sex and incest, the film was obviously too strong to be shown to the congregation as a whole. But it did an excellent job of showing the twisted psyche that results from sexual violation, from the betrayal of trust, and from the shame and sense of powerlessness that comes with being a victim.

The film gave Keith and me the insight we sorely needed to keep working with Vicki because the story of the little girl in the film was almost an exact overlay of Vicki's. It provided validation, along with a shot of energy and compassion. It told us that Vicki wasn't crazy, that her acting-out behavior was typical for what she had been through. This affirmation from another outside source was precisely what we needed to keep going forward.

Near the end of the film my wife broke out in tears when the father killed his daughter's pet goat. The neck of the cute beast was slit and the father told the terrified little girl that if she ever revealed anything, she could expect the same fate. On the way home from church that Sunday my wife told me that the same thing must have happened to her. She felt certain because of the strength of her reaction.

Days later Vicki had a dream and then a series of vague intuitions. She told me the story of being three years old at their house in Atlanta. Her father took her new white cat from behind the front tire of their car . . . .

'. . . . I was three. My cat was laying behind my parents' car. (It was white and there was a garage.) It was dead. The car did not look like it had moved enough to run over it. My father held the dead cat under my nose. Later he picked me up to take me to my grandparent's car. On the way he said, "Remember the cat. That's what will happen to you if you tell."'

"You know, I am not sure the cat was run over. I'll bet he killed it—just like in the film."

This was stretching her credibility. By now, I knew better than to say, "Are you sure you're not imaging this?" But I couldn't help but wonder if she hadn't picked it up from the film. That made more sense than adding this new debit to her father's character. But we had read that killing a child's pet to ensure silence was not uncommon. That was the point of the film. My mind had a difficult time stretching to keep up with these new attributions to Tom's character. It just did not seem like her father—the one that I knew— although radical change was certainly possible. Could he have changed from the mean man of her memories to the seedy but generous and engaged father that he was today? I guessed it was possible . . . . ?

That spring we got word that my mother's cancer was in total remission; that was an answer to prayer. She was scheduled for radiation treatments in May; my sister would help with those and then in June she would go back to work sporting a wig. It was a remarkable turnaround.

But before we could celebrate, we started getting bad news about Vicki's brother Stephen.

April 22,1989. Journal entry. Steve had a stroke and is in the hospital with his left side paralyzed.

May 24, 1989. Journal entry. Stephen had another stroke. His third in six weeks. His speech is affected and so is his right side. He can't walk. He's very upset and so am I. Oh, I wish that he had the peace that only God can give.

Stephen was almost thirty-seven years old. He had been diagnosed with childhood diabetes when he was seven, and Vicki remembered much of her childhood being tempered with his diagnosis. His diabetes had always been a family affair. She and her siblings were only allowed two cookies at a time and once a week there was desert which was always made with *Sweet & Low.* Stephen always had to use an artificial sweetener. He had been to a special summer camp for young diabetics where he learned to give himself shots.

The whole time I'd known him he'd been angry and ill-tempered; it was not explosive but rather seemed to be constantly smoldering. The anger seemed to ooze out of him. He could not hold a job for any length of time even though he was a skilled carpenter. On more than one occasion—during his down times—Vicki had suggested that I hire him, but the hostility that he radiated was too strong for me; I couldn't be around him.

In addition to his sporadic work history, he had minor health problems that were a constant challenge. He medicated these complications and his mood with illegal drugs and alcohol. This reached a climax some ten years earlier when he blacked out while driving to work one morning, crossing the center line and colliding head-on with another car. The young woman in the other car was disabled for life. (While Vicki's parents visited the disabled young woman, Stephen never could. He felt horribly guilty.) The police found that his blood was full of alcohol.

His troubles were multiplied exponentially when he was pulled over several weeks later for weaving across the center line. When searching his car for drugs, the police found a loaded revolver under his seat. The district attorney went after him for hard time. It was only an expensive lawyer and a tearful courtroom plea from Tom that saved Stephen from prison.

For a time he swore off his dangerous lifestyle. But after his probation ended, Stephen was back with his old friends and heavily into drugs, headed toward self-annihilation.

After that first stroke, Vicki immediately wanted to see her brother. But we had started to notice a pattern: Whenever she was around her father, I was inevitably pummeled by her anger afterwards and that destabilized our house. I said no to the visit with Stephen.

After his second stroke, Vicki was on the phone with Stephen every night. She claimed that she had the intuition that he would soon die and she wanted to see him one last time. That only amped up the tension between us.

With the third stroke I knew we were going to have to go and visit, but I still dragged my feet. Abruptly, Vicki changed her tack in dealing with me. Knowing of my interest in her memory work, she came up with the idea of researching the old family photo albums. These were the traditional source of clues. In particular, she wanted to investigate the incident at age three with the dead cat. Had her memory of such a cat been accurate? I was intrigued but skeptical; she wanted validation. But the timing seemed to be critical and we began making plans.

Our arrival was memorable. Just as we got out of the car, there was a small pop and then a long whistling sound as a very worn tire I had been keeping my eye on went flat.

Our kids crashed through the front door, excited to be at Grandma's. Vicki shepherded them downstairs. I entered with trepidation, not knowing what kind of mood or state of infirmity to expect from Stephen. My apprehension was immediately justified. Virginia whispered that Stephen was in a foul mood and that she had no idea what to do. He had just gotten back from the doctor and would not talk to anyone. Virginia expected the worst.

I retired to the living room while my wife went to Stephen's bedroom. Twenty minutes later she returned. The look on her face told me she'd had a workout.

"Boy, have I got some news . . . ." she said, goading my curiosity.

"What?"

"First, you've got to tell me some things."

It was time for twenty questions. I sighed but was in a relatively placid mood. She had three women she had to check off her list. With that satisfied she told me the bad news that her parents were unable to get from Stephen. The doctor confirmed that the last stroke had taken a permanent toll on his masculinity; and with his ability for work, at best, already seriously impaired, what was there to live for? Big sister tried to answer those questions but nothing she said mattered. Stephen's response was loose talk of suicide.

Vicki also said that her father had stopped her as she existed Stephen's room. Tom, well-read in diabetes, had guessed the diagnosis of impotence from Stephen's belligerent attitude on the drive home. He also guessed that Stephen would talk to Vicki about it. He just wanted confirmation. Later, when I saw Tom, his face mirrored Stephen's grief. He now had a son who could not function in life in the only two ways that mattered. I remembered the sign Tom had posted on his flea-market booth from a decade and a half earlier: "Life is a good woman and a good paying job." With the hope of either seriously dashed, I wondered just how long Stephen would hang on.

After the meal Vicki pulled out the old family albums. Feigning innocence, she cruised back through time. It was interesting to note that the plump child of two, who at the time refused to wear anything but dresses, had turned into a steely-eyed wraith at six and seven. It was easy to transpose the information we were gleaning from her memories onto that older child. But was it true? Was there a sense of desperation behind that knowing smile— that smile that said it knew too much for her age?

When she got to the photos of herself at age three, she exclaimed, "There's our old car. I remember that." She elbowed me and nodded conspiratorially. It was a black De Soto. She whispered, "Just like I remember."

Virginia followed with an account of their life in what had now turned into a downtown Atlanta slum. She was careful to point out that it had been a nice place to live thirty-five years ago. She seemed to love reminiscing and was effusive with information.

"Mother, didn't I have a cat back then?" Vicki asked. We both held our breath.

Without skipping a beat Virginia acknowledged that Vicki had had a white cat and continued with her history lesson.

"Whatever happened to that cat?" Vicki interrupted.

Before Virginia could answer, Tom got up and growled, "Shut up, Virginia! Let's talk about something else."

Both of us were dumbfounded by the timing and the sharpness of Tom's reaction—his overreaction. It not only seemed to answer the question that was on our minds, but it did so with an exclamation point. Her memory was accurate! And if this farfetched memory from age three was true, the other ones probably were as well.

An hour later, after I finished putting the spare tire on the old station wagon and we were loading the kids, Tom pulled a credit card out of his pocket. He gave it to his daughter.

"Get some new tires on that car," he said in his usual gruff voice. "I saw in the paper just a minute ago that Sears is having a sale. They have your size." And then in a much softer voice, which came across as artificial, "And if the kids need anything . . . ."

Once inside the car and on the road, I asked, "What do you think?"

"I think my father didn't want to talk about the cat," she said with a smile that spoke with new assurance that she knew she was right—and had been all along.

THAT FABULOUS FATHER'S DAY

May, 1989

Mother's Day of that year was a sad day. For several weeks Vicki had been bleeding with a miscarriage that she didn't want to admit to herself. It was the second one since Bethany's birth. The implication was obvious: This baby-lovin' momma was running out of baby-makin' days. I was sympathetic, which Vicki appreciated. While I didn't understand the emotions involved with her memory work, I knew my wife well enough to understand that this change of life would be distressing for her. Personally, I had ambivalent feelings. Under Vicki's tutelage I'd grown to love having babies around, but I wouldn't miss her slightly underhanded way of filling our house.

Her OB doctor, who by then knew us well, agreed to meet us at his office that Sunday afternoon. There he did a D & C, and then wasted his breath telling Vicki not to get pregnant again for at least six months. Without realizing it, the good doctor had issued a challenge to my wife.

The next day Dick echoed the same caution. He told her that her therapy was too demanding and it wasn't a good time for her to get pregnant. He too was wasting his breath.

The only upside to that sad day was that our church responded. The women did not understand her strange behavior and the therapy she was going through. She had become a pariah in the congregation. But they did understand a miscarriage. They understood how much Vicki loved her babies; we had a pew full. They responded by providing us with meals, trucking them out over an hour to our house. That was gratifying, especially for Vicki.

When Vicki heard that her sister was going on a family vacation to the beach with their parents, she met with her sister and explained what she'd remembered from her childhood. Several of her memories (not noted in this story) occurred at the beach. While she had not seen any indication that her father's deviancy was still ongoing, Vicki urged caution based on what she'd learned from Dick and the Parents United group.

Her sister did not take this information well. She considered the very thought of anything so heinous to be a betrayal of the family trust. It appeared to Vicki that her sister was going out of her way to put her kids in jeopardy. Her sister apparently did not remember their childhood the same way.

In early June, after missing several appointments, Vicki returned to Roanoke.

There had been a gradual attenuation of new memories over the last several weeks. Dick took this as a sign that, along with the validation Vicki had gotten of her memory from the dead cat, it was time to move to the next phase of her therapy.

"It's time to confront your parents: your father for what he did and your mother for not protecting you," Dick said.

This was standard procedure in the healing paradigm for incest at the time. Vicki immediately ruled out a personal confrontation. She was terrified. Dick concurred based on her father's violence in some of her memories. Vicki would have preferred a phone call, but Dick ruled that out as too impersonal. While a call was safer than a face-to-face encounter, it too easily evaporated.

"The most common method is sending letters," Dick continued. "There is something indelible about ink on paper. And that makes sense with the distance. Write a personal letter to each of your parents giving specific but not graphic detail. Mention some of the places. The more minutiae you can add, the more convincing the effect will be. Tell them how it has affected you over the years and how you feel about it."

Even though she knew it had been coming, Vicki was stunned. It was only then that she fully understood Dick's previous comment that the hardest part of therapy was the part you were in at the time.

Dick added a caution: "I guess I need to warn you that your father is not in a therapy group like the offender's group that you attend. He may not react the way you want him to."

Vicki had come to know those men and trusted them. They could acknowledge the pain that they had caused, and that's what she was hoping for with her father. Dick reminded her that much of their attitude was the result of therapy. And that therapy had been court-mandated. None of the men had started therapy voluntarily; rather, they did it to get out of jail early or to stay out of jail altogether. Dick pointed out that this was not the case with her father. She needed to temper her expectations.

I was absolutely terrified of writing these letters. I had something going on in my subconscious that said if you ever tell, something bad will happen to you. I'm sure the dead cat was part of it, but I was committed to doing what Dick said and overcoming my past, so I first spent time panicking and then figuring out how I could write them. Praying at the Temple had worked well for loosening the blockage, so that it seemed like a good place to start with these letters.

There was a youth Temple trip coming up, so I volunteered as a chaperon. I felt like I would be able to gain the strength I needed there.

June 9,10, 1989. Journal entry. Went to Temple with church youth group without Jody, had a wonderful relaxing time. Swam, ate gourmet food. Had the best night's sleep I've had in ages. Went to the Temple and did an initiatory session and then prayed for:

1) *uplifted self-esteem*
2) *help with the letter to my parents. Was told to pray every day and God would tell me the right time to send it.*
3) *another baby*
4) *my brother Stephen to receive the gospel*

The gourmet food Vicki mentioned was a swordfish steak. It was her reward for the commitment she was making to write these very difficult letters. She sat alone in the restaurant at the *Marriott*. She picked an isolated table in the corner so she could concentrate. With her notepad beside her plate she looked like another lonesome business executive on a Friday night.

Her waiter, about a decade younger, was being especially solicitous and before long it dawned on my wife that he was trying to pick her up.

"Do you have any plans for the rest of the evening? I get off work in just a little bit."

Flattered and taken back, Vicki collected her thoughts. It had been years . . . .

"I've got to get my eight kids together and off to bed and then call my husband . . . ." she said with aplomb. The waiter was stunned. His plans and his countenance plummeted together. Vicki smiled as she heard him mumble to himself after turning around "Eight kids . . . ."

The next morning Vicki went over to the visitor's center and put together the letter to her father. When she returned from Washington, she showed me the letter. It consisted of three handwritten pages detailing the abuse she had remembered. She described her feelings at the time of the violation and her present confusion of emotions. At the end she held out an olive branch if he would accept responsibility. In particular, she was hoping that he would help defer some of the costs of therapy.

To her mother she was planning to send a photocopy of her father's letter along with a brief note explaining her culpability: A mother should protect her daughter. Both Dick and Vicki believed that at some level Virginia knew the incest was occurring but chose to ignore the clues.

With no new memories we were flush with excitement that she really had moved to the second stage of her therapy. Maybe there hadn't been a core memory. We relished the idea that someday this would be all be over and behind us. And we *would* live happily ever after.

We debated her father's possible reactions to his letter. I appreciated Tom and hoped he'd have the guts to admit his faults and begin the healing process with his daughter. I knew doing so would make a world of difference with Vicki's healing. I knew how much my wife wanted her father to be like the men in her therapy group. But Vicki was not hopeful; it seemed out of character for him. She was also worried about her mother. Virginia was over seventy years old: could she handle the stress? Would it be too much for her? How would she feel when she saw the profound cost of her maternal neglect?

Sending the letters proved even more difficult than writing them. She found one excuse after another to postpone going to the post office. My wife felt a need to protect her mother. Dick tried to balance that feeling with the obvious fact that if her mother knew, she had some culpability. And how could her mother not have known? Still, Vicki had strong misgivings about the grief that the letters would cause. The situation was further complicated by Stephen's dependent medical condition. Tom was giving Stephen his daily insulin shots, his numerous prescriptions, and driving him regularly to the doctor and to physical therapy—no mean task with Stephen's ungrateful and belligerent spirit. It was hard for my wife to throw a monkey wrench into that delicate equilibrium. This confluence of emotions created a lot of tension at our home and neither one of us was handling it well.

By Father's Day, both of us were working hard to bridle our potentially explosive feelings. The tension of the letters was always with us. I wanted her to get rid of them—be done with it. But she was dragging her feet and I was catching the backlash. Now the day to celebrate her father had arrived. We had fought on Saturday evening and started again on Sunday morning. Vicki had already decided against playing the game—that would be self-betrayal— and giving her father the traditional call. (The thought of calling my father never crossed my mind.) She also knew what to expect from church and she could not tolerate the syrupy tributes to other dads. Vicki would start crying when other women told sentimental stories of their dads, but it didn't take much before her emotions transformed into rage. I usually felt hollow at such times and wondered if I'd grown up in an alternative universe. I mostly didn't remember my father being around.

As a child Father's Day was a tradition in our family. We went to church and sang special songs celebrating fathers and then we came back and my mother prepared a special meal. Then we moved to the living room where my father sat in his special chair and we kids came up to him bearing gifts. My mother always had a present from us kids and my father would always say in his false humility, "I really don't deserve this." And that was it. I never hugged my father and said, "Happy Father's Day." None of us kids did. I wasn't upset; I wasn't mad. I was numbed out. But now I wasn't numb anymore; I was angry.

We were each laying stiffly in bed that Sunday morning and had been awake for hours. There was a battle line drawn down the middle of the mattress between us.

I grumbled aloud, "Let's forget about church today." It was hard to say. I was compulsive about it like most other things, and it was usually my only social outlet of the week. There was also a vague uneasiness left over from my Catholic upbringing where missing Sunday mass was a mortal sin. And I got something out of church—a fill-up that is hard to put into words but nonetheless significant.

"What'd you say?" My wife's voice was tentative with a flicker of hope.

"We both know that church is going to be miserable today. Why don't we stay home?"

Vicki dived across the line of demarcation and hugged me. This day suddenly had more potential than I'd ever dreamed. Without realizing it, I'd given myself a Father's Day gift.

"Let's go for a hike. I'll pack a picnic lunch," Vicki said. I hadn't heard that kind of excitement in her voice in ages. I liked the idea and briefly wondered where all of our family hikes had gone; they had been so much of our life before . . . . I guess much had to do with Vicki's therapy.

The kids were exhilarated by the sudden change in plans. After a quick breakfast and some preparation we drove five miles to a link in the Appalachian Trail. We started up two and a half miles through the woods to a bald summit. Seven frolicking kids, thrilled at the idea of skipping church, were enough to distract our attention from the pressure of the letters. When we stopped for lunch, she granted permission to the kids to go exploring. The little ones tagged along with their older siblings and we were left by ourselves.

After eating I laid beside Vicki in the thin alpine grass. The billowy white clouds were accented by a cobalt-blue backdrop. The air smelled green with hope. It rekindled the anticipation that her therapy was almost over.

"I think Dick's right. I think it's almost over." Her voice had a dreamy quality in it that made me want to believe. We were holding hands and staring into the clouds scurrying by. I couldn't remember the last time we had held hands.

"Do you really believe that?" I asked, hoping she was right.

"Even if my parents don't respond well, it's still almost over." She paused, pointing out a cloud that looked like a dog chasing a ball. "My healing isn't dependent on them. No matter what, I'm getting over this. I'm tired of the memories and I don't want to keep being strung out."

"What's the next step?"

"Getting better. Putting all the pieces together . . . . I'm not exactly sure. We haven't talked about it. But things in our family will start to mend; I'm sure of it."

I so wanted that Indian summer feeling back. I wanted that perfume, the scent, the excitement of when we first met but with the settled maturity of those intervening dozen years. And maybe we wouldn't live happily *ever* after, but certainly things would be better: we would live partly happily ever after. And that was certainly better than what we had now.

We took turns pointing out pictures in the billowy white clouds. The fragrance of that hope on top of that mountain with a light breeze and a breathtaking sky overhead was refreshing and then intoxicating. We talked of trivial things and laughed. We shared our dreams which had too long been relegated to a secondary status—so long that we'd forgotten them.

"The first thing I'm getting is a new van," Vicki said. "I don't know whether you've noticed but the station wagon is getting a little crowded. Besides Bethany in my lap, there are four in the back seat and two in the very back. Plus successful decorators have a van; they all do."

"I want to get our bathroom finished," I said. "We've got that old clawfooted tub in there; I need to hook it up. I can't wait to take a bath in it."

There was a lengthy pause. Then Vicki's voice took on a deep, vulnerable sincerity. "And I want a new baby. I'm not ready to quit. I want one more baby."

Her voice stirred deep feelings in me. My wife loved her babies. Our children were lucky to have a mother like that—and I was grateful for our babies as well.I heard the kids close by. The older ones were rounding up the younger ones.

"You ready to hike back down, Sweetie?" She rolled over and gave me a kiss.

We needed that time! We so needed that time off on that fabulous Father's Day.

THE LETTERS

June, 1989

Shortly after Father's Day Vicki discerned it was time to send the letters. She decided the incest was her father's responsibility. He would have to deal with the inconvenient timing. The abuse had been inconvenient for her as a child and she was still suffering from it. But she was bothered by the frank language and graphic detail her mother would be reading in her copy of her father's letter. Vicki wanted to buffer that. After reading the letters Dick thought she ought to send them as is. I concurred and so did Keith. But again Vicki was hesitant and the days dragged on . . . into weeks. I wondered if God had calculated my wife's stalling into His timetable.

The second Sunday in July brought several area leaders to our small congregation. Vicki had made up her mind to send the letters the next day and asked for a blessing after the block of meetings. Along with Keith and these men, I laid my hands on her head to call down the power of heaven. I was surprised at the encouragement that came out of my mouth. I told Vicki that in the future the work she would do in the area of sexual abuse would benefit many. I tried to say "thousands" but had to correct myself to say that "millions" would be helped by her work. In addition, I promised her a complete healing, which is what I desperately hoped for. I felt after some initial resistance that her father would cooperate, and there would be a family restoration. After I finished, one of the visitors asked Vicki about the letters she was sending.

"Are you sending the same letter to both of your parents?"

Vicki explained that she was.

"During the blessing I felt impressed for you to minimize the detail in the letter to your mother," this individual said.

I thought my wife had discussed the matter with him earlier, but she told me later that she hadn't. She was grateful for the inspired counsel and decided to greatly abbreviate Virginia's copy of the letter she was sending to her father. [5]

> *Dear Mom,*
>
> *This is a hard letter to write but it's become a matter of life and death— mine. I am fully aware of the good things you did in my life. The time and sacrifice you put into all of us children and how hard your life must have been. And about the money you've lent us several times including the last.*
>
> *I don't know how aware you were of the incidents in the letter, but I remember one time when I was thirteen and you made me model my first bra in front of Dad; you must have played a part. I resent not being protected by you. I feel I was made the family scapegoat. Even now you leave me out of lots of things. For example, the recent family beach trip. Everyone knew and was invited but me. I wished as a child I could have told you, but I was afraid Dad would kill me if I did. And you would stand by and watch.*
>
> *Maybe now you will understand why I don't let my children visit . . . . There is hope though. I'm in a group with men who have abused their children, and their wives. They are getting counseling and we're all getting our lives back together. I am enclosing the names and phone numbers of people in your area who deal with this. Call them; they can help.*
>
> *Love,*
>
> *Vicki*

Vicki was too nervous to eat on Monday morning. She called a Raleigh detective looking for a therapist with experience in sexual abuse so she could

---

5   We do not have a copy of Tom's letter.

include it in her letters. The detective said that incest was running rampant in the area and there was no effective method of dealing with it. There was no local program like the Parents United program in Roanoke. He told my wife of a recent story that was in the newspapers of a man who had been convicted of incest and was given two life sentences. That call almost broke Vicki's resolve.

Then we argued for the tenth time whether to send the letters certified-restricted.

I said, "If your father gets his first, your mother will never get hers. I don't want to go through this again. Do you?"

"It's just so incredibly hard."

Finally, Vicki acquiesced.

(The green post office receipts are taped into Vicki's journal. Ironically, on the next page the birthday card that her mother sent to her that spring is taped in.)

With the letters in transit, we put the finishing touches on our plans for a camping trip. Our goal was to be lost and out of touch on the Appalachian Trial when the letters arrived on Wednesday or Thursday. Vicki had scheduled this excursion when she first decided on the letters. The kids were farmed out to church friends, and we were walking out of the door of my shop when the phone rang.

Vicki shot me a questioning look.

"If it were me, I wouldn't answer it," I said.

But she wasn't me. Vicki's primary goal was restoration. She answered.

Virginia was distraught on the other end of the line. She was careful to mention at the onset that Tom was not around. Vicki was grateful that I had pushed to send the letters certified-restricted. It soon became obvious that her mother would have taken Tom's letter and subterfuged the plan—something we hadn't counted on.

"I've just talked with your sister," her mother said. Her voice was frantic and Vicki immediately felt her pain. "You must be crazy. We're just going to have to come up and deal with you." By this she meant putting Vicki in an institution.

Vicki was impressive to listen to. Despite the tension on the call, she was calm and rational. She was prepared for this opening volley. More than once we had read that victims were often treated as the culprits. To her mother's numerous charges that she was fabricating the story, Vicki flatly answered, "No."

"It's impossible. I was always there. Your sister was always there . . . ." Virginia reiterated. She had a way of talking in which she pasted one sentence after another, giving Vicki no time to respond. "You're making it up. Why do you want to destroy our family?"

"I don't want to destroy it," Vicki finally interjected. "I'm trying to heal it. Do you have any idea how difficult that letter was to write?"

"You don't know how it feels to hear your daughter say something like that."

"No. But I can imagine. Can you imagine what it's like for me . . . to have lived through this?"

Virginia changed her tack. She pleaded for Stephen. "Your father's taking total care of him. Nobody else could do the job he's doing." She went on and on.

Vicki interrupted. "Stephen's not the only one in bad shape. I've been having suicidal thoughts for months."

Virginia again talked of commitment to an institution.

"Why don't I give you the name of my therapist?" Vicki interrupted again.

Virginia was surprised that her daughter was already in therapy. She readily took Dick's name and number. By prearrangement he was on emergency standby.

Fifteen minutes later Dick called Vicki. He reported that Virginia was in denial, which was common. He thought she basically believed the matter and would eventually come around. Vicki gave a grateful sigh.

My impression from listening to my wife's conversation with her mother was that Virginia did believe Vicki's story, but a life of compromise in that area had weakened her resolve. Denial was so much easier.

We hiked a ten-mile stretch of the Appalachian Trail that afternoon and returned the next evening. The time off was needed—the fresh air, the comfort and stability of nature, and the impossibility of another telephone call allowed some of the tension to dissipate.

On Friday, I drove Vicki into Roanoke for a special session with Dick. She needed the extra support. On the way home we stopped at a yard sale. I got a few obnoxious questions on the spot, and then I was peppered with more questions about every woman she saw on the side of the road as we drove home. Then she fell apart, alternating between crying and violent bursts of anger.

Life was miserable for the next several days. I didn't know how to deal with it. Slowly, I recognized her vehemence as a thin veneer for the terrible pain she was in. She could not rid herself of the anguish: There had been no further communication from her parents. The worst of all responses was no response.

Late Tuesday she came down to the shop and told me she had finally talked with her mother again. She took the call as a sign of reconciliation; her mother was lining up on her side. I was surprised and asked for details of the conversation. Vicki said that it had started with the usual pleasantries, as if nothing had happened just six days before. Vicki finally broke in to ask how her father had taken his letter.

"He denied it," her mother had said. But Vicki felt an alliance with her mother who continued by saying that Stephen was acting up and almost intolerable. "We just can't deal with it now." My wife heard a conciliatory note in her mother's voice.

The conversation then abruptly changed. Virginia said that she and Tom wanted to see Tripp before he left for his church mission, but because of Stephen and "this other stuff" they would be unable to come up. Then the conversation ended suddenly.

I was skeptical of Vicki's analysis. It is common upon the exposure of incest for the mother to suddenly enjoy a superior position in the family structure. Whatever way she leaned had a lot to do with the final outcome. Virginia had mentioned that Tom, normally gruff and sometimes verbally abusive, had totally changed. He was now solicitous and was taking her shopping the next day. And she did not fail to mention that he was a saint for taking care of Stephen. My opinion was that her plea of "let's not deal with this now" was just a sophisticated denial. Virginia wanted to close her eyes for a while longer. But she had been closing her eyes for years; that's how the incest occurred. It took some time for my wife to see what I was saying. She desperately wanted to feel like her mother was on her side.

The next Monday Vicki drove herself to her regular therapy session and then to the men's group. She got a standing ovation from the group as she relayed the story of the past few weeks. They understood—as much as anyone could understand. They commended her courage for sending the letters. It had been heroic. And when I wasn't being badgered by questions, she was a hero in my book as well. But most impressive was that her motivation was reconciliation; more than anything she wanted a *real* family.

AFTERMATH

August, 1989

August was full of canning, getting Tripp ready for his two-year mission and the funeral of Vicki's cousin, who had finally succumbed to multiple sclerosis. Vicki's parents refused to acknowledge her at the funeral, and Vicki said that it hurt—like she was being raped all over again. We also decided to homeschool our kids, chiefly because they brought so many viruses home from school.

These items were part of the brief splurge of writing in Vicki's journal after she sent the letters. The writing was Dick's idea, to take some of the tension out of her life. While Dick may have guessed the probable outcome of sending the letters, Vicki was deflated because her parents' initial reaction was to distance themselves from their daughter. We had read that this was a common reaction and should have been anticipated it. But most notable in her journal was that there were no new memories, which substantiated Dick's belief that that part of her therapy was over.

Her journal does mention that a fifteen-year-old girl had moved in up the road, invading our sanctuary. She was in the habit of walking up and down the road, and even though Vicki knew that the girl was fat and unattractive, I was pestered with questions. Frustrated and angry I began to refer to these as "JD" attacks—a derogatory euphemism for "Jealous Dog." Beyond her usual strident invasiveness, I was troubled because I expected— since the memories had ended—that the questions would attenuate and then gradually disappear. That was not happening and it was disheartening as well as confusing and irritating.

Her questions seemed to fill the void where hope had previously been. It was perfectly obvious to me that the seemingly endless questions were now slowly draining the good will that had been engendered from that unforgettable Father's Day and her heroic act of writing the letters. Her questions were siphoning off of my energy, creating a vicious downward cycle and replacing the camaraderie between us with friction. With the questions seemingly much worse than before, we finally decided to let Dick arbitrate.

Vicki reported that he did not see the questions so much as jealousy, but rather as a control issue. On a very deep level—deeper than my ability to comprehend at the time—she was doing everything she could to make sure I didn't turn out like her father. She did not want to be married to a man like her father. It was a perpetual fear because that was the kind of man she knew best from her formative years. I didn't see that she wanted to be able to trust me, and that her questions were the litmus test she was applying before she could feel secure. While the information she wanted was important, the most significant part for my wife was being able to ask and get an answer. It gave her a sense of control. I was always surprised that she inevitably believed what I told her. I could have lied and she would have accepted it. She wanted to be able to ask; the act of being able to ask and get an answer was reassuring in itself. It separated me from her father and her childhood, where such questions were off-limits.

If Dick had given her any suggestions to remedy the impasse, she did not pass them on. We tried to negotiate a trade where I got something in exchange for answering her senseless questions or she got something for not asking them. But as in times past, she didn't keep up her end of the bargain. During this particularly unsettled time Vicki's journal notes, *'Divorce is always on my mind. Will things ever get better?'*

In mid-September Vicki's journal mentioned her first memory in three months:

September 17th, 1989. Journal entry. Had another memory. Jody got violent a couple of weeks ago. Grabbed me, pushed me, pulled

me. Left me very upset. My uterus hurting a lot. Thought maybe it
was connected with a memory. It was:

Daddy, when I was 14 or 15, pulling me upstairs from LR to
bedroom hall. Backing me into a corner between Steve's room and
linen closet. Then raped me . . . .

My baby Bet will be 2 tomorrow. It's the first time in 13 years
I haven't had another one already born or on the way. Some parts
of getting older are hard.

Two weeks later she wrote: '*My period didn't start today. Maybe I'm*
pregnant. If so two weeks along.'

October 10th, 1989. Journal entry. I've been losing my temper a lot
lately and the way I've decided to deal with it beside talking to my
therapist and group is to
    1)   take 1/2 hour each day to myself
    2)   write in journal each night
    3)   make love more
    I sent another letter to my Dad telling him I need a response.
He sent me $200.

Vicki then called her father to tell him thanks. She explained that she
used it to cover some of the travel costs to therapy. From that point on he sent
a hundred dollars a month. "Just don't tell anybody" was his only requirement.

October 19th, 1989. Journal entry . . . . I'm pretty positive I'm
pregnant. About 4 1/2 weeks.

November 15, 1989. Journal entry . . . . Change in attitude towards
my father. I will no longer force him to admit incest. Instead, I will
take him as he is & try to forgive.

My mom has admitted it—that he did it—and our relationship
is at least pretty honest.

Vicki wanted to believe that by sending money her father was admitting
to the abuse. And by defraying part of the costs of therapy, it was a way of

him taking responsibility. Money was the principle way Tom knew how to relate to his kids. She told herself that it was the closest she was going to get to an admission and an apology.

But her relationship with her mother wasn't that simple, and certainly not that honest. Vicki had previously told her mother that she didn't want to see her father until he had admitted to the incest. Virginia had simply rescheduled the annual Thanksgiving get-together from the mountains to Raleigh and not invited our family. When Vicki heard that in early December from her sister, she was irked. She felt left out, like her sister and mother were colluding behind her back. My wife confronted her mother.

"You said you didn't want to see your father," Virginia responded.

Vicki exploded, hammering her mother about how the sexual abuse of two and three decades earlier was still effecting her. "And do you know that Daddy is sending me a hundred dollars a month?" There was a lengthy pause.

"Please don't mention anything about it to your brothers," was all Virginia could say.

Hurt by her mother's paltry concern Vicki made plans to retaliate. She ruled out talking to Stephen. His health, although better, was still too fragile. She decided to meet with her very successful younger brother for lunch. I warned her to go easy. There was a good likelihood she would simply alienate another member of her family. With her brother picking up the tab at a posh restaurant my wife realized that truth: Her whole family was wearing rose-tinted glasses.

In the next conversation with her mother, Vicki again brought up the issue of incest. Virginia reported Tom's latest stance:

"Your father said that he would take responsibility for the incest but would never admit to something that he didn't do."

"Just what do you think that means?" Vicki asked pointedly.

Virginia rehearsed the history of Tom's generosity, including paying off Vicki's several-thousand-dollar loan after she dropped out of law school. Her point was obvious: Giving money to his children was not necessarily an admission of guilt.

"But honestly, Mother, what do you think?"

Virginia hemmed and hawed. She could not actually say that she believed her daughter. It would mean that she had been a failure in one of her most important jobs as a mother: protecting her children. "Can't we just let the past be . . . . I haven't many years left. I want to enjoy them with my family."

My wife had to accept that as an admission and be satisfied; she wasn't going to get anything more than that.

Vicki came into Dick's office for her usual Monday appointment complaining about Sunday. Unexpectedly, Dick told her he wanted to try hypnosis. Overwhelmed by the previous day, she did not have the energy to refuse. He sat across from her in the now-familiar office and told her to get into a comfortable position.

"Now I want you to relax . . . and when you feel comfortable, go ahead and close your eyes. You're safe here and you won't remember anything you can't handle . . . and you're safe now . . . ."

In a soothing, professional voice Dick continued the themes of safety and relaxation.

"Now let's go back to an average Sunday in your childhood. You pick the time . . . ."

Images began flowing into Vicki's mind. She told Dick she was about fourteen or fifteen years old and had just gotten back from church. She walked into the small kitchen where her mother was putting the finishing touches on their traditional Sunday dinner. Her sister, a year younger, was setting the table in the next room. There was clique between the two of them and Vicki felt ostracized. She felt the reason was jealousy: her mother and sister did not like the special attention she got from her father. But it was not something that was talked about; perhaps it was not even on a conscious level.

Vicki went to her bedroom and closed the door and took out her books. School was the one area where she excelled and got her mother's approval. Minutes later she was startled by the doorknob turning rapidly back and forth. It was her father, reminding her that the lock didn't work. Then his strong hands were on her shoulders. She stifled her immediate reaction of fear as he continued massaging. His right hand casually slipped down her blouse and fondled her breasts.

"Dinner's ready, Honey," her father whispered in her ear and then outlined the words with his tongue. Vicki was inundated with a wave of disgust, then fear.

At the dinner table her mother and sister tag-teamed a constant barrage of criticism:

"I wish you could help with some of the chores around the house. Your sister does everything." (Now, almost twenty-five years later, Vicki remembered that because of her severe allergies that she had been restricted from everything but ironing.)

Her sister began talking about her date the previous night. Her mother then took up another familiar theme: "Your sister's been dating steadily since she was thirteen years old. What's wrong with you? You're doing too much babysitting . . . ."

The next day Vicki recounted her session with Dick to me. If my wife's memory was accurate, her relationship with her mother and sister made more sense. There *was* some collusion. While the two may not have known exactly what was going on, on some level they would have sensed it. They certainly apprehended the special attention Vicki got from her father. Over the years I had noticed the competitive relationship that Vicki had with her sister. Her sister was not bashful about letting Vicki know that her family was better off financially than we were and that her parents always stayed with her when they came to the mountains.

Summing up her thoughts, Vicki said, "That's what it was like at my house. No wonder I don't like my sister or mother very much."

"What about the part with your father?" I asked. That aspect of the everydayness of the scene was chilling.

There was a long silence and I could feel the shame wash over my wife. She answered with a voice that was small and flat. "I think he came into the bedroom that night." It dawned on both of us that Tom's nighttime visits may have been much more frequent than either one of us had realized, and certainly much more often than Vicki wanted to admit to herself.

CHRISTMAS TIME

October, 1989

I have an image in my head that comes from a later conversation with my brother. It is of Mother silhouetted against the reds and golds of a late-summer, early-evening sky. My sixty-four-year old mother has a drink in one hand and a cigarette in the other. She is boasting: "I'll take on cancer any day."

That October my mother flew up to visit my sister. Denise noted that Mother hardly ate and that she was covertly smoking again. "She was weak, depressed and drank quite a bit," my sister reported. By Christmas, her doctor suspected the cancer was back.

After missing two periods, Vicki went to her OB doctor in late October. And, yes indeed, she was pregnant. That was exciting—for her at least; it was an answer to prayer. For me it was one more unplanned pregnancy, but I had gotten to the point where I didn't feel like I needed to get upset by it. There would be another baby and I would learn to love it. I had gotten kind of partial to babies by then, especially when they were young and cuddly. Also, there always seemed to be some blessings—I noted the financial ones—that came with each new birth and we always needed them. One of the blessings with this one would be a lifesaver.

Her OB doctor was well over an hour away—in the opposite direction from her therapy. This mandated a change in her schedule. Not only would she not have the time to make one more long trip each month, she wouldn't have the energy; she was forty years old. Vicki was also being very careful because she didn't want to have another miscarriage. With the memory work diminished to almost nothing, she decided to cut Dick and the Parents United group back to once a month, and then once a month she would go to her OB doctor in Boone.

With a little networking, she found a therapy group for survivors of sexual abuse in Boone that met in the evenings, and she coordinated those meetings with her OB visits. Vicki took our older kids and occasionally dropped them off to visit with their cousins who were the same ages. She was able to quiz her niece about whether anything sexual had happened between her and her grandfather. When she got a negative response, it greatly eased my wife's mind.

I relished the support of a group. I was hoping for something with the give-and-take of the men's group in Roanoke. This Boone group was different though. It was all women; there were six to eight of us seated in a circle in the back conference room of an office building. It was moderated by Sally, a local social worker, and her husband, Tony. Both of them had master's degrees in therapy. It did not have the anger and hardness of the women's group in Roanoke, but it had something else that I didn't like. It was dark, occult-ish. I was one of the few participants who shared, but I needed to talk. I'm not sure Sally and Tony liked that. They were used to doing all the talking.

The few memories that beset my wife that fall were from her teenage years and she shared them with her new group. She was fourteen, fifteen, perhaps sixteen years old and allowing her father to rape her. Why wasn't she fighting back? Why wasn't she telling somebody? Maybe not her mother, but why not her aunt? She was afraid that the answer was that she was enjoying it. Her father made sure that she had orgasms, and once she remembered falling asleep comfortably in his arms. That was horrible! While no one in the group had a problem understanding the dynamics involved, her shame was intense—and very, very difficult to accept.

As Christmas approached, Virginia began pushing for her and Tom to make a visit. Vicki understood that it was all for show. Her mother would take a few pictures so she could report to her bridge club and other friends that all was well with her number-one daughter, the one with all the kids. Neither one of us thought the timing was good, but we didn't know how to say no. There wasn't room for them to spend the night and Vicki wouldn't have it anyway. It was an in-and-out visit that lasted no more than a couple of hours. But it left quite a residue, upsetting our house for days.

December 27, 1989. Journal entry. Another memory. This one triggered by a visit from Mom and Dad. Preceding their visit I had a week of nightmares. On Christmas I had one that really bothered me: Jennifer was standing in the bathroom with only a towel wrapped around her and Jody was reaching across her in a seductive manner. There was a look of terror on her face.

After waking and reflecting on it several hours, I realized it wasn't Jennifer in the dream but me and I had projected Jody on my father. The man was my dad and most likely it was a trigger for a new memory.

I just remembered it. It was me on Christmas Eve after taking a bath. I was standing in front of the mirror with a towel wrapped around me. My father opens the door and reaches his arm across me. While pulling his arm back, he pulls the towel off me and scrapes his fingers across my breasts. I feel terror!!!! and some titillation, lots of sadness and shame, shame, shame.

I put on my chaste new Christmas flannel gown feeling totally helpless and weighted down by the world.

I go to bed. Laying there. Waiting. Dreading the inevitable.

He comes in. Raises my gown over my head suffocating me. Does oral sex on me . . . . Then me rolls me over . . . . . He comes. And pulls down the gown and leaves. I am overwhelmed with emotions. Some arousal during oral sex. Terror that I will suffocate while the gown is over my head. Pain during intercourse. Total feeling of worthlessness, sadness, and shame.

January 9, 1990. Journal entry. Jody was mean to me off and on all day. At bedtime he started saying unless I did things his way he was going to quit doing things I liked or wanted. It really upset me and I started feeling physically afraid. I decided to sleep upstairs where I felt safer. Sometime in the night I realized that as tense as I was, I must be having a flashback. As a teenager I remembered my father becoming real hostile if I would become rebellious about his raping me. He told me either I cooperated or he would not let me do this, that, or the other . . . . And to emphasize his point he did anal intercourse so hard he made my spine turn stiff as a rock.

REEVALUATION

January, 1990

These latest memories—on top of what Vicki had been through for the past year—forced me to reevaluate Tom. I knew he was generous and concerned because I had lived it. Even though he was brusque, he had given me an idea of what fathering was all about by simply being engaged—something that I had missed on the home front growing up because my father was rarely around. Vicki had told me often enough of his foul and violent moods during her childhood that I now believed her. But I hadn't lived them. The new picture that these once-buried memories painted was very difficult for me to accept.

Slowly, and with some reluctance, my gut told me that he was not simply a grumpy but benign old man with an excess of twenty-dollar bills. But what was he? Was he a grumpy old man with some serious baggage, and for the most part that was behind him because his daughter was no longer around to molest? Statistics that we had read indicated that sexual predators were voracious and their appetite did not go away on its own. They usually had scores of victims. Was he a predator? So was it still going on? We certainly hadn't seen it—and we had been looking.

Rather, I wanted to believe that the twenty-dollar bills he had given us through the years were overindulgence; that Tom's help had been genuine paternal concern; that the painting of Tripp I gave him that first Christmas after Vicki and I were married and the reciprocal moisture I saw in his eyes was evidence of a much softer heart than the one her memories portrayed. I didn't want to believe there were people like that—even if they could change.

So I was left with a big question mark that had been gilded by his generosity over the years.

And Virginia was also an unanswered question. She seemed to be AWOL at too many critical times. Her eyes were mostly closed, unable to see what was going on right in front of her. It didn't make sense of the educated woman that I had gotten to know. She did have an unbelievable knack for putting up with Tom's unsavory moods. It was obvious from her demeanor what she thought of her husband at such times. She didn't say it; she didn't have to. Tom always came out looking like the fool.

But where had she been during Vicki's childhood? And why had she married Tom to begin with? Had it been desperation? She was certainly an unanswered question, but one that had treated me better than my own mother and that had mothered my wife, who was now mothering my children.

GROWING UP
IN HELL

STRANGE NEW MEMORIES

January, 1990

In her Boone group Vicki continued to vent her experiences to get validation, even though it irritated Tony and Sally, the therapists. As she was relating her recent memory of anal rape, Tony abruptly rose and quickly exited the room, but not before my wife saw a pained expression on his face that she could easily identify with. When he didn't return, Vicki asked Sally about the matter during a break. Sally told my wife that her husband had had a very difficult childhood. He suffered from flashbacks and he was simply protecting himself and his professionalism. It was then that Vicki understand the look on his face; he was simply getting out of the room before he had a breakdown.

Sally gave his condition a name—something called PTSD—Post Traumatic Stress Disorder. We were slightly familiar with the term when it was applied to war veterans, especially those who had seen the horrors of combat. There was something innately atrocious about war that often affected veterans years later with intrusive thoughts, flashbacks and nightmares. They would have a spontaneous reaction to present-day stimuli, as if they were living in the traumatic past. A Vietnam vet, upon hearing a car backfire, might hit the ground and reach for his gun as if under enemy fire. These present-day reactions to stimuli that mimicked the past were virtually uncontrollable.

Vicki had all these characteristics, but up until this point we had never heard the term applied to victims of abuse. It occurred to Vicki that this was what she was suffering from. In time, we began to hear it applied to victims of sexual assault, especially in severe cases such as with violent rape. It was validating to know that what she had been overwhelmed with for the last year had a name, and that it was an official psychological disorder. She was not acting crazy: rather she was reacting normally—just like many others—to a crazy, violent history. Amnesia was also a common characteristic of PTSD. The fact that she hadn't remembered most of her past for several decades was not unusual at all; again, it was normal.

Curious, Vicki asked Sally about Tony's childhood. "What kind of abuse did he suffer as a child?"

From comments in the group, Vicki knew Tony had a problem with compulsive masturbation, and that Tony's and Sally's sexual relationship was sketchy at best. My wife decided that he might be more dysfunctional than she was; he couldn't hold down a regular job.

"Ritual abuse," Sally said, answering my wife's question. She would not elaborate except to indicate that it included sexual abuse but was much more severe than just that.

Neither one of us had heard of that term before; nor could we imagine anything more damaging than sexual abuse. We surmised from the name and what little bit Sally had said that it was sexual abuse done as part of a ceremony, perhaps a religious ceremony. It sounded weird and possibly associated with the occult. It was strange that in the many books we had read, we had never come across the term before.

It didn't take long before we made the association between the ritual abuse Sally had mentioned and Satanism—the slang being "satanic cult" or just plain "cult." My initial problem was that I didn't believe Satanism existed. I thought that it was what we would now refer to as an urban legend. Perhaps there were people who played at worshiping the devil, but I could not imagine normal everyday people taking it seriously. Over the past decades there had been a steady decline in the percentage of people who believed in God. Who in the world would choose to worship the devil? His credibility had to be seriously lacking if God's was on the decline.

Reliable information on the subject was sketchy, bordering on nonexistent. But we found a paragraph on Satanism in a brand-new book on sexual abuse. As more and more therapists worked with patients on sexual abuse—especially incest—rumors of something more sinister arose:

organized sexual abuse involving religious ritual and usually multiple perpetrators.

For the first time in over a year Vicki's therapy was not the primary thing on our minds. An entry in my journal dated January 12 notes our family goals for 1990: get a van; go on a vacation; have a baby; finish the house; keep Tripp on his mission and get money. I was gratefully flush with sewing work from the several decorators we did wholesale work for, and the previous autumn Vicki had landed our largest job to date: a hundred, hand-pieced quilts for a new hotel—$20,000. I did note in my journal 'the time surrounding flashbacks she is especially violent. Anything can set her off,' but that we were learning to disengage better. And finally that my mother indeed had another tumor, that she had 'started smoking again exemplifying that negative attitude about life—it was probably the same that I fought against in my late teens to be able to enjoy life.'

We got an emergency call from my sister in late January. Mother had been hospitalized with a collapsed lung. The cancer this time was in a different spot and this time it would be fatal. While Mother was in the hospital, they had radiated the spot enough to allow her to breathe easier. Mother had overheard the doctors saying she had six months to live, but the message relayed to us was tempered with the power of modern medicine— the same power that had reversed the course of the inevitable a year earlier.

With my mother on our minds, Vicki told me that she felt certain that I'd been sexually abused as a child. With all the reading and therapy she had done she was becoming a real aficionado on the subject. With her enhanced self-awareness she became almost clairvoyant when it came to seeing it in others. While I initially discounted this new skill that she claimed, it became evident she had gained something: as she befriended women she suspected had been abused, they would eventually confide to her that it was true. It was uncanny; she was never wrong. But I was resistant when she put her all-seeing eye on me. I told her I didn't remember anything like that with my mother—and I would have remembered it! And then we both laughed at how ridiculous that statement was in light of what we'd been through for the previous year with her memories.

Recently, I'd had a vague impression that she used as evidence. It occurred during a leisurely nighttime bath in our claw-footed tub: It was of me being a very small boy and someone sucking my penis. I would have thought nothing of it except for the fact that often when I was first sexually excited I sneezed for no reason at all. I had the sensation of hair—that wasn't there now—in my face and nose. I didn't want to believe it because that's not the kind of thing mothers are supposed to do.

We attributed the spike in the intensity and number of Vicki's memories that occurred after Christmas to the visit by her parents. After the uproar calmed, she said she wasn't going to see her father again until she was finished with therapy. Even though she was thoroughly infused with a sense of family and its accompanying duty, it just wasn't worth it. She was getting too upset and the house had been upside-down for days.

Looking back at her journals—with the gift of hindsight—I see a gradual transition in her memory work after that point. The intensity tapered off and her age in these new memories also changed. Her worst memories had been before and just after Christmas—of her teenage years. Because of her age and the sense that she was more culpable, the shame had been intense. In a sense, those memories had exploded into her consciousness, ravaging the house. Now there was a shift to being five and six years old and living in Hawaii. Shame was no longer the dominant theme; it was replaced by fear. Her brother Stephen was also in these new memories.

The buildup of tension that traditionally had preceded new memories and upset the household was mitigated to the point that the memories almost seemed incidental—that is, compared to what we'd just been through. Vicki wondered if some of the hormonal changes related to her pregnancy might be affecting this process of remembering. We were both assuming that the worst was over and these last memories were tangential. We blocked out any other possible meaning.

January 20,1990. Journal entry. More memories of late. Woke up on a Friday night scared and very upset. Tried to call Keith after Jody wouldn't deal with me. He wasn't home, so Jody finally dealt with me. Later in the day, I remembered a memory. My father taking me and Stephen to a sandy, isolated beach. I was standing there with my head hung. Dad had a sharp pointed knife & sliced a nick in Steve's penis threatening to cut it off if he ever told. Then he made Steve lay on me, simulating intercourse.

We're in Hawaii and Dad is putting on mine and Stephen's coats. Puts us in the car and takes us to the playground. Takes us back into the woods. Undresses us. Ties us to trees. Stimulates— does oral sex on Steve. Sticks a banana up me. Sticks penis in my mouth & comes to the point of almost suffocating me. Then releases us, dresses us, and we leave. I look like I'm almost dead.

February 27, 1990. Journal Entry. I had a doozy of a memory last night. It started with a dream the night before. (I was scuba diving under water with a group of people. We came up on a deserted island. I went a different way from the other people. Jody followed me carrying a baby. I was going toward a blonde-headed 4-year-old boy in red swim trunks. A wave came and took the little boy away. I was screaming for Jody to come rescue him, but I couldn't make a sound. I was so frustrated.) The next night I was acting like a memory was coming up so Jody pushed me to remember it. I thought of the dream and realized the group of people were frightening to me. When trying to remember back, all I felt was extreme terror. Finally was able to remember a group of people building a fire on the beach; they were using rocks as ends on which to set a wooden door. Beach was rocky with strong surf. People had on masks—costumes. One was a devil, another a 14th-century king, one was a hawk, one—dog, one—fox. My brother and I were standing on the sidelines. The fox came & took Stephen and carried him to the table. Then the men did all kinds of sexual things to him. I watched in total frustration & terror, wanting to rescue him and not able to do anything. The fox brought him back and a few drops of blood from his anus fell onto the sand. The fox took me over to the door & the men stuck penises in all my holes. I looked up as the fox placed me on the table and realized it was my father. The ultimate betrayal!!! Words cannot express it. End of memory.

I had a difficult time believing this memory. It followed all the familiar lead-up patterns and had an immediate let-up of the terror feeling when it was over. But it was so bizarre. Went over it with Boone group and Tony and Sally (who have personal and clinical experience with cults) felt it was a valid memory.

Yesterday morning I had a dream (memory) where I was pushing a blonde-headed boy (about 4 yrs. old) down on me . . . . I enjoyed it. I think this may be something my father was having my brother and I do. Maybe in front of the group.

I couldn't make heads or tails out of the Hawaii memories—if memories were what they were. What was her brother doing in them? Had he too been a victim of her father's lust—a plaything of his like Vicki had been? If that was the case—and Vicki was inclined to believe it was—then that might explain some of Stephen's self-destructive behavior over the years. And what were the other men doing in her memories?

DARK SPOTS

March, 1990

Because of her pregnancy and the severe winter weather Vicki missed most of her appointments with Dick. She made one in early March and related her recent memories. As she was describing the scene of her and her brother being tied to trees, she blurted out, "I think someone was taking pictures." She recalled her father looking back over his shoulder several times into the woods surrounding the clearing. Dick looked at her askance. He told her she was being influenced by the other group.

"Your other group's leader's background is being infused into your memories."

Vicki accepted Dick's analysis—at least when she was in Roanoke. She had been working with him for two years and greatly respected his judgment. It made more sense than the alternative: believing this peculiar twist in her memories. The strange scenes seemed out of character and so foreign. But when she went to the Boone group she got a different opinion. And she wanted to believe her instincts, which told her that these new memories were as valid as the others.

This jostling of viewpoints continued into March when we entered an extended calm with regard to new memories. Again, we wanted to believe that the first half of therapy was over. The problem was that both of us were expecting some release from the compulsive behaviors that had driven her to therapy to begin with. In particular, we expected to see more conscious control over her fears: less jealousy and fewer questions and especially less trouble at church. But that was not the case, and we were perplexed.

Vicki had already told Dick that she might not see him until after the baby was born. And she thought nothing of missing her OB appointments; she had been to so many of them over the years. With the latter she also missed her group in Boone. We decided to take up the slack in her therapy by doing some memory work together. Vicki was hoping that by sharing this therapy time I might develop more empathy, and I was game simply because I was fascinated with the process of retrieving the buried memories. Both of us wanted to search for any other stray memories that might be blocking the healing that we expected. Vicki coached me on the hypnotic technique that she had learned from Dick, and it worked well because our life was relatively calm. Several days a week Vicki would come down to the shop and we would journey into her past.

"I want you to close your eyes." I used Dick's words and Vicki combined them with the centering exercises she learned from the Boone group. In less than a minute she was ready.

"Let's go back to your home in Hawaii. . . ." And my wife would immediately find herself in the house she had not seen in thirty-five years. Walking through the rooms she would describe the floor plan, the color of the walls, the furniture and especially the places that were important to her as a child. I could ask questions and get answers. Like Dick, I was amazed at the clarity of her memory. She always knew the clothes she was wearing and could often describe the weather.

Over the following weeks we toured the houses of her childhood. There were a couple of poignant scenes from the one in Louisiana. Vicki was eleven years old as she looked out into the back yard at two of the neighborhood dogs mating. She was giggling to herself when her mother came up.

"Don't you know anything about sex?" Virginia scolded. Although Vicki had felt humiliated as a child, now both of us got a laugh out of the irony.

My wife also remembered the embarrassment of her mother trying to explain to their neighbors her younger brother's fetish. Four-year old Jack went around pulling all the girls' and women's underwear off their clotheslines.

Vicki also recalled walking into the living room of the large ranch they lived in that year and seeing her father crying. He was alone. Word had just come that Stephen, at eight years old, had diabetes. She watched the heavy slobs coming from her father. She was spying. It was the only time in her life that she ever saw her father cry. Again we wondered If there might be a correlation between Stephen's sexual abuse—if those memories were true—and the onset of his diabetes.

We also visited via hypnosis the houses in Richmond and Hershey, Pennsylvania. What intrigued me about those two homes was what I called "dark spots." As Vicki walked from room to room giving me a tour, she suddenly stopped.

"I don't want to go upstairs," Vicki said as she looked up into her attic bedroom at the Richmond house where she lived when she was seven. "Something bad happened up there."

Was that something beyond what she had already remembered? I wondered. But that was the only thing that made any sense. What would it be?

I suspected if I pushed her, Vicki would just quit and the session would be over. I escorted her elsewhere and then returned to the stairs a second time. With more emphasis she repeated, "Something awful happened up there. I'm afraid to go up there."

It was an eerie feeling for me and Vicki promptly came out of her trance. I was perplexed.

"What do you think it was?"

"I don't know, Jody." Her voice was insistent. "But it was something awful and I don't want to think about it."

The same thing happened in the house at Hershey where she lived when she was eight. She was walking down the hall when I asked her to find her bedroom. She got to the first door and immediately came out of her trance and opened her eyes. It was the same fear.

I didn't know what to make of those "dark spots." If they needed to come to light, I figured they eventually would. It was obvious that I wasn't going to push Vicki to remember.

Several times we worked on the two houses that she had lived in in Texas. Her father had been transferred to the missile program at Fort Bliss near El Paso when she was nine and ten and also later when she was twelve and thirteen. My wife talked freely of her life at age thirteen but it was conscious memory. She was a young teenager with school and boys on her mind. There seemed to be nothing hidden. Of ages nine and ten she remembered absolutely nothing. I spent little time trying to access those years because she had remembered no incest episodes from that period during the previous year and a half of her memory work. There were no specific incidents at Hersey except the one "dark spot."

Altogether it was puzzling. Vicki remembered incidents from age three to age seven minus age four when her father was in Korea. There were several scenes at age eleven and then it picked up again at age fourteen after her father exited the military and the family moved to Raleigh. She was not sure when the abuse ended. Her last memory of it was at sixteen: we postulated there may have been other episodes after she started dating Jim, but they were just too painful to remember.

Neither one of us could account for the "empty" years. I wondered if there was some kind of battle in Tom's conscience, and some years he had more control over his behavior than others. But nothing seemed to make a lot of sense.

The memory work that Vicki and I did together continued into April. It had been over two months since her last full-fledged memories, and those were the strange ones at the beach with the men wearing animal masks. I put these in the "maybe" category. Like Dick, I believed they seemed out of character; Vicki was ambivalent. To me it made more sense to discount those and believe things were just winding down. Maybe those "memories" were fantasy, full of unconscious symbolism, rather than real events from the past. In time, maybe some as-yet missing pieces would complete the puzzle. Maybe not. It was possible, probably likely, that we would never understand everything.

A GLARING PAIR OF EYES

March, 1990

J ournal Entry. *My mom called and said she and dad want to drop by our house for an hour on my birthday even though I don't want to see her. Those were her words not mine. I told her I'd have to think about it.*

I told my mother I didn't want to see Daddy for a while although I would like to see her.

Virginia meant to have it her way or not at all and backed out of the visit.

I had a dream a year or two before this time of watching a tornado in the distance. In the dream a second tornado joined the first, making twin tornadoes. I marveled at them dancing with each other in a valley and then over a range of mountains. I was grateful for the space between us. The scene suddenly switched and I was at the ocean at Virginia Beach where I'd grown up. The tornadoes were upon me and I ran down cement steps leading from the boardwalk to the sand. I crawled into the cavity underneath the steps for protection from the fierce wind and flying debris.

The meaning was obscure, other than the obvious—that tornadoes are very destructive and Virginia Beach was my childhood home. Tornadoes are almost unheard of at our mountain altitude of 3500 feet, but I later read that twin tornadoes do occur even though they are extremely rare. What I didn't recognize initially from the dream was that the distance represented time. And that now that time was almost up.

March 7, 1990. Journal entry. Might have had my first 'memory' today. In reflecting over preceding signs. (1) Most obvious was a certain tension between my shoulders just below my neck. It wasn't physical, yet in a sense it was in my body. (2) My mind's been running x-tra fast the last few days. (3) Perfectionistic streak driving me crazy. (4) Violent episode with Vicki on Sunday when I verbally threatened her & held her with my feet.

After going to the shop and praying, a strong sense of being small—2 to 4 yrs. old & crying till I choked—while in crib. Tears of grief came to me as I relived it. As I walked up to the house, I imagined the face of my father & was overwhelmed with <u>strong</u> love feelings (very simple as a child) for him, which is very out of character for our relationship.

When I was young my mother crooned about my father's singing voice being so much like Perry Como's; she looked forward to their weekend dancing dates. He had an easy, outgoing sales personality and he loved to talk; and looking back it's not surprising that if he couldn't handle my mother's mental illness, he would have been oblivious to my inner workings. He was a traditional father who left raising the kids to his wife while he took all the responsibility for bringing home the bacon. He gradually spent less and less time at home, until as a teenager I saw him only every other weekend. Besides taking us to mass on Sundays, I have very few memories of spending time with him. I also had an innate antagonism toward him that ran deeper than my ability to remember.

I was also having periodical flashes of being left in the crib for too long; and to make matters worse for my infant self, when my mother finally appeared, I would have messed my pants, which brought on her wrath. The feeling that came along with this quandary was an existential distress: "This is not right; life is not supposed to be like this." This created anxiety and a wariness of life.

I suggested to Vicki that being an infant may have distorted my sense of time and thus escalated my fear of abandonment, but she was more practical: "Your mother was an alcoholic. She probably got drunk and left you in your crib for too long. And like you've said, you messed your pants and she took that out on you. Your father was negligent leaving you with her. He should have known better."

It wasn't a very flattering picture of either of my parents.

March was another unusually busy month as I finished up the quilts and tried to stay caught up with the decorators for whom we did wholesale work. Vicki had no new memories; that bode well for the entire family. And it looked like we were going to have the money to buy the van she wanted; it was just going to take a little more time. With no new word about my mother, I was willing to give that inevitable trip a little more time. Our resolution to make concrete plans at the end of March drifted into April when we did not get any further updates on my mother's health. With Vicki due in two and a half months, if the trip would wait, we would wait as well and visit after the baby was born.

Then Vicki got a brusque phone call from my step-mother. She pushed Vicki to shuttle me down to Florida by air to be able to be at the bed of my dying mother.

Vicki was noticeably shaken when she reported the call to me. "I think she was speaking for your father. He probably feels guilty."

"They weren't willing to invest anything, were they?" I asked sarcastically.

But before we could make plans, we got an Easter card from my mother. There was a check to buy each of the kids a small gift. In a hand-written note, Mother said the cancer was in full remission and not to worry about coming down. She said she understood how hard that would be as pregnant as Vicki was. "I'll come up in July, after the baby is born."

With a sigh of relief we surmised that we were off that roller-coaster. By and by, we bought the van after living for three months on our canned food storage and almost nothing else. It now was time to fluff the nest for one last baby. Vicki was forty-one years old.

Early in April Vicki made her usual trip to the OB doctor with the kids in tow. Then she went to her therapy group. It was late when she began heading home. Several miles outside of Boone on a meandering two-lane road, her attention was arrested by the headlights of a car suddenly drawing up behind her. A continuous string of petty fears welled up to trouble her: They're following me. Why? Why are they following me? She slowed to a crawl on a long, straight stretch, hoping the car would pass. But it didn't. Her fear then escalated and started to take over. She was alone with the kids, and it was a long, forty-mile trip to our house on increasingly more isolated roads. Her imagination made the worst of this situation.

She asked the kids, "Do you think that car is following us?"

Her question, her tone of voice and the darkness outside immediately drew them into her panic. The kids ducked down and peered into the blackness behind the car. They saw only two bright lights following them around every bend. The car behind slowed as Vicki slowed and accelerated when she increased her speed.

"I don't know, Mom," said a wary voice.

"It's catching up," a frenzied voice said.

"Now, it's slowing down." There was a communal sigh.

Mile after dark mile, Vicki inched along with the car behind coming closer and then fading. All the while, the kids' intermittent panic echoed her own.

Finally, as she approached West Jefferson, she turned down Main Street and the glaring eyes of the car behind did not follow.

The rest of the ride home was uneventful, but her system was filled with too much adrenalin. Finally, it hit her: It must have been a flashback.

"What do you think?" she asked me, relating the scenario after returning home.

Seeing her safe and sound and wanting to put memory work behind us, I told her that it was just her imagination.

"I think it was part of a memory. The feelings were incredibly strong. I *knew* I was being followed. You can't believe the fear I felt."

That night Vicki did not sleep well. In a nightmare the fearsome scene was recreated, but the surrounding scenery was different. Vicki felt herself to be a child. She was in the back seat of a car and terrified by the glaring pair of eyes following her.

Over the next few days her anxiety did not go away, but instead increased. My wife cancelled a late-afternoon trip into town that would have brought her home after dark. Her sleep was terrorized with strange images.

There was a fox and several other animals; real animals out to get her. The hawk was particularly vicious. Each night Vicki increased her dose of herbs to help her sleep, but she was only partially successful.

It had been so long that we did not recognize it at first, but her symptoms were the traditional pattern of a new memory coming on. Looking back, I think what threw us was the new, dominant element of fear. Fright had been present to some degree in the past, but now it was overpowering and its origin was different. It was not associated with the physical and emotional pain of violation or the shame that vexed the memories of her teenage years. This was a heightened version of the same fear that came with the last few memories that I didn't want to believe were actually memories.

The exotic images that troubled Vicki's sleep soon interrupted her daytime consciousness. There were flashes of different animals, bonfires and the ocean. The lack of sleep took its toll; she was soon screaming at the kids, and she got vicious toward me. I withdrew to the shop and the boys came to visit, complaining about Mom.

Vicki's own life became disorganized and with it, the entire household. This hadn't happened in months. By the time we acknowledged that another memory was coming, our house had reached a new state of chaos. Another difference in this new memory was that it kept coming and coming and never seemed to arrive. All the while things kept getting worse at home. As Vicki's fear increased, her mood fouled. Turmoil reigned at our house. It was worse than anything we had been through before; my wife looked like she was coming apart at the seams.

"I've set up an emergency session with Dick for tomorrow," she finally announced when I came up for lunch.

"Thank goodness," I thought so loudly that it leaked out of my lips.

"I may be part of the problem but . . . ."

I turned my ears off as she started into her familiar litany of my numerous degenerate shortcomings.

She stopped herself suddenly. "I want you to drive me to Roanoke."

I knew it was supposed to be a question, but it didn't sound like one. I stalled, pretending to mull the situation over. I didn't want to be pushed.

"If I could drive myself, I would," she added defiantly.

"I was trying to decide if we could survive through that much time together. You can't wait until next Monday for your regular appointment?"

"Does it look like I'm handling this very well?" she asked. I didn't bother to answer. With a sudden change in her voice she continued with a bribe: "I'll take you out to dinner with my father's therapy money."

It wasn't much of an incentive. "I hate to tell you this, but you're not the only one having a hard time around here. You've been making life miserable for everybody." I didn't say it, but I knew that a day away from her would be heavenly.

"That's why I'm going to therapy," she screamed through clenched teeth.

"Let me think about it."

She began a whine that pressed my guilt button. Then she changed her tack. "Besides, you'll get to hear this memory straight from my mouth. And this is going to be som-m-m-e memory." She had me hooked and she knew it.

"Have you remembered anything else you haven't told me yet?"

Vicki lied and said yes. She then strung me along, embellishing the same flashes she'd already told me. My curiosity got the best of me and it wasn't long before I had committed myself to being her chauffeur. I was dying to hear one of her memories in its raw, original state. While I had done a lot of hypnosis with her, we had never processed a memory.

Dick had to shift some appointments around to make room for Vicki. We arrived promptly at one o'clock, and Dick apologized for not being able to round up more than one hour. I was impressed with the prosperous changes in his business. Gone were the days with an almost empty calendar. He was already making plans to move down the street where he was going to head up a clinic with several other psychologists and psychiatrists.

With minimal pleasantries Dick opened up the conversation. Soon he was repeating the words that Vicki had taught me. Within minutes she was ready.

"I want you to go back in time . . . ."

My wife settled in the loveseat beside me as if she were placing herself in a nest.

"Let your feelings be your guide . . . and tell me where you are . . . ."

Vicki suddenly bolted. Her hand shot out to grab mine. "This one is scary." Her voice sounded almost childish.

Dick's response was strong and soothing. "There are two of us here to protect you."

Vicki mimicked a line I often used with the kids when it was time to work in the garden. "I hope you're wearing your muscles today."

She straightened up and then fluffed herself back into her nest. She intertwined her fingers with mine.

"I know where to start. With those headlights that scared me." She was silent momentarily as if she were getting her bearing. "I'm in the back seat of our car in Hawaii. I think Stephen is in the seat with me again. We're driving down a dirt road. I'm afraid. The headlights of the car behind us are scaring me." Vicki's voice took on a childish tone of genuine fear. "We're going down this dirt road. The car is bouncing. I almost hit the ceiling."

"It's a rutted dirt road?" I interjected.

Impatiently Vicki answered, "Yes, it's a dirt road with deep tire tracks . . . and ruts."

The emotions became intense. As if watching a movie, I could see the bobbing head of the little girl. There was a terrified look on her face as she kept turning her head from the rear to the front and back. She wanted to protect her little brother. She was franticly trying to figure out where she was going . . . and who was following.

"It's dark outside. It's the same road we went on last time." She seemed to come up for a second with an adult voice. "Our destination has sinister purposes."

"You're safe. There's nothing to be afraid of." Dick's voice was professionally reassuring; I suddenly wished mine was like that.

"I'm bouncing in the back of the car with Stephen. We're going down a long drive that opens into a pineapple field. The car stops." Her voice abruptly changes. "They're trying to scare us." She was close to shrieking.

"What happened?" I blurted, unable to help myself.

"When the car stopped, Daddy got out. He got something out of the trunk. Now, all these animal heads are beginning to peer into the windows. They're trying to scare us . . . . It's working. I'm totally scared." Her voice was oscillating back and forth between her adult and child selves. Her younger voice continued, "There's the hawk and the king and the fox. My daddy's the fox. Stephen is petrified beside me. He won't even look out the window." An older voice. "They're purposely trying to scare us."

She continued, "The men are wearing those masks. They get Steve and me out of the car and carry us out into a field. There is a big bonfire. It's dark. It's the only light . . . . There is something roasting over an oblong barbecue pit." Vicki later wrote in her journal that she hoped it was a pig. "There is a long table with chairs on both sides."

The hawk was holding little Vicki. She was taken to the head of the table where her face was pushed in and out of a pan *'full of brown mush, maybe feces.'* Then she was pulled away and something was forced into her mouth. The same bobbing motion continued. The leader climaxed. He undressed Vicki and stretched her out on the table. Stephen was forced to do oral sex on her.

My wife continued talking intermittently. She relayed only part of the information that she was reliving. There was no doubt about the terror she was experiencing. Her voice occasionally gagged with the sobs and muffled screams of a little girl being terribly abused. It appeared that she jumped in and out of the memory to keep from losing control. The balance comes from her journal:

'. . . . *Then the men at the table slid me along as each of them did oral sex on me. Then the final scene. They got up from the table and took their clothes off. (There were six or seven of them.) They lined up along the table and moved me down from one end to the other taking turns raping me vaginally and anally. The third one was my father.*

'*Then they put us back in the car and we drove out. I passed out. I woke up as my father was carrying me in the house. His words were, "Pretend like you're asleep."*

'*As we walk down the hall my mother timidly pokes her head out of her bedroom door. "Tommy, is that you?"*

'"*Just go back to sleep, Virginia. I'll take care of the kids." She disappears into her bedroom acting scared to death of him.'*

By the time Vicki had finished reliving the scene, the session was over. I had no idea of what to make of the memory Vicki had just relayed. "Blown away" probably comes closest to describing my feelings. Both of us were cognizant of the time. Dick gave her a compassionate smile and told her how courageous she was. He said he would talk to her about the content when he saw her on Monday.

Over the next few days there was a rapid deceleration of tension in our household. By the next Monday Vicki was feeling much better and drove herself to Roanoke. Dick retracted his previous statement of doubt about the last few memories.

"It's either a satanic cult or a pedophile group," Dick surmised.

My wife was disappointed when Dick did not want to dwell on the subject. Instead, he talked of the impending delivery of the baby. Vicki mentioned that we were thinking about using his name if it was a boy.

Using his same hypnotic technique Dick told Vicki he wanted her to take some time off.

"You've earned a break. You've been courageous; you're a sweetheart. I don't want you to remember anything until July. Have an easy delivery too."

I was disappointed with my wife's report the next morning, but what Dick was doing made good sense. We had been through a lot with that memory. It was a good time for a pause.

The only thing that troubled me was the strength of that last memory. It was hard for me to believe that a few words—no matter how professional Dick's voice sounded—could stop something that powerful. Her memories had always seemed to have a mind of their own.

One thing that we did not notice at that time was the correlation of this last memory and the calendar: It was just a few days before Easter.

TWIN TORNADOES

May, 1990

We were in a celebratory mood as we took some time off to go to the Temple in early May. We just felt the urge, not really understanding why. We were honoring our thirteen-plus years of marriage and what would certainly be our last baby. We prayed for a safe delivery, and on the way home we talked of withdrawing from life to get ready for this new addition. Vicki's therapy was on hold and everything was in order.

We hadn't been back in the house more than two hours when I got a disturbing phone call from my brother. He said that Mother had only two to three weeks left to live and asked was I coming down or what? I didn't believe him. I told him of the Easter card we'd gotten from her a few weeks earlier. He assured me he knew what he was talking about. Our life suddenly turned into a panic.

Vicki called my mother's nurse and confirmed what my brother had said. This new found panic turned into a whirlwind. Church friends who had watched the kids while we went to the Temple agreed to take them for a few days while we went to Florida. Vicki called her successful younger brother who flew all over the world and asked him to put our two tickets on his credit card and we'd reimburse him. (He did it but refused to be paid back.)

We drove three hours to Charlotte and then flew to Fort Lauderdale. Vicki had to lie about how pregnant she was to get on the plane. Not-quite three-year-old Bethany still qualified as a freebie.

This was Vicki's first flight, and it was traumatic with the mild turbulence triggering into the memories she'd just had. We were also squeezed tightly in coach with people all around us. They were too close for Vicki—way too close. She was anxious and hyper-vigilant. She was supposed to be my support person and she knew it, but this was almost too much.

I grabbed the window seat, which suited Vicki; I wanted to be in my own world. I reminded myself that this was a once-in-a-lifetime event: that one's mother dying was supposed to be a real tear-jerker. But it was hard to garner up much feeling for this impending emotional loss.

I couldn't figure out what was wrong with me, but I had only seen this woman twice in almost fifteen years. I tried reviewing my childhood, going back as far as I could. I remembered a story my mother told of when I was five years old and she was driving me and another boy to kindergarten. She had burned him with a car cigarette lighter for something he'd done to anger her. (It would be some time before I would finally admit and then understand the reservoir of anger she possessed.) But mostly there was a void; I hadn't had much of a relationship with her. Finally, as we flew over northern Florida I felt some moisture in my eyes; that was going to have to do. Maybe I was more together about this than I thought I was. I then thought of the last words my sister had told Vicki when my wife explained about the Easter card we'd gotten and why we hadn't made any plans to visit: "If she doesn't know she's dying yet, she will when Jody shows up."

With my brother's directions we pulled into a modest neighborhood of mobile homes, and we wandered around, not sure of where we were going until we saw an old lady walking a dog and decided to ask her. That old lady turned out to be my mother. My brother later told me that she hadn't walked her dog in ages. Apparently, my sister's assessment of what my visit meant was correct and it gave her a burst of neurotic energy.

We sat outside in lawn chairs and talked of our kids and other light topics for a while, but there was nothing light about the mood. I was astounded at how much my mother had aged since the last time I'd seen her less than two years earlier. She kept interrupting the conversation and scolding her dog, who wanted to get up and move. Finally, the mosquitoes forced us inside. Vicki whispered in my ear as we stepped into the screened porch that she would not be able to stay long because of her allergy to cats; my mother had several.

I thought back fifteen years to my first visit home with Vicki. I told Mother that Vicki was highly allergic to cats, and Mother said she'd clean and prepare a room. After a vicious allergy attack that forced us to sleep in my van, Vicki swore my mother must have locked her cats in the room in preparation of our visit. And that set the tone for their relationship.

Inside her trailer, Mother asked if there was anything that I wanted—a going away present, I assumed, although she didn't use those words. Without the money for a second trip down and with the space constraints of an airplane ride, I couldn't imagine taking anything home. Being the family's "black sheep" who never visited, I didn't think I was entitled to much until I saw an old lithograph of *Little Red Riding Hood*. This framed artwork had hung above the handsome mahogany bureau in the dining room in my childhood house in Virginia Beach. Often I had gazed at it and the scene had resonated deeply within me.

I hadn't recognized it as a youth and wouldn't for a few more years, but it was a perfect Rorschach for my experience. Little Red is in the deep dark woods on her way to Grandma's. Dressed up, including a red hooded cape, she is holding the basket of goodies with one hand and suddenly stooping down to pet her little terrier with the other—probably to get comfort herself. Her head is cocked; she has just heard something in the distance—it came from the direction of Grandma's house—because she is looking anxiously over her shoulder. She didn't know it, but as a child I did—it was the wolf, and she was heading straight toward him.

The scene, with the aid of my untamed imagination, perfectly pictured the anxiety that often pummeled me as a child and now still reared its head in me as an adult. I asked about it and Mother was thrilled that she had something I wanted. It was only much later that I would recognize that she, too, carried Little Red's baggage, but that she had been medicating it for years with alcohol.

The next day Vicki and I tried to vacation a bit. We started with a gourmet breakfast, and our hotel had a walking tour through a tropical garden that was crowded with vibrant flowers and polychromatic-leafed plants.

My brother came by; he was getting his doctorate in psychology at a local college. We talked for a couple of hours, catching up with life. He had the easygoing personality of my father. He apparently had not inherited some of the more debilitating baggage from my mother's side.

Then Vicki and I got in the car and headed to the ocean to walk along the sand.

"I'm getting triggered," Vicki said after we got out of the car. "Maybe it's those last few memories, but I can't take much of this."

The palms were swaying in the gentle afternoon breeze and even as preoccupied as I was, I could see how this scene might remind her of Hawaii. Having grown up at the beach, few things were more soothing and grounding for me than walking along the ocean's edge amid the waves lapping on my bare feet. That's what I wanted to do. I needed some grounding.

"You know, your mother didn't even ask to hold her namesake."

I thought for a moment. I couldn't remember.

"I don't think she really likes kids," Vicki continued.

"Yeah, you're probably right."

"And she's mad." I looked askance at Vicki, who continued, "She's probably angry that she's dying."

I hadn't seen that, even though I considered myself rather sensitive to the moods of other people. I thought my mother had been in a good mood.

"Jody, you're not here," Vicki said without much sympathy. "You're not. And you're not the only one having a hard time."

As we got closer to the water, Vicki got noticeably more upset. It was reflected in her increasingly sharp tone of voice—a tone to which I was oblivious to. She brought up several vignettes from her last memory as our tropical surroundings reminded her of them, and it slowly dawned on me that I was not going to get my walk along the shoreline. The entire episode was difficult: I was dealing with my dysfunctional mother's impending death while my dysfunctional wife was threatening to go off the deep end. And my dysfunctional self had no clue how to handle any of it.

We again visited my mother that evening after her doctor's appointment. It appeared that Vicki was right about my mother's mood—at least now. She had paper and tape and pushed me to wrap up *Little Red Riding Hood*. Something didn't seem right about her attitude. While I was wrapping the picture, I was glad Vicki was there to keep up the conversation because I had nothing to say and couldn't think of anything even when I tried.

I did have a simple childlike glee because I was getting something important, something that I really wanted. It was like being a kid at Christmas, except as a child I'd never gotten that special something that I really wanted; it was strange that now I was.

After I sat down, my mother left the room for a minute and returned and dumped something heavy in my lap. In a brown grocery bag was my penny collection of twenty-five years ago. I was dumbfounded. I'd asked her about it several times over the years and she'd apparently lied, saying she knew nothing about it. She said she'd gotten it out of her safety deposit box earlier that day. The only thing I could think of was that she greatly overestimated its value and didn't trust me with it.

Vicki gently reminded my mother that Bethany was named after her, but it didn't seem to click.

Recognizing that it would be the last time to get information about her childhood and perhaps insight into mine, Vicki and I had strategized a series of questions. We asked her about growing up. Mother said she'd been hurt terribly when her mother had died; she was just a young teenager, perhaps twelve. I asked about her parents but she didn't go into any depth.

Suddenly, something came to my mother. "When I was getting a massage recently, I remembered something." She smiled to herself as it came back. "My mother used to give me enemas all the time. Even when I was ten or twelve years old. I don't even think I was sick." Mother continued saying that she hadn't liked it and used to fight her mother. And then I remembered getting enemas as a child and fighting my mother. My memory was that they had more to do with her anger than anything therapeutic.

Vicki and I looked at each other and wondered if that may have been sexual abuse. Unexpectedly, I saw my mother in a new light: that mean spirit that sometimes rose in her, she had inherited from her mother.

The conversation lightened up, but she still didn't hold Bethany. As we were getting ready to leave, Vicki suggested I give Mother a blessing. Mother pulled off her wig—Vicki thought for emphasis—and I saw the pitiful, nappy fuzz that showed the ravages of her chemo. My already conflicted emotions got even more tangled.

The next day we picked her up to take her to the hospital for a transfusion. My journal notes that she was 'basically cold and rejecting. Not much of a hug good-bye as we left for the airport.'

On the airplane heading back home I held *Little Red Riding Hood* as if it were my life support. I considered how foolish I looked—and I know how foolish I felt—but I couldn't let go. It was an umbilical cord to my childhood. At the same time, I gave myself kudos; I was handling the situation well. I hadn't fallen apart and become an emotional wreck.

My mother died thirteen days later on Memorial Day. She did not have a funeral or service of any sort. She was cremated and had her ashes thrown in the ocean.

> *June 11, 1990. Journal entry. A new journal. The baby was due Saturday but isn't here yet. We're almost ready. Jody and I are at a real stalemate. Apparently his mother's death is really upsetting him. There have been 3 violent episodes in the last 3 weeks. I have been told he would leave me at least 10 times for a variety of reasons . . . . This doesn't even cover the fact that he's totally uninterested in me & my feelings and has broken his word to me on several things as if they were totally unimportant. I've handled it okay, but the last couple of days have been very depressed. We got no compassionate service from the church at his mother's death . . .*

Things only got worse a few days later when I got a copy of my mother's will and a check for ten thousand dollars. (The money went to pay Vicki's parents back.) As I was reading through the text, I saw how unevenly the money was divided between me and my siblings and I again saw my mother's anger. I understood her insistence that I take the lithograph, which she mistakenly thought was worth quite a bit of money. It was to appease her guilt.

A sibling later filled me in on some of my mother's mental gymnastics, and I saw the consequences of being the black sheep. Mother had taken back stock that she had initially put in the names of our older children. She did not compute that *she* had moved one thousand miles south and refused to cultivate a relationship with Vicki.

My mother's most basic failure in life had been her inability to generate the gravity to hold her husband and children in orbit and create a family. I suspect she hadn't learned it as a child; I'm sure her mother's untimely death hadn't helped, but it was more than that. I suspect it was related to her severe anxiety and it went back generations—as well as the habit of self-medicating with alcohol and tobacco. Her last will and testament only accentuated her anger by creating ill will among her children, reiterating how much she didn't care.

June 23, 1990. Journal entry. A piece of good news. One new daughter, Hannah _____ Dalia was born June 18 at 6:35 p.m. after a 9 1/2 hour labor . . . . And it was a girl, a girl!! How could that be? I had known all along it was a boy. We don't even have a complete girl's name. She weighed 8 lbs. 1oz. and is beautiful black-headed baby. We went home at 3:30 a.m., exactly 24 hours from when we left home.

I started a new journal in June but didn't have an entry until Christmas Eve. However, this hardly meant that nothing important happened. Rather, I see it now as a forty-year-old man coming apart at the seams because my long-gone, forgotten childhood, is haunting me. The death of my mother was the trigger.

Dealing with my mother's death was interrupted in late June when I got a call from my father. That was rare in itself. He usually had his wife handle any necessary contact through Vicki. We had visited him occasionally (and sometimes with the kids, who liked his swimming pool) because he was close to the Atlanta Temple. I was further surprised when he said he wanted to come and visit. He wanted to see the house I'd built. He hadn't been to see us in ten years—since just after Erin was born, and then only to give us a lecture on birth control. I remember it well because it was only three words long: "Buy a TV."

I didn't take this call seriously because he wasn't dependable. I had learned this lesson over and over since I'd left for college. But he called a few days later to confirm: he had a business trip in the area and would stop by. He told me to think of a few work projects around the house that we could do together and he would spend a few days. I told him I was terracing the hill behind our house with railroad ties. He laughed and said he was almost sixty-seven years old and to think of something less strenuous.

I couldn't help myself; I started to get excited. Part of me knew this was foolish, because he was not good at keeping his word. But even knowing that, I found myself getting mildly exhilarated trying to think of things I could do around the house with him. There was a little kid inside of me that was getting animated because his daddy was coming home and wanted to spend time with him.

My father also told me he'd had something of an epiphany: If my lifestyle suited me and I was happy, that was okay with him—being happy with your life was what mattered. This too was an eye-opener. He'd been judgmental about the way we lived from the time we'd moved to the mountains. His idea of success involved money and status. I didn't qualify because I was kid-poor and grandkids didn't count in his book.

He called me one more time a week later to tell me that he'd gotten a doctor's appointment, and that was forcing him to postpone things just a little bit. He was having some trouble with his stomach; it had been going on for a while. This doctor was a specialist and renowned and it was difficult to get an appointment. And he would get back up with me immediately afterward.

That next phone call never came. His promise to call back would be the last time I ever talked with my father. The next communication came from my step-mother to Vicki several weeks later to say that it appeared that his cancer, fifteen years in remission, was back and his condition was serious. My father was in the hospital and the doctors were doing tests and preliminary treatments. She would give us an update when there was more information.

The tests soon showed that my father's cancer was not only in his stomach but had spread all over his body and there would be no reprieve.

'We got the call that his dad's melanoma had come back. He was given 3 months to live and then Joe died quicker than anyone thought he would, and we did not make it in time to see him. We did then pack up all the kids including the newborn and truck down to Atlanta for the funeral.

'I did enjoy showing off all my beautiful children to Jody's relatives. Jody again had to deal with the emotional ramifications of losing both of his parents in 3 months. He had a hard time talking about it. All I remember him saying was how absurd the Catholic priest's eulogy was, asking for contributions to redeem his father's soul—as if money could recompense a lifetime of sins.'

In early September when we returned home from my father's funeral, I noticed a nervous tick in my left eye. I knew it meant I was emotionally constipated and couldn't process my feelings, but I didn't know what to do about it. I didn't feel like crying about these two people that I felt I barely knew, who over the years through their actions had demonstrated they didn't care about me or my family. Gradually, it hit me that this was exactly the source of the pain: the loss of not having those relationships. I had grown up feeling like Little Red Riding Hood, alone in those dark woods and suspicious and fearful that there was danger up ahead. Neither one of my parents had seemed to notice or care, so entrenched were they in their own worlds.

A bit later my older sister sent a package of mementoes from my mother's house. It included an old photograph of my mother sitting in her father's lap. She was about eight years old and squirming to get off, looking like she'd rather be any place else in the world. He seemed oblivious to her anxiety. We again began to wonder about sexual abuse—whether it was a family tradition, because I was beginning to accept it in myself.

Years later, another piece of the puzzle of my mother fit into place when I got a birth certificate, and it showed that my mother had had a previous pregnancy. I understood then why she had been kicked out of college—that was the awful something that she had done. It accounted for the touch of shame that came when she obfuscated that bit of her history. She had been a rebellious kid from the beginning; sexual abuse will do that.

INTRODUCTION TO SATANISM

June, 1990

T he upset with my parents' sudden deaths was not happening in a vacuum. In early June we finally put on our bed a set of sheets that I'd given Vicki for Mother's Day. It had a large floral print with a tropical flair and within a few days Vicki recognized it was triggering her. One of the flowers—an iris—brought up a memory from Hawaii:

> *'I was laying on this table naked with my hands tied & legs tied. The leader walked up & gave me a bunch of irises . . . . Then they had me get up—again holding me tightly by the back of the neck— & had me wipe blood on the leader's erect penis. Then I was forced to perform oral sex. I was floating in & out of consciousness. Then they put me back on the table & he did oral sex on me . . . . '*

> *June 29, 1990. Journal Entry. Another memory. As related to total fear I feel when Jody sees anything about another woman.*
>
> *Was at a cult meeting. Leader acting affectionate towards me. Sat me on table—naked. Told me to watch & I'd see how real women acted. Scene before me was men & women. Women dressed in all sorts of seductive costumes. Some dressed modestly. They & men were doing all possible kinds of sexual acts on each other. Leader kept coming over to me repeating over & over they were real women & I ought to copy their actions. Had someone hold me on their lap & do anal sex while someone else performed oral sex. He*

kept insinuating I ought to be willing & able like they were. Then he laid me out on the table—I think my legs were tied & he vaginally raped me. It hurt like I was being ripped apart. I bled afterwards. Then he made me stand in the circle & he made me look at him while he repeated over & over if I ever told I would be killed or kill myself....

As soon as she felt well enough after Hannah's birth, Vicki set up an appointment with Dick. With these new memories, so different in character than the incest memories, she was desperate to talk to him. She made the two and a half hour drive to Roanoke without me and settled the kids in the waiting room, the older girls taking care of two-week old Hannah. While his furniture was familiar, he was in his new office just a mile down the street from his old one and appointments were now scarce. She had to take what she could get. But Dick looked the same, perhaps with a few more pounds—success pounds.

She related to him the last few memories she'd had since their previous meeting and how fearful she was. It was obvious that his post-hypnotic suggestions to take a break from memory work had not been effective. My wife wanted comfort and reassurance. She wanted him to tell her she was courageous and call her "sweetheart" and for things to be as they had been for the last two years. She didn't want this growing sense of fear to metastasize; she wanted him to excise it, or at least reassure her that it was transient and she would make it through.

With about fifteen minutes left in the session, Dick dropped a bombshell. He was stuttering as he said, "I'm not equipped to handle ritual abuse. You're going to have to find another therapist."

Vicki was devastated. At her most vulnerable, Dick cut her loose. He apologized but said firmly that this was out of his league. As Vicki related the story to me the next day, she said that he had another patient that was admitting to ritual abuse. This new patient was from the area and trying to escape from the cult and Dick was afraid. He had been doing research on ritual abuse and discovered that the cult didn't like losing one of their own. They sometimes went as far as to threaten the therapist who was treating a member who was trying to escape.

Dick didn't want that in his life. Several times he said that he wasn't equipped to handle that. He didn't know whether or not Vicki's father was still involved in the cult and warned her to be careful. And good-bye, it was over.

"Dick was afraid?" I said with incredulity. "Ex-military Dick, who took his pistol when he went camping?"

The fear that my wife had hoped Dick would assuage was instead amplified. We began to wonder if her father *was* still involved. Could it be possible? We hadn't seen any signs. These incidents had occurred thirty years earlier. Was that enough time to let it go?

> *August 6, 1990. Journal entry. 2 more horrible memories. The last one first since I just remembered it. I have been in tremendous emotional and physical pain since I started remembering this one. I've barely been able to keep it together. Now I feel a lot clearer. I recall what happened.*
>
> *I was playing in our living room in Richmond, VA. It was daylight. The doorbell rang & I opened it. A man holding a baby walked in. The baby was dressed in a christening dress. A woman trailed behind. Things started getting very dark looking and somewhat blurry (I think I was drugged. I remember earlier drinking some Kool-Aid in the kitchen—maybe laced with LSD). My father came out & in a very friendly manner greeted the man. Some more men came in like a typhoon of Darkness. Shortly we all went upstairs. The leader of this group took me in front of him and as he undressed me, told me I was going to be privileged enough to help in this sacrifice. Then he handed me a paring knife & told me he wanted me to chop off the baby's finger. (The man looked like my uncle and I remember I hated him with every ounce of my 7 yr. old body.) I told him no. That was a baby & I wasn't going to hurt it. He kept saying his part, getting more and more furious each time I refused.*
>
> *Then he had them lay me down on the bed closest to the window. They stuck an electric shock gadget (it looked similar to a curling iron) in my vagina and proceeded to use it. When I started screaming from pain, they put a pillow over my head. After doing*

this for a while they got me up. Since I was about to collapse, one of them held my neck & kept me on my feet through sheer force. The leader started his thing with the knife & the baby again & I gave him the same response. He put me back down on the bed & used the electric shock gadget again, this time in my anus. The pain again was intense, but I didn't scream this time. I didn't want the pillow. This time when they finished someone had to carry me over to him. He started with the knife thing again & again I said no I wouldn't hurt the baby. Then in a rage he kicked me in the belly. When I fell on the floor, he stomped my belly. He had them pick me up, carry me to the baby who was on the trunk altar & then hold the knife in my hand while they used my hand to cut its finger off. It was shrieking at the top of its lungs and I was screaming no, no, no trying to make them stop. They handed me the finger and said I was one of them and I collapsed. I have vague memory of the baby being dismembered and at one point its tiny arm and fist being placed in my vagina.

Thanks again Dad for a lovely childhood!

This next one is the memory I had 2 weeks ago. It & the one I just told happened when Jack was born & my mother was in the hospital for month afterward because of hemorrhaging. Daddy was "taking care" of us.

Steve & I were sitting on little chairs in the living room. The doorbell rang & a crowd of men came in. A few minutes later it rang & a little girl came in with a man. She looked like a little Shirley Temple in a white chiffon dress. She sat in a little chair beside me. The men were in a group doing something. Maybe taking some kind of drug. Soon we all went upstairs & they made me undress. I was sitting on one of the twin beds. The girl sat on a footlocker draped in black (the same altar they used for the baby). The men lined up & proceeded to vaginally & anally rape her. I looked & felt exceeding sorrow until they came & started anally raping me over & over & over. Very painful. Then they had us line up & had someone hold her up as she was too hurt to sit up by herself. They had me go up and kiss her vagina. Then they laid the backside of an axe on my head so I could feel its weight & told me they wanted me to watch because if I ever told the following would happen to me. Then they whacked her over the head and split her skull. Then they chopped off her arms & legs. Later they put her in the footlocker & hauled her out when that set of men left. Oh, the extreme sorrow I felt!

With these new memories Vicki began furious networking in the hope of trying to find someone to help her understand them. We learned that these groups were vicious and obviously criminal, and as Dick had said, didn't like losing one of their own.

An insidious paranoia ensued around our house. Vicki wondered whether our phone was tapped. She wrote in her journal just after the memory noted above that she was no longer going to talk to anyone about Satanism over the phone. *'If I have to talk about it, I will get in the car & go see someone. I will only discuss it in person with the following people.'* She limited these conversations on Satanism to Keith, me, her therapists, her therapy group and a few chosen friends from church.

She also began noting her blood pressure, which had begun going through the roof. For years of getting it checked at every OB visit, I had been amazed that she was able to keep it around 105 / 70. Now it occasionally jumped up to 140 - 160 / 90 - 100. It was dangerously high at times, but usually dropped after she felt safe enough to talk about what she was remembering and get the tension out of her system.

She began to worry about our children. One of them could easily be kidnapped and used for extortion—if "they" wanted Vicki back. I tried to look at it rationally, but her consuming paranoia was contagious. From what little we had read, stories of cult vengeance were rare but a few seemed to have validity. Playing it safe made sense.

We were certainly vulnerable. We decided to restrict the kids' play area to a section close to the house, and we had them tell us if any strange cars came up or down our road. It would be obvious because our dirt road only saw a half-dozen vehicles a day. For the first time in our lives we began locking the doors at night and when we left the house. And we were grateful that we had dogs—dogs that barked, and especially at strangers.

I tried to reason my way through Vicki's infectious fear. Her father was nearly seventy years old. The other cult members from Vicki's childhood days would be about his age. Were they still involved? Were they watching us out in the remote area where we lived? It seemed unlikely. They would be too old. Had they been keeping an eye on us and we hadn't known it? Had her father's regular visits with Virginia been a method of keeping track of us over the years? That was a possibility, but it seemed farfetched. Or had her resistance to comply with the leader in those sacrifices mean that she was a failure and a dropout and they didn't want her? I liked that possibility.

It seemed preposterous to me that they could have kept up with my wife's crazy life, but it wasn't totally contrary to what we'd heard. We lived in the middle of nowhere; it would take an enormous amount of energy to maintain any kind of surveillance, and we had never had any hints of our lives being monitored. But perhaps Vicki going into therapy had been a trigger. Her father *did* know that she was remembering, but he didn't know how much. At the time when the letters were written and sent, she had only remembered the incest. Perhaps those letters had been a mistake. Much of a cult's ritual consisted of illegal activities and being exposed was what they were trying to prevent—and prevent it at all costs. Just the constant thinking about it laced my caution with fear.

That time in my life was so . . . hard. I was telling, not only Jody but my therapist also. The memories were pouring out of me faster than I could process them, and I was an emotional wreck. The fear was a pulsating being that stayed with me always. My children saved me. The daily care of so many bright faces grounded me in a way nothing else could, other than perhaps the arms of my husband. But we were not always getting along very well. We fulfilled our parental and wage-earning roles, but in the middle of the night when I was waking from terrifying nightmares, it was not Jody I called. I had tried that a couple of times and had been met with anger about waking him up. One time I woke him up to ask for a blessing because I was so afraid. He put his hands on my head and started out with the right words and then blessed me with the strength in my arms and legs to vacuum. I thought I was going to kill him until I realized he was still asleep.

It was our branch president, Keith, who eventually became my 911 answering service in the middle of the night. But that was after some reluctance on his part. To begin with, he didn't want that role. It was certainly not in the Church handbook. It was only after his wife suggested that maybe that's why he was called to that position that he got his own testimony. And later I remembered having a flash of inspiration that said, "When you see him, you'll know it's time to remember." And that's why Keith was in my life. Keith and the phone and the steps leading up to the second floor were my solace and my grounding.

I had been brainwashed in very emphatic terms as a six-year-old that if I ever told anyone of the horrors I was being subjected to, I would kill myself. They had a young woman act out this very thing at one meeting. She stood in the middle of the circle of people who had come out to this isolated pineapple field to participate in this frenzy of sex that included us children. The leader produced a knife, a long one, and gave it to her. He screamed at her about telling and then told her that she knew what to do. She then proceeded to stab her belly over and over. There was blood and she collapsed. As a child I believed it; as an adult I am skeptical. But whatever . . . That spring I was now a pregnant, forty-one-year-old woman and I was telling. My brainwashed inner child came out, and I fantasized many times in the middle of the night about grabbing a knife and stabbing myself. Hannah literally saved my life. No way could I stab a baby and there was definitely one in my belly, and therefore I forgot about the idea of the stabbing myself.

I would pick up the phone, settle on the steps and call Keith. He was always patient and caring and was able. He was what I needed at that time in my life. His wife Sharon was too; she probably woke at my calls and was supporting her husband in his role as my 911 person. How long this went on for, I don't know. They started up again just before Hannah was born and lasted months afterward, months that felt like years. Those 2 a.m. calls sometimes lasted for two hours. I remember the fear pulsating inside of me for several years afterward until it finally dawned on me that these people were not going to appear out of the darkness and harm my family.

There was little information available on Satanism at first. Over time we gradually learned there were three levels of those involved with Satanism. First were the dabblers. In general, these were teenagers and young adults who were playing at it. They might have meetings in the woods, dress up in robes, sit in a circle, do chants, even profess worship of the devil. They might even sacrifice an animal—a stray dog, a member's old pet, or in some more ambitious cases, someone else's livestock. These groups were transient and not particularly cohesive. This was not the kind of group that Vicki had been in.

The second group were serious and their pursuits included illegal activities. They were not playing; they were dedicated, not so much in the religious aspects of their practices, but about the secrecy. They could not afford for their disciples to come and go because of the criminal nature of some of their activities. There were threats and blood oaths and consequences for betraying the trust of the cult; the more stalwart disciples could be upstanding members of society. They were involved with prostitution, drugs and other underworld activities. There was a profit motive as well as the bacchanalian nature of their meetings, which included lots of drugs and sex—including sex with children.

The third group was the most serious and dangerous and secretive. They had very effective methods of member retention, which were reputed to include murder. There were few to speak of their doings, and they made sure of that. These were the groups that threatened therapists when one of their own sought counseling. These were the generational cults. These were devotees who were serious about their religion and the ensuing Darkness that came with it. They were involved in the same illegal activities as the serious group mentioned above, but these groups had been in continuing existence for several generations. The members married and had children who served as new recruits. These children were physically and psychologically damaged and indoctrinated from the earliest ages until they fit the profile for cult membership. These cults used a combination of intimidation—often through brute force, positive and negative reinforcement, and brainwashing—to get what they wanted. Because of the long-lasting nature of these groups, over time their members and then their children got jobs in the public sector as policemen, judges, doctors, and became influential people in society— people who needed to keep this aspect of their lives secret.

We would later guess that most of the cults Vicki was involved with as a child fit the profile of the second category, except the Richmond group, which took their religion much more seriously.

From a religious perspective, the word "Satan" comes from the Hebrew meaning "adversary." Most of the theological tenets form an antithesis to traditional Christianity, often mocking Christian values and ordinances. Sex, including homosexuality, was a sacrament in this creed through which enlightenment was to be achieved. The concurrent use of drugs fostered this notion.

As Vicki was networking, looking for a new therapist, she talked with a psychologist experienced with ritual abuse. He was too far away to work with, but he said he had worked with a number of victims and every one of them had been associated with the military. Over the years we would hear this often from both therapists and survivors. What was the connection between this type of abuse and the military? Had that been how her father had gotten involved? He had been in the army for twenty-plus years.

Some time later Vicki got the name of an expert in the area of ritual abuse from one of the books she found. His name was Dr. Dale Griffis, Ph.D., and he had been working in this field for decades. He was an ex-police investigator and now an independent contractor who did trainings and seminars for police departments across the country. He inevitably got an initial call for assistance when a local police department came upon a scenario that didn't fit any previous identifiable profile and had an occult leaning.

Vicki got his phone number through information. (My first thought was that he must not be that afraid of cult retaliation or he wouldn't have a listed phone number.) Then she made a cold call. She got him and he was willing to listen. He first asked a question and Vicki answered that, yes, her father had been involved in the military. He listened and validated the scenes of sacrifice that she had remembered and the nature of the groups. When she mentioned the little town of Hersey, Pennsylvania, known only for its chocolate factory and its amusement park, he stopped her.

"I was just called in to work a case there," he said. "Where else did you live?"

Vicki mentioned Richmond, El Paso, and Shreveport.

"I've worked cases in every one of those places."

And Dale became a believer. Tom had been transferred by the army to one post after another, and every post had a history of cult activity. It had to be more than coincidental. That knowledge was incredibly validating for Vicki.

As the conversation wound down, he told Vicki he was busy and not always at home, but he would be glad to help. He was not a therapist, but he understood the cult mentality and would help where he could—mostly in validating and giving her information. Over the next several years he told us more as Vicki made intermittent phone calls. He was writing a book on the involvement of the military in ritual abuse. Some of our country's clandestine agencies were involved with mind control—a topic that the Nazis had been researching. When our government brought over German scientists after WWII, their complicity with war crimes was overlooked and their records were doctored to allow them to enter our country.[6] The government rationalized that we needed their knowledge of missiles, space medicine and much more, and decided to overlook the fact that these men had been involved with heinous crimes against humanity.

Vicki's father had been in post-war Germany. Was there a connection there? After his stint in Korea, much of his military time had been spent with missiles. He had said that he knew Werner von Braun personally. Was all of this coincidental?

Dale gave her the name of a local investigator whom he trusted who might be able to find out whether her father was still involved. Dale also told her to be careful; local police were sometimes infiltrated by the cult.

6   This recruitment of German scientists was known as Operation Paperclip.

A NEW THERAPIST AND
A NEW VOCABULARY

August, 1990

After Dick dropped Vicki as a patient, she felt adrift; she was without mooring in a sea of terror. We had no map or guidebook or any way for us to discern direction. We didn't know where we were or what we were supposed to do. Without Dick, she now had no one to hold her hand and escort her through this fearful panorama of new memories. She had no sherpa who had been there and back to lead the way.

This new place in her memories was so foreign and horrific—much more so than before. This place didn't make any sense in our normal day to day lives: people worshipped the devil, killed and cut up infants and children, and forced her to participate. And these people often reminded her that if she ever told anyone about what she'd seen, the same thing would happen to her. There was also no escaping; and to the child who was doing the remembering, even though she was in the body of a forty-one-year-old who was married and had nine children, these dark figures seemed to be omniscient.

And now she *was* telling. She was telling me every time we had a therapy session down at the shop, where reviewed her miserable past. She was telling Keith in those middle-of-the-night phone calls—those many lengthy phone calls that he should be canonized for dealing with. And occasionally she would tell our whole congregation an abbreviated, censored version during a testimony meeting. (That did not go over well at church.)

My wife was a talker and talking was how she released the roiling inside of her. And talking about her past was the one thing she had been thoroughly brainwashed against. Now she was revealing what she had seen, and she was scared beyond her capacity to manage.

We really needed some help—someone to walk us through this new stage of therapy. And miraculously, within a month, she had one.

Neither one of us remember how Vicki got Peter's name or phone number, but we somehow learned that he was experienced in the field of ritual abuse. That's what we needed—someone who understood what Vicki was going through.

That initial phone was memorable. Vicki explained her reason for calling and a little bit of her background, but before she could continue, he took over the conversation.

"Do you find that you sometimes lose time and don't know what happened for a period of several hours or days?" he asked.

The volume of the phone was loud enough for me to hear. Vicki and I both looked at each other, wondering what that question meant. Finally, my wife answered, "No."

"Have you ever had someone come up to you and call you by a different name? I'm not talking about a nickname. I'm talking about a stranger calling you by a totally unrelated name?"

Vicki and I exchanged questioning glances again. "No," she said a little warily.

"Have you ever been called a liar by someone you don't know?"

We again looked at each other.

"Do you ever find strange items among your possessions that you have no idea where they came from? Like someone else's keys or clothes?"

These were very strange questions. "No."

"Have you ever had the sense that there is more than one person inside your body?"

Vicki said no. I thought for a minute and realized that she had her normal part that functioned well, keeping the family running smoothly and pulling her weight in the business, and then she had her crazy part that blamed me for everything wrong under the sun. And I laughed a little too loud.

Peter apparently heard me and asked Vicki if I was her husband. He asked to talk to me and asked me the same questions about Vicki. With the last one I fudged a little bit and downplayed the difference between those two parts of herself. I was pretty sure I knew what the right answer was supposed to be.

"No, that's just standard dissociation. What I'm trying to sort out is whether Vicki is a multiple. Whether she has multiple personalities. I've got one such client and I can't handle another. This woman calls me up at night. I've told her I'm not available after hours, and I'll review that with her during the next therapy session, and she has no knowledge of having called me a night or two earlier. She's not lying. It was another personality that made the call."

Vicki took the phone back. The conversation continued and then came the hard question. "Would you consider bartering?"

There was an anxious pause on our end of the conversation.

Peter was very matter-of-fact. "I'm in a practice. I can barter my half, but you would have to pay the half that goes to the practice. Call and set up an appointment and we'll see how it goes and take it from there."

We learned two new words in that one conversation that sent us to researching: multiple personality and dissociation. These new words, along with multiple perpetrator abuse and PTSD, were part of the vocabulary of ritual abuse. We also learned another word that would explain many of the problems that Vicki and I had encountered: transference.

Even though as part of my Introductory Psychology course, many years earlier, I had had to learn the psychological defense mechanisms, I really did not understand what dissociation was. It would take some time to comprehend this particular word, because I was swimming in it and had been for much of my life. I think that is why neither one of us remembers much of our time with Peter—even though Vicki did many, many sessions and I did several. At that time we were both drowning in it: Vicki for the terror that came with her new memories and me for the detachment that I felt from the sudden deaths of my parents.

Dissociation is that sense of being disconnected from your body or emotions—the reality around you—and is a normal defense mechanism that we all have against stress. It is now presented on a continuum where on one end we might find ourselves daydreaming to escape boredom—in a classroom or long distance driving—and on the other, the most severe end, the personality is fractured into different selves that may not even be aware that other personalities exist within the same body. The latter state is the multiple personality that Peter specifically asked about before taking Vicki on as a patient. I had seen the movie *The Three Faces of Eve* and was fascinated by the concept of multiple personality but wondered what precipitated this severe dysfunction.

As we studied we would eventually come to understand that multiple personality was caused by severe and repeated physical, psychological and especially sexual abuse, particularly at a young age. Here the victim experienced intolerable stress and being able to compartmentalize it was a method of coping with and diminishing the pain. This compartmentalization of pain (facilitated by the fracturing of the personality) allowed for some alters (different personalities) to have amnesia with regard to the experiences of other alters and thus hide from the pain. We learned again that traumatic amnesia (not remembering a traumatic event) was a common method of dissociation, of keeping the pain of the past at bay. In multiple personality disorder, these alters could have different names, ages, backgrounds and even genders. This severe dissociation was a normal defense mechanism in the case of very severe abuse, but the most chilling thing we would learn was that with regard to ritual abuse: cultivating multiple personalities within a victim was done purposefully. The perpetrators wanted to fracture the personality to make the individual experiencing the unthinkable abuse malleable to his or her handlers, but could also pass as being normal to a casual observer by switching to another personality.

This information seemed incredible. But it did make sense—those who were involved in criminal activities wanted pawns who were malleable. They wanted pawns who were convincing liars; pawns that could do a filthy job like prostitution, and then not remember it or its degradation; pawns that could simply change selves and appear normal to the casual observer.

There was another aspect of dissociation that we would find woven throughout Vicki's memory work: the ubiquitous use of drugs. These drugs actually induced a form of dissociation. Drugs increased the revelry of the ritual by heightening sensuality, which could be interpreted as spiritual.

Since wanton pleasure was a satanic sacrament, the use of drugs made sense. The perpetrators used drugs to help create the faux spirituality that surrounded the orgies, tinting them with a religious hue.

Over time, as the public became more aware of the activity of satanic cults, professionals preferred to use the terms "multiple perpetrator abuse" or "ritual abuse" because of the baggage that came with any reference to the word "satanic." The religious overtones of the word could easily obscure the more fundamental abuse being perpetrated on children. And it was obviously horrific abuse. Other survivors were remembering it much like Vicki had—as PTSD. They were having intrusive thoughts in the form of flashbacks or nightmares and basically going crazy with fear—the fear that was still buried from their childhood.

Through networking Vicki was able to talk with a few of these other survivors, but their fears made for very short conversations. It was the same paranoia that Vicki had: the fear of talking and the fear of retribution. They too had been brainwashed to believe that if they told, the cult would kill them. Vicki did learn that the stories they were telling of their childhoods were basically the same as hers. There was some connection to the military and there were religious ceremonies reverencing Satan coupled with the abuse, especially the sexual abuse. There were sacrifices; there was blood, and the ceremonial drinking of blood, and the eating of flesh. And these survivors were all heavily invested in therapy, as Tony at her Boone group had been.

From the very first meeting it was obvious that the nature of Vicki's memories did not bother Peter as they had bothered Dick. He had heard similar stories before and that offered a form of validation to Vicki—to both of us. That in itself was very comforting because the strangeness of these new memories—we had never heard of this kind of abuse—was initially the hardest part for us to deal with. But apparently other people had been through these kinds of experiences before. It was real. However, Peter maintained a strict rule about not calling him after hours.

"This memory work is going to be very difficult," he told Vicki in a form of understatement that we didn't appreciate at the time, "and you need to get together a support team—people you can call day or night to listen to you and help you work through this; friends whom you trust who can handle the kind of information you are going to tell them."

This was Vicki's homework assignment after her first meeting. Peter wanted her to pick five people she trusted whom she could talk to when her fear became unmanageable. I was grateful that I was not allowed to be on the list. The idea was to take some of stress out of our personal lives and to prevent it from invading his.

Keith was at the top of her list. He was her "go-to" person in the middle of the night. She didn't trust anyone else to do that job. During the day she inevitably came to me, even though I wasn't on the list. If she pushed too many buttons, too often, and I became unglued (this did not take much right after my parents' deaths), she would need to have some backup support from friends and she found several.

Within a couple of sessions Vicki tackled the uncertainty foremost in her mind. Was her father still involved?

Peter was thoughtful for a moment. "From my experience, I would say, it's best to assume that he still is."

Vicki was terrified at his response. That was the most frightening thing he could have said to her.

"Now, your fears of your phone being tapped are unrealistic. But I think for the sake of precaution we should assume that he is still involved." He paused before continuing. "If we assume that he is, he's not going to do anything to bring attention to himself. Exposure will be his greatest fear."

Vicki replied, "It's my fear that I'm worried about. I'm terrified by what you're saying. I don't want to believe it."

"I think it's best to take precautions . . . ."

Vicki interrupted him and pressed. Her voice was frantic and earnest. "Do you think he's still involved? We've never seen anything to indicate that he is."

Peter warned, "You've remembered over a decade of criminal activity. He didn't get caught. He's obviously smart about it."

Vicki replied, desperate: "I don't want to believe it. I'd never visit my parents again. And then my mother would be heartbroken."

"Your mother had to know what was happening. On some level she was collaborating."

That thought was heartrending to Vicki. She didn't want to believe it either.

Peter asked, "You're currently refusing to see your father, and your mother is lining up on his side, is that right?"

Vicki knew this but didn't want to believe the implication.

"I think it best that you continue to avoid your father. You have eight children at home that you're responsible for. You can't afford to fall apart. There is something else that we should consider. I know the money you receive from him is a help, but I think the best idea would be to write him a letter and tell him that you've finished therapy, at least for the time being, and you no longer need the money."

While the intent of that deception was obvious, this was too much at one time. Vicki was petrified with fear. And now the money. The money *was* helpful, but it was also a tangible signal that her father was taking responsibility. It helped the world make sense: her father did care; he was taking responsibility for his past actions.

"Of course, don't let your children visit. In fact, I'd advise eliminating any contact with him at this stage of your therapy. This is for your own benefit. Any contact is liable to trigger memories and as much as possible you want to control that. At some future point you can change your mind."

The fact that her father might still be involved played on our worst fears. It created a sense of panic that did not go away—despite Peter's assertion that exposure would be Tom's worst fear. Did this have something to do with all those twenty-dollar bills that he so freely handed out? Had the incident with the pig several years back *really* been a come-on, an invitation, a way of feeling me out? Had he been keeping an eye on us and the children with those regular visits with Virginia? Was it possible that he was involved with some kind of group, even though he had always seemed to me to be a loner? While he was very friendly with an expanse of casual acquaintances, neither of us had heard he had any close friends. Was there something going on that we didn't know?

And what about her mother? Vicki had now had memories that spanned thirteen years during which her mother was conspicuously absent. She had been home to pick up the pieces, but she didn't seem to have known what was going on. She didn't seem to want to know, other than to ask a few feeble questions. In Vicki's memories Virginia appeared to be blind—to a fault: unwilling to demand answers of Tom and certainly not willing to confront him.

I agreed with Peter's suggestion that Vicki write that letter. The money was helpful; it covered the cost of the half of Peter's therapy that he had no choice but to charge. But the letter would be an excellent decoy. If her father believed that she hadn't remembered any more than the incest, it would give us a cushion of safety that we both felt like we needed.

Peter helped us better understand the problem of Vicki's incessant questions and her JD attacks. She had never been able to convince me that they were simple questions requesting information, especially when I felt battered by her compulsiveness. Dick had clarified them as a control issue: I had no trouble believing that. They were actually quite effective. I noticed over time that it was often easier for me to just avoid the initial imputes of her questions than to deal with answering them. I generally found them affronting and hurtful, because they obviously belied a lack of trust. In the short run this strategy worked for Vicki, but it created resentment on my part as the hurt accumulated. This could later come back to haunt her, because my anger was always more volatile than hers.

As Peter came to understand the nature of her constant questions, he had a different slant: he blamed it on transference. Because I had spent so much time doing the memory work with her, I had inadvertently played the role of Vicki's therapist. Part of the natural process of going to therapy was for the therapist to take on the role of the problem person in the client's life. In Vicki's case it would be her father. Peter said much of the emotional baggage that belonged to her father had been "transferred" to me instead of a therapist. If she had lived closer to Dick and could have gone to sessions every week, or twice weekly if needed, then much of her anger could have been placed Dick as the surrogate perpetrator. He would have been trained to handle it and then the two of them could have explored those issues together as part of the healing process. Also, since I was taking the heat of Vicki's anger, that allowed Keith to be the Good Guy, the Rescuer. He was never the recipient of any of her anger.

As I thought about what Peter had to say, I realized that the early violence in our relationship also contributed to this transference. It, too, mimicked her relationship with her father. Looking back, Vicki had from the beginning tried to "straighten out" her relationship with her father by manipulating me. That had been the source of much of our friction.

"So what did Peter say to do about it?" I asked Vicki when she returned from a session dedicated to exploring the issue. Dick had been no help in this regard. I was hoping with Peter's insight that we might really start to make some headway with this issue that had plagued our relationship for so long.

"He said that the transference had already happened. It was too late to try to change that. He could be a therapist in the sense of counseling me, and he said if you wanted to talk to him that would be fine, but that transference was too firmly set. He said I couldn't possibly make it to sessions twice a week and process the memories in the office. He's right. It's just too late."

I discerned that Vicki felt relieved, that Peter's answer had been a reprieve for her. She would not have to give the questions up—not that that was possible anyway. And I had to smile at the childlike simplicity of her thoughts. The incessant questions were so much a part of her that I couldn't imagine a Vicki who felt safe and not plagued by a deep inner insecurity. (That benefited me. Her profound sense of need assuaged my own deep insecurities.) And while this insecurity may have created some transference difficulties, it also created an intimate bond between us. It was something very personal that we did together. Keith once mentioned to me that he envied the closeness of our relationship. He knew us well and I took that statement as a compliment, but the intimacy that we had achieved had come through years of hard work.[7]

The memory work we did together was healing not only because she was exorcising her past and hopefully getting it out of her system, but our time together also provided a counterbalance to her shame. I knew all about her childhood and was nonjudgmental. And if I could accept her, knowing what I did, then maybe she would be able to accept that part of herself as well. This was an inherent part of the healing process.

---

7   Vicki has a placard on our bathroom mirror that says: *You will always be my friend; you know too much.*

Although there was a period after my parents' deaths during which I was emotionally unavailable, I didn't want to give up doing memory work with her. And Peter did not see a problem with us working on it together the way we did. I was enthralled with it; it was like looking into a crystal ball or some kind of seer stone. Through a small aperture in her mind, we gazed into her past—her polluted, filthy past. In a profound way I sensed the process as being spiritual. I was gazing at a rare slice of the human condition that was invisible to most people. It was horrible, yes; it encapsulated the negative potential of human nature.

NEAR DEATH AND DEITY

August, 1990

August 19, 1990. Journal entry. Had another memory 3 or 4 days ago. A very scary one. My blood pressure is also high. 140 / 98. I need to take it for a while.

*Memory. In Richmond. At a house for sale. I think it's Halloween. It's a party. I'm taken up to a cage next to a table. Something on the table. I think a dead man. Next to table is a cage with rats. Big ones. The leader & his wife — blonde hair in french twist — are sitting at the front behind the table in king / queen costumes. He calls up all the kids. We are nude. Has them stand on table in front of him while he kisses their genitals. He asked my father where his kid was. I had run off & hid in a big round drainage pipe. They found me & brought forth me & drainage pipe. Put me in it & closed ends with wire mesh stoppers. Then put in 2 **big** rats. They were pretty tame & only sniffed me all over. Scared me silly. Then they started turning the thing around & around. Rats started scratching me. One bit me on small of my back. (Jody found a scar in the exact spot). Then they took me out. Took me to doctor table & he nursed hurt back. Then they took me off (I could hardly walk & kept falling against my father who was nude). My father forced me to do oral sex on him. Then showed me table where woman lay on table & mice running in & out her vagina. They laid me down and put mouse in my vagina. I screamed. They taped my mouth. They kept doing the mouse trick. When they let me down,*

I walked towards outskirts of party. Someone grabbed me & forced me to do anal intercourse. Then I crawled to our car & climbed on floorboard of backseat & passed out. Dad woke me. Dressed me in clown costume — blue w/ yellow trim & we went home.

I remembered Mother earlier dressing me in costume griping to Daddy that I wouldn't get to go trick-or-treating if he took me with him. He said I'd have fun & took me.

I remembered the beginning of this memory. We arrived at the house for sale. There was some maggoty dead person hanging from a cross they kept trying to make me look at. I wouldn't & they forced my head with their squeeze-the-neck trick. Then they had a feast & tried to get me to eat cubes of what they said were the man on the cross. I wouldn't eat it & they slapped my face & ear so hard I can still feel it.

I also remember another time where they put me in this cage that went round & round. It had bars that I tried to climb as they turned it, trying to keep up with them. They went too fast & I would lose hold, falling against the bars & getting very dizzy.

No date. Journal Entry. Another memory. This one in El Paso, Texas. I was 13 & I was going off with my father. I was very rebellious & sulky about going & kept saying I didn't want to go. My father kept pushing me to get in the car. When I finally got in the car, I had a moment of intense fear of being alone with my father. (This is the same fear I feel about Jennifer and Jody.) We drove off in car & left neighborhood & got on 4 lane. Parked in front of pancake house. I looked over at a hamburger joint across the street wishing I was just a normal teenager. Two men in a shinier, fancier car (I think red) pulled up & we got in their car. We drove off & they passed around a Coke & a little pill we all took. Sometime later (about 20 min.) we were outside El Paso in the desert. We turned off down this long driveway. We came to this unattractive adobe house with other cars at it & got out. I was still acting somewhat defiant. We went in to this room that had funny carnival-type mirrors & then into a dining room that had racks to hang clothes on. We took off our clothes, hung them up & went out.

There was a circle of people standing around a ring. The drug they had given me was starting to take effect & things in the ring looked bizarre. Someone naked riding a horse. Something like a high altar with maybe a body on it. Then they wanted a "volunteer" and I got volunteered. They dragged me to the center of the ring, put me face down on a door & strapped down my arms & hunched up my butt. Then put door under the horse who was standing . . . . I left my body as soon as pain got unbearable. I watched the rest happen from above.

(Vicki included a crude illustration in her journal showing her spirit outside of her body.)

When they pulled the penis out I started hemorrhaging. They panicked & hustled me into my clothes & into the red car. They rushed back to the station wagon. Daddy got scared—I guess because I blacked out. Next, I remember I'm in Army hospital & everyone asking "What happened?" & everyone saying "I don't know." My mother came in & asked the same thing & got the same answer.

So what happens when the fear or pain becomes unbearable? We learned that a victim typically dissociates. When the abuse is very severe and happens on a regular basis, especially when the victim is young, they can learn to dissociate by fracturing into different selves such as a multiple personality. While Vicki had several episodes of severe dissociation, she never became a multiple. We wondered if victims didn't necessarily have to split into different personalities, even with the most severe trauma. Could a victim, as in Vicki's case, learn to dissociate by leaving their body?

I was well-read on the subject of out-of-body experiences (OBEs), often reported as near-death experiences. But Vicki had no interest in the subject. For her it fell into the category of the occult, and she hated anything that even smacked of the occult. She hated Halloween and was conflicted about taking the kids trick-or-treating. She didn't like costumes and would not allow the kids to wear masks. In our early days together we had often gotten into fights if I brought a book home from the library that leaned in that direction. She claimed it brought a negative spirit into the house, and if I wasn't paying attention, she'd put the book outside.

I say this to point out that she had no background or knowledge in this area. She had never read anything about it. When it started showing up in her memories, I was surprised—and fascinated. She simply postulated that being able to leave her body was better than splitting into a multiple. She certainly did not think of it as spiritual; rather, it was a survival technique.

No date. (Probably mid-September) Journal entry. After going to Jody's Dad's funeral I came up with this memory.

This one was in Richmond, VA. Dad & me drove up to the cult meeting at house for sale where they had the Halloween party. Just a few cars were there. We went in & Fat Guy took my hand & held it so I wouldn't bolt. There was a coffin in front of us. In it was a black witch. She got out. They put me in. Then closed the lid. I felt something at my feet. Mice. I was so terrified I had to leave my body. They left before this. My spirit hovered outside the casket the rest of the night until they came back in the morning & got me out. I couldn't walk or even move. I was a zombie. They told me if I didn't go get in the car they'd put me back in the coffin. I got in the car. They drove me to school. I went to the principal's office as I was late. They told me my mother had called me in late. I went to class. Teacher put arms around me & said she was glad to see me. After school my mother picked me up. Jack in car seat. She never commented on me being gone all night. Acted as if all was normal.

I did not work with Vicki to retrieve these memories above; she did these on her own. The fact that there is no date is indicative of the stress she was under. She mentioned to me in passing that she had had them and that they were in her journal, but we were getting along so poorly I never accessed them. The fact that I was not familiar with these memories, which would have normally fascinated me, is indicative of the stress I was under.

No date. Journal entry. 2 more brief memories.

This came as I was sitting on the couch feeling very dizzy. I remembered being hung upside down & being pushed back & forth like a swing & twirled around & around. This was the Richmond cult.

Another memory. Again of the Richmond cult. The leader — Fat Guy —bringing me over to him, looking me in the eye and saying,

'You'll never get away from us.'

I looked confused as I already knew I wouldn't get away. He got mad because I didn't look afraid and he said, "Did you hear what I said? You'll never get away. We'll always know where you are & we'll be able to get you anytime we want."

He got madder and madder because I wasn't being terrorized, the reason being I already knew all of that.

Those several months after Hannah's birth were the most difficult time with Vicki's memory work. While she would have more difficult memories in the future—the general pattern was for them to get worse and worse— we were unprepared for these, perhaps because we were thinking a few months earlier that the memories were almost over. It was a shock that the memories got so much worse, so quickly. Looking back, the fact that I was overwhelmed with my parents' deaths kept me off-balance and I was less of a help. And again, these memories had a physical component. For the first time since I had known her, Vicki started having dizzy spells. Sometimes these were overpowering and she would spend a few hours or sometimes a day in bed.

During this time Vicki asked for a blessing to help with her memories. While I was there, I don't remember who gave it to her. The blessing told us that her memories were being ordered and that she would not be overwhelmed. God, who knew her limits, was controlling them. Neither one of us understood the last part since both of us felt overwhelmed. But as I look back now with hindsight, her memory work often pushed us to what we thought of as the brink—and then over—but we still managed to run the house and bring in enough money to pay the bills. The kids got to their activities, so at a superficial level most things were functioning. We were just at our wits' end—stressed out, and consequently fragile. And now, looking back, I must concede, the memories were certainly being ordered. As they became more difficult, the strength to deal with them also came. And that Someone who was ordering them had to have a writer's flair because the storyline would have been fascinating if we hadn't had to live it.

As had been with the onset of the incest memories, a primary battle with these cult memories was believability. Peter did not discount these memories. As had Dick with the incest memories, he had heard them before and that was incredibly validating. These latest memories coincided with the publication of the first books on ritual abuse and Satanism; apparently, it really was happening to other people and that too corroborated what Vicki was remembering. But we wanted more validating proof before admitting them into our lives and giving them credibility. Vicki did this by calling her mother every time a new detail—something previously unremembered—from her childhood came to light in a new memory. Each time Virginia validated it. Like the incident with white cat these tidbits slowly formed a foundation for belief. If extraneous details of these memories were valid, the memories as a whole were probably valid as well.

Vicki's next journal entry recounts an incident from her childhood that she partially remembered the old-fashioned way. It included a broken living room window in the house where she had lived when she was thirteen. She had grown up with her mother telling her that Stephen had broken the window with his baseball bat; he would have been about ten years old. Now Vicki was remembering it differently. She was in the living room with Stephen and her mother and father. Tom announced that he was taking Vicki out for the night. She remembered it as the first such outing since the incident with the hemorrhaging from the horse.

'I'm bucking. Being surly — rebellious, etc. Anything not to go. He's pushing me toward the door & Stephen grabs his arm. Daddy slings him back & Steve goes thru glass window (my mother always told us Steve broke it with a ball bat) Daddy pushed me on out telling mother she can handle it. He pushes me in car & I tell him I hate him. He looks crestfallen and is in a very somber mood the rest of

*the evening.[8] We drive to the pancake house parking lot where we
are met by his buddies. One, obviously high on drugs, dances over
to me and clucks me under the chin with a "Hi Doll," hands us
white pills and a drink. I'm spaced out before we go any distance
at all. Very dizzy & disoriented. We get to deserted house & go in.
Past funny mirrors to where we undress, then outside.'*

We were too busy trying to survive these cult memories to notice any
regularity or pattern to them at the time, but that was about to change. With
hindsight, it is obvious that there was a certain consistency to her memories
and to our reaction to them. As with the incest memories there was enough
time between each major cult memory for Vicki to process them. Again,
they sometimes included corollary memories that seemed to spin off from
the major memory. They would fill in details that Vicki might have missed
or tap into another scene that was similar in content or closely related along
the timeline. After each memory there was a span of days for us to repair
our relationship.

I had to let go of the hard feelings that came with the sense of being
battered, and Vicki had to get enough clarity of mind to separate me from her
father—so that I was no longer the bad guy. Then she had to forgive me for
being human—possibly less than human she sometimes said—and not able to
be a better support person. During this particular period just after my parents'
deaths I was much less emotionally available. A workaholic by nature, I had
a tendency to hole up in my shop. I would sew because any hands-on activity
was grounding for me. I also started writing again, which was an emotional
release for me. We still made an effort to continue our date nights even if they
only consisted of a hike at the nearby park. But mostly we were going through
the motions—attending regular church activities and a homeschooling group
the kids belonged to—and that was the best we could do.

If I was going to surface from my funk to breathe and reconnect with
my surrounding life, it would be during one of our date nights. It was our
best chance to rekindle our friendship. This particular Friday afternoon
Vicki interrupted my hibernation and suggested we go for a hike at the

---

8   This was not meant as irony.

park. We started talking and gradually I began to thaw. She asked what I was writing and I told her it was a recap of my parents' deaths. She thought that would be helpful. She then talked of the memories she'd had recently— the ones I didn't know about—and how difficult they were. Certainly they had to be near the end; they couldn't get much worse.

Before long we were joking about the preposterousness of her alternate childhood. It was almost impossible to believe. It was the most light-hearted moment we'd had in some time. We began speculating anew about whether her father was still involved. While Peter advised that he likely was, we tended to believe he was not because we had seen nothing that even intimated that he might be.

I let Vicki read what I was writing and then we went for that hike. It was the closest we'd felt to each other in weeks.

Soon afterward I noticed her mood starting to change. At first, I was offended that she was already starting to tear down the closeness that we'd just struggled to rebuild. What started out as her typical pesky insecurity questions were turning into what I felt like was battering. As we drove up our dirt road several days into this unfortunate about-face in our relationship, we were greeted by an almost-full harvest moon cresting the horizon. It was a huge and spectacular butter yellow in a cloudless sky with a few pinpricks for stars away from it. Then it clicked. Based on her present mood, her next memory would arrive in concert with the full moon. That was about how often they were coming—about every four weeks. And then I remembered the satanic calendar: full moons and new moons were a big deal as well as specific holidays like Halloween, Christmas and Easter.

While I didn't like the reminder—full moons would keep on coming and that was the antithesis of our deep desire that her memories were almost over—being able to anticipate new memories would be a help. Knowing that she was going to go crazy for a few days, I could steel my emotions. I could tell myself that there was no point in feeling hurt; she was not being herself. Full moons might never again be romantic, but I wasn't the romantic type anyway. If I could talk to myself enough, possibly I could respond to her verbal pummeling with Buddha-like calm and compassion. That was unlikely, but I relished the thought.

I longed to be above the uproar that she engendered just before she remembered a new piece of the puzzle of her past. Perhaps if I could temper my reaction, it would calm the household down. I hated it when she and I got into it and she hustled all the kids into the car and raced off down our dirt road. While in the flashback she saw herself rescuing the children from me, the truth was that it rattled them. They didn't feel safe when she was acting that crazy. And then she would "come to" about a half mile away and slowly return home as if nothing had happened.

As I had guessed under that almost-full moon, the tension in our house steadily increased over the next few days. I tried to keep my cool, even though it was in short supply. Unexpectedly, Vicki showed up at the shop early in the afternoon. I could tell by looking at her that she was in a foul mood.

"I want you to work on a memory with me," she demanded.

It was the first time she had asked in quite a while. I was irritated at her demanding tone of voice but flattered that she would come to me. Maybe it was because I had tried hard to keep it together this last time, or perhaps it was because of that date night she'd instigated.

With my hesitation, she added, "It'll be a good one. You'll want to hear it."

Wary but curious, I arranged a couple of chairs facing each other in what had been our old living room. It was moderately dark because windows were at a premium when this house was built a half-century or more ago. "Where do you want to start?"

"It's another Richmond memory. Those are the worst. It starts at the dinner table. I'm seven years old. My father announces that he's taking me out with him again." She had remembered that much already. With her eyes closed she feathered herself in the chair as she was accustomed to do. She got herself into that peculiar state: part in the present and part in the past. "At the dinner table Daddy looks at me and announces that he and I are going out tonight. My stomach turns in knots and I quit eating. The other kids look up, look at me, then at Daddy and then look down. My mother protests but he rebukes her and she pushes her plate away. I go to the bathroom and vomit. The next scene I'm in my parents' bedroom. My mother is dressing me. My father's gone out for a few minutes to get something.

"I tell my mother that I don't want to go. I say, 'Please, don't make me go.' There is urgency in my voice. My mother's face is confused. 'It's not fun. They put people in cages with rats and hang them upside down.'

"'That's silly. Nobody does that. You'll have fun.' I furiously shake my head no.

"She pushes me through the door into the hall. My father is standing at the other end of the hall. He is waiting for me. Did he hear? His face is inscrutable. I try and assess if he heard me tell mother, and if he did, what he will do about it. It is a *very* long walk down that short hall. The need to know if he heard is overwhelming."

Vicki came out of the trance-like state of remembering and said, "This is the same need I have when I ask you a question. It's the feeling of *I've got to find out or I'll die.* It's the anything-is-better-than-a-secret." The urgency and sincerity in her voice was almost overpowering. I suddenly wanted to be better at answering her endless questions. I felt sorry for that little girl. I was afraid something bad *was* going to happen. It inevitably did in her memories.

Vicki went back into her trance. "My father takes me by the hand and we go to the car. All the way to the meeting I wonder if he knows. He has to stop while I vomit again. We pull in to the same old Richmond house and barn that's for sale. There are ten to fifteen other cars. We go in the barn and Fat Guy's wife takes me into a stall to the left and takes my clothes off. There are twenty-five to thirty people."

I interrupted the flow. "Did you tell me before that she was your Sunday school teacher?"

"Yes." Vicki stopped as if considering something. "She was mean as a snake. But not on Sundays. She was my Sunday school teacher. In the cult, the women were often worse than the men. They could be more cruel."

I paused for a minute trying to take in this charade. It was not just her father who was duplicitous; this couple who were leaders seemed to be as well.

"When I reenter the main room, I see a big platform up high at the back and my dad is talking to Fat Guy up front. I'm real nervous wondering if my dad is telling him. Then Fat Guy comes up to me and pokes me in the eyes with his index and middle fingers. 'You told!' he says loudly. Then he shrieks in my ear, 'You told!' I know I'm in big trouble."

I was captivated by my wife's story and my heart was aching with sympathy. I knew it was going to be bad for the little girl who would somehow survive and grow up to be my wife. These men and women were vicious and cruel in a way I couldn't understand. Why did they want to treat children this way? What was the origin of their debased motivation?

"Two or three men take me up the steps to the top of the high platform. I'm in front of the group. They start putting ropes around my neck and underarms. While they are doing this, they are pushing me off the platform and then grabbing me before I fall. They do this about ten times before they completely push me off and the ropes catch me. I hang about halfway to the ground.

"The pain gets bad. I leave me body. I'm free of the pain."

As Vicki continued talking, the deep weariness that life was a struggle abruptly departed from her voice. Although she didn't say it in words, it soon dawned on me that she was a spirit flitting around. She was much more animated, exulting in the feeling of release, and I realized that she was indeed relating an out-of-body experience. I was awed.

"So what's going on?" I asked, full of curiosity but carefully modulating my voice to show no emotion. I wanted to know what it was like.

"My body is hanging by the ropes, but it's unconscious. I must have passed out from fear. I'm in the back watching everything. Fat Guy is telling the group that he had to wipe me out because I told. My father is sitting at the table with him and his wife. He's being treated like an honored guest because he brought me in and reported that I told."

I asked her to describe the setting.

"It's that same old barn. The chairs are arranged in a semi-circle facing the front. There's a coffin in the front and a fire off to the right. There's always a fire. The table with Fat Guy and my father is between the fire and the coffin. I'm in the back watching everything. I can see my body hanging. And there are stalls off to the left, just after you walk in the door."

"It's a two-story barn?" I asked trying to make sense of the scene.

"I guess. The ceiling is pretty tall." There was lengthy pause. "Before my spirit left my body they cut my heel and between my toes for blood to use in their ceremony. They passed the chalice around and everyone stuck their tongue in. They said several prayers—incantations really—and my spirit went back in my body at that point. There was liturgy and some Christian hymns turned inside out to demean Christ and worship Satan. There was the usual orgy. I remember looking down and thinking that at least I would miss that."

"Were there other kids?"

"Yeah, there were four or five.

"After everyone left, Fat Guy told my father they were going to take me down and revive me. They used something under my nose and lightly slapped my face. After reviving me, Fat Guy said they were putting me in the coffin because I told. I was scared silly again. They put me in and closed the lid. It was padded and I felt like I was suffocating. I left my body almost immediately—just after they left the barn. I sat on the wooden bench up in the front and looked at the coffin. Jesus Christ came and sat down beside me."

I was flabbergasted and yearned for details, but I also did not want to interrupt the flow and bring her out of the hypnotic state. Lots of questions sprang to mind: What was He like? What was it like sitting next to Him? What was he wearing?

As if reading my mind, she continued, "I felt totally loved and protected by Him. There was no pain and no fear. I just knew that the world was okay and that one day I would have a life of joy and peace. He sat with me through the night. As morning approached He told me that He had to go: He couldn't abide the presence of evil men and they were coming." Her journal continued:

'I told Him I didn't want to go back into my body and He said I didn't have to. I could go with Him. I almost did; He was so loving. He told me if I did go back in my body, I'd be able to help Him fight against Satan, but I could do whatever I wanted. I decided to stay & work with Him against Satan. They—the evil ones, including dear old Dad—came back & got me out. I was about dead. Dad thought I was. He kept wondering what he would tell Virginia. Fat Guy told him I wasn't dead. He acted like he knew what he was doing. Dad dressed me, put me in the car (laid down in back), drove me home, carried me in. My mother met him in living room, looked at me and I at her. No words were spoken. He laid me on my *bed & then left the house. My mother spoon-fed me as I couldn't lift my arms & treated me like I was sick, but never asked where I had been or anything else.'*

I was a sweet seven-year-old girl trapped in a living nightmare. I had been going to church and learning about Jesus since I was a baby. Now my adored Jesus was sitting beside me. It was a wonderful, innocent feeling of adoration that I felt. It was very real. He was my hero and of course I would do anything for Him. So when He told me that I could help him fight against Satan, I wanted to help Him.

I know it was remembering this out-of-body experience that was the turning point in my healing. I have never doubted for a minute that it really happened. This last memory gave me energy to heal. And heaven knows it was going to take a lot of energy. It gave me a testimony of Christ that is totally precious to me—one I can turn to again and again when needed and the same feelings of warmth, love and ultimate safety will return. It secretly gave me feelings of "self-worth," something I was seriously lacking in: That Christ loved me enough that He would take time from His busy schedule and sit overnight with a seven-year-old girl who desperately needed Him.

IT'S CHRISTMAS TIME AGAIN

November, 1990

Sometime after my father's death Vicki persuaded me to begin seeing a therapist. I'd forgotten about it until I saw it mentioned in one of our journals. She felt there was all kinds of hidden abuse below the surface that just needed that therapeutic touch. She may have expected memories to mushroom for me as they had with her, but they did not.

Bill, the therapist that I started to visit, was someone for me to talk to but it never went anywhere. The recent deaths of my parents had left a hole, but I had little idea what exactly was missing and even less of an idea of how to fill it. The bits and pieces that I'd remembered seemed to be too ephemeral to be of much importance. And I don't remember him having much of an opinion about the most troubling issues in my life, which would have been Vicki's incessant and vexing questions. But that fall—as I was slowly coming out of my funk—I did have something of an epiphany—one that I'd had before: If someone in our relationship was going to flex, it was going to have to be me.

Vicki seemed incapable of flexing. I suspected she did not even think of it as an admirable quality, particularly in dealing with me. I was irked that she could do it in professional relationships; she was an excellent salesperson, knowing just when to give and take. But she was unable or unwilling (or both) to do it with me.

No date. Journal entry. Not being able to ask Jody questions is like making love with my father. Asking the questions and getting an answer is my key to safety. Since I couldn't ask my father any questions, I ask Jody. If he answers, I know deep down he's not my father.

The congeniality of our relationship rested on Vicki feeling safe. She couldn't feel safe without being able to ask questions. What I got out of it was the house running smoothly and her mood being civil. That was usually enough. With eight children at home and our modest income it took a magician's touch to keep the logistics operating. I didn't appreciate that enough at the time. But I had another incentive outside of keeping the peace at home: I wanted to birth the memories with her. After that last memory with the out-of-body experience and a night spent with Jesus Christ, I was hooked. That memory rang true to me. From what I'd read years ago, OBEs generally occurred in painful or life-threatening situations. And if Christ did come to sit with her, I wanted to find everything I could about who He seemed to be. This was the turning point in my reaction to her memory work, nudging me out of my depression and at the same time giving me an incentive for answering her endless questions, which was in essence the same question asked over and over again: Can I trust you?

She now often talked about her inner child—her seven- or thirteen-year-old self—as if it were one of her birth kids. (She picked this jargon up from one of the books she was reading.) She was emphatic that this child needed to feel secure before she could remember and then pass the information on to her forty-year-old adult self and then onto me. I thought of this as a psychological gimmick she used for leverage for more questions, but I eventually came to accept it as one of the rules of the game.

Vicki was very protective of her "inner child," as she came to call her. She even gave her a name: Tori. If I wanted to go back into her past with her, I was going to have to placate Tori. I was going to have to find a way to force myself to not get upset with her invasive queries. It required a lot of talking to myself. (Also, I think the writing I was doing helped. It was a way of expelling that emotional constipation, which allowed me to be more focused on the present and more able to remind myself not to take the questions personally.)

Admittedly, I wanted to be there as future memories erupted; especially if she had more encounters with deity. I wanted to understand what was going on and why. But to do that I could not offend little Tori or she would refuse to talk. I needed to remind myself that, above all, she needed to feel safe. This was another battle I wasn't going to win any other way than by conceding.

It was just in time, too. Vicki was tired of writing her own memories and I soon took over. I don't think she wanted to go back into her past, which is what it took because she wrote down her memories in a coherent narrative. She had to go back in her mind, into her past, and relive the scenes a second time, and then she would write them down. She didn't want that responsibility anymore. The new pattern would soon be for her to come down to the shop, and I would scribble in one of our journals, trying to gather as much information as possible while she relived a childhood that chilled me to the bone.

> *November 9, 1990.* (This was the last memory that she wrote in this journal.) *Another memory. This one from Hersey, PA. On the hill where we went sledding. A cult meeting. Everyone in black. About 12 people in a circle. I'm in a chair in the circle. There's an altar of stones & they are slitting the throat of a tan dog. They stick their hand in the blood & I have to taste it. They make me feel partly responsible for dog's death. At same time I feel very sad about it. We move to a table with dead puppies on each plate. They cut mine up & try to get me to eat a bite. I won't. They force me & I vomit it back up all over the leader. The leader gets furious. Tells my father to take me home & not bring me back until I'm more obedient. He takes me home. No one is there. They're at church.*
>
> *He lays me on his bed & tells me I'll be sorry. He goes & grabs a broomstick & thrusts it up me several times. I pass out & wake up in my bed & my mother & siblings come in. Later that night I discover blood in my urine. I'm very sick. Feverish, etc. Go to doctor.*
>
> *Am told later it was a kidney infection caused by sulfa drug.*

(I added in Vicki's journal.) 'This memory was triggered by the death of the runt puppy of one of our dogs, and then the death of one of our other dogs and a cat—all within a week. Vicki was close to hysterical.'

Now I understood that dark spot we'd found when we were doing therapy the previous spring.

As Thanksgiving passed and everyone's focus turned to Christmas, Vicki was no exception. I didn't like Christmas and wasn't much help. There was usually a minor spike in our business as well, so she carried all the responsibility for turning Christmas into a noteworthy holiday for our kids while I worked long hours. But as the full moon approached and climaxed in early December, her mood got predictability pugnacious. Several days later we cooperated to retrieve the first of two Christmas memories. These are written in Vicki's journal, but they're obviously in my cryptic handwriting.

The actual trigger for the memory was a program I occasionally listened to on the Christian radio station called "Songs in the Night." Three women were singing traditional Christmas songs and hymns.

Vicki was again seven years old in Richmond at the old barn where her previous memories had taken place. She was wearing a red velvet dress. And everyone else was dressed up as well. Her father was in his winter dress uniform. Fat Guy was wearing a suit and his wife was in a formal dress. Vicki and her father were sitting on folding metal chairs. There were approximately ten rows of chairs with eight in each row. Vicki and her father were in the middle of the second row.

Vicki couldn't keep her eyes off the baby lying in a manger in front. He was about five or six months old, and he was lying in a real feeding trough stuffed with hay. The baby was naked, his tiny penis obvious, and he looked undernourished. Her mind was fixated on plans to rescue the baby. She had an idea of what was about to happen.

To the side were three women singing, accompanied by a portable organ. They started with "O Little Town of Bethlehem." The prayer that followed hailed Satan. The small congregation joined in the second song "God Rest Ye Merry Gentlemen," and the third song was "Silent Night." The words in the songs were strategically changed to ridicule Christianity and applaud Satan.

As the chorus echoed ". . . sleep in heavenly peace . . ." Fat Guy skillfully cut the baby's stomach with a small knife—possibly a surgical knife—and with both hands took out his guts. The baby wasn't crying. (Vicki's adult self suspected that he was heavily drugged.) Fat Guy presented the bloody mess to the congregation who responded by symbolically touching it with their tongue.

Directly afterward the organ started playing again. Fat Guy's wife began stripping and the audience followed. Vicki had a creepy sensation as she felt her dress being unbuttoned from the back. She turned and it was her father. She resisted, slapping at him and then scratching at his eyes. He laughed. Others turned at the commotion and a chant began: "Father—daughter, Father—daughter . . . ."

Fat Guy signaled for Vicki to be brought up the front. He finished undressing her and then raped her vaginally and anally. And the frenzy started. Surrounded by a raucous turmoil, she was repeatedly raped. It was beyond counting. Seven- or eight-year-old Vicki was flipped over from top to bottom and back again many times. With her face ground into the barn floor she wanted to become part of the dirt, to crawl into it—anything to escape the skin she was in . . . .

The next thing she remembered was her father getting dressed. She noted that his clothes were in good condition.

"Time to get dressed. Come on. Time to get dressed." His voice was sweet and solicitous.

He took Vicki to a tub of warm water.

"You're such a mess. You've had a big night."

Vicki was confused at his tone of voice and gentle treatment. He washed her face and wiped her bottom. She was surprised at how bad it hurt. Her father had to hold her up; she couldn't stand on her own. She felt disoriented, like a child awakened in the middle of the night.

Fat Guy was pushing the satiated bodies sprawled on the dirt floor with his foot. It was time to leave.

Vicki's father dressed her, cradled her in a blanket and carried her to the car. He put her in the front seat but she was too sore to sit on her bottom. She laid on her hip with her face against the hard arm rest. That hurt. Everything hurt.

It was a short drive to the house. Tom carried her in. Virginia tentatively came out the bedroom into the hall.

"She's all worn out. She's had a big time." He was in a jovial mood.

Virginia took advantage of his mood to ask, "Exactly, what do you do at those parties?"

"Oh, just have fun. Kind of thing you do at any party."

He took Vicki to her bedroom.

It is unclear when the second memory was retrieved. Her journal notes that we started talking about it down at the shop and finished up in our bed.

Vicki was thirteen years old and living in El Paso. She was standing in the living room with her dad. There was a wooden panel over the window where Stephen had been thrown against the glass in that previous fight. Vicki again resisted her father's overtures to leave with him, causing a commotion. The rest of the family scrambled to their bedrooms while Vicki picked up something heavy to battle with her father. Tom went to the kitchen and returned with a long knife. He deftly swung it and nicked her hand, and her resistance melted. Tom quickly hustled her out to the car. But at the edge of their neighborhood, he turned right instead of left. A few minutes later he parked at the rear of an abandoned school with about thirty other cars. They passed through a set of double doors into an auditorium. There were lanterns spaced along the perimeter for light. It was dusty and there was debris all over. The ceiling was caved in and timbers were lying across some of the seats.

Ten to twelve girls about Vicki's age were forced to change into white outfits. Tom had brought one for Vicki and ushered her off to the right of the stage to change. Soon the girls were paraded across the stage. Vicki was third or fourth.

A voice from the audience hooted out, "Hey, there's Tom's daughter. We know she's no virgin. Ha, Ha, Ha."

The most humiliating feeling permeated Vicki from head to toe. She heard several rowdy voices from the audience agreeing, enumerating previous gang rape scenes.

The audience picked out an older girl to play Mary. She had a Shirley Temple look and was escorted to the center of the stage beside a boy playing Joseph. While Vicki was changing back into her old clothes, a manger scene was set up in front of an altar. There was a live baby in a manger and a roving satanic figure dressed in red. He had a devil costume made from a scuba diving suit with horns and a tail added.

Vicki noticed from the audience that no one was paying much attention to the baby. He did not appear to be well-kept to begin with, but he was plumper than the one in the previous memory. Now, he was crawling around in the dust, wearing only a T-shirt and a droopy diaper. Mary took the baby and brought it to Satan at the altar. Vicki was angry with Mary for cooperating. She knew what was going to happen. The baby began crying as Satan took a knife to his arms and legs.

This started a sexual frenzy. Everyone else's focus turned to Mary, who was being gang raped. Vicki did not want to see that. She began to strategize about rescuing the baby, but she was pulled into the frenzy. She remembered hearing the baby crying, but it was beyond her ability to help. Soon she was out of it.

When she woke up she saw people in various stages of dress and undress sprawled on the floor and bloodied parts of the baby strewn all over.

After those two memories both of us were supremely grateful that this Christmas was much quieter than the previous year. We had made the decision not to allow Vicki's parents to visit and it was a wise one. There were also fewer presents under the tree than in past years with both my parents gone. But my journal notes on Christmas Eve that we relished the peace and quiet.

I was in a reflective mood: 'No (extended) family meals or other get-togethers. And no big blow outs.

'Older girls basically stay upstairs & I rarely see them . . . .

'There's been a lot of sickness now & at Thanksgiving which we almost cancelled. Accumulation of stress from XMAS season & my parents' deaths. Vicki's had 2 grade A cult memories. So we're both on edge.

'I guess the basic thing I'm thankful for is that, in general, the family is amenable to allow the craziness of PTSD to expend itself & tries to cooperate & not generate any more flashbacks than necessary.

'Vicki feels that memories are coming close to end—possibly more at Easter but then time to work on grieving.'

December 30, 1990. Journal Entry. Am going to try to start a new habit of journal writing every Sunday along with working on my photograph album. Had a pretty nice Christmas. Jody really worked with me and it was mutually cooperative. We didn't deal much with either one of our families.

We've started a nonprofit corporation for helping families deal with sexual abuse. I ordered a couple of books for our groups . . . . .

I have searched our journals in vain for any reference to personal contact with Vicki's parents since the previous Christmas. In early March when Virginia had purposed a get-together for Vicki's birthday, Vicki told her mother she would like to see her but not with her father. Her mother then begged off. We did finally find a photo of Virginia taken several weeks after Hannah was born—probably in August. Virginia would have wanted to see the new baby. But Tom was conspicuously absent. Later we found a second photo taken in April of the upcoming year, 1991, again without Tom. An explanatory caption said that Tom had dropped Virginia off and was up at the park visiting. Although they were infrequent, this became the new pattern with visits from her parents.

We did not recognize it at the time, but Vicki's cult memories changed her mindset with reference to her father. A year earlier she had been grasping for reconciliation, even to the point of being willing to settle for less than a verbal apology. She had also been willing to accept the money he was sending as a form of restitution. But those days were gone. Now, she adamantly refused to see her father. But, as Peter had cautioned, in her many conversations with her mother, she never blew her cover and only referenced the incest. She never mentioned the ritual abuse.

When I pointed out this change in attitude to Vicki—it was obvious when I was combing through our journals and putting this book together—she said that it was the memory of the cruelty of her father that changed her mind. "I could never countenance cruelty. What kind of man would do that to his own children?"

She didn't see her father for over two years. That only changed when Stephen had a series of insulin overdoses, and Vicki discerned that her father was trying to kill her brother.

TOO MANY CHAIRS

2016

As I was writing the last chapter, reading and rereading our old journal entries, I was surprised by the number of chairs in the Richmond cult memories and the apparent size of the crowds in the El Paso scenes. I had initially pictured the cult meetings as necessarily small and secretive, with perhaps a handful, or at the most two handfuls, of people. What was going on was too illegal to take chances, especially in that much more conservative culture of the 1950s and early 1960s. But Vicki's memories seemed to indicate a robust party atmosphere with lots of bodies, including those of other children.

At the time we were processing the memories—twenty-five years earlier—these details escaped our attention, I'm sure because of the stress and uproar that inevitably came as these memories saw the light of day. At that time we were captivated and overwhelmed by their strangeness and missed some of these features. I now asked Vicki what she thought.

"You need to start talking about trafficking," she said emphatically and probably for the tenth time in the past three months. She had been telling me this since I started writing the section on ritual abuse. "This is about my father and his cronies selling their kids. You're focusing too much on the religious aspect, but it was really about making money. Sex with little kids was the service provided. I'm sure there was alcohol . . . ."

"In addition to the drugs?" I asked. This was new.

"Yeah."

"Did you ever see any money exchange hands?" I asked because she hadn't mentioned it in her journals either.

"No, but that's what was going on. There were people who came for no other reason than to have sex with kids. I'm sure they were paying."

"But you don't remember anything specifically?"

"Let me meditate on it and I'll talk about it with you tomorrow."

The next day was a predictably busy Monday. Vicki was on the phone much of the day being what I considered one of the world's best mothers—the type of mother that I wish I'd had. One child who lived two-thirds of the way across the country needed therapy and another at home needed life-skills training. My wife was making it happen. She was also recovering from a mild flu we'll picked up at our family get-together over the New Year. As evening drew near, I asked her about the trafficking conversation again.

"I don't want to talk about it this late in the day." I started to object, to remind her of what she'd said the day before but stopped. I'd finally learned to accept this very typical response. "I had nightmares last night. I don't want to talk about it now," she repeated firmly. She had learned not to read or to talk about anything related to her memories when she was tired, especially at the end of the day. It had a tendency to dredge up too much muck from her past.

The next morning, before the kids were up, she told me she'd put some thought into it. "It's a little fuzzy but I remember there being someone that collected money from cars in Hawaii as they drove up, and in Richmond there was someone at the door collecting money." She had no more details. The fact that her memories were vague was not surprising because she did not want to go back into the past. I think she feared the possibility of getting stuck there and overwhelmed. Also, her attention as a child was focused on safety—or the obvious lack of it. She may have taken the collection of money for granted because it had always been that way. She'd mentioned more than once that just skimming through the manuscript I was writing and coming upon her old journal entries was too much; she didn't want to remember again. "I was in intense fear when I was a child. I wasn't paying attention to the collection of money." I could see that, but being a natural skeptic I decided to put it in the wait-and-see category.

"Do you think your father was benefiting financially, or were you his ticket into these events?"

"Some of both."

"Was there a hierarchy and if so, where was your father in it?"

"Yes, and my father seemed to have some authority. It's not coincidental that my father always seemed to find a group like this every time he was re-stationed. I think he was being sent to organize and bolster those groups. There was an inner circle—like when they killed little Sue Mandle in Richmond—the little girl that they sacrificed and then dismembered when I was seven and my mother was in the hospital when Jack was born. There were four or five men . . . . Perhaps he was in training."

As you might expect, Vicki was right. The next memories, which I had forgotten over the intervening years, make it plain that the religious aspects were much less important to the participants than the wanton party atmosphere, which included sex with children. It only made sense that the people were paying and that soon became obvious. Except for the Richmond group, the Satanism was just a garb, the backdrop where everyone got in character. The Richmond group seemed to take the theological aspects more seriously. Perhaps the extreme torture that seven-year-old Vicki experienced was just an excuse to exercise cruelty—I don't know.

It was surprising to find with this next memory that these groups were not independent.

Again, her memories over the next several months make it obvious that Vicki was right: This was all about money. The organizations that her father was involved with were primarily interested in making money. And sex with kids was the service provided.

DAWN

IT'S A DOOZY

January, 1991

y journal on December 26th notes that Vicki hadn't slept much the last three nights. The least little sound startled her awake and her dreams were bothering her. Five days later she noted the following:

'I'm suffering under the weight of a new memory. I need to list what I know about it: it's heavy duty; I had a flash of being 11 onstage and doing some provocative dance in t-shirt, sheer knee socks with garters; I had a flash of the terror of being buried . . . and being at a house were Jody & I were doing some (drapery*) work for the Crandells.* (The Crandells were a current drapery client of ours.) *. . . . Then the Crandells arrived and I saw them in a room sitting on a throne: him on the left—her on the right . . . . She had straight black hair—shoulder length—about 40 years old. They opened a door to a secret room—a huge bedroom—porch—that had tons of windows w/ floral-print pleated shades on them. It looked out over a beautiful lake—grass—trees. I got into a discussion w/ him & he got irritated. Slung me over his shoulder and started swinging me around. Then threw me down and started doing sexual things to me in a rough manner. After, he let me up & ridiculed what he had done to me to a group of men. They acted disgusted with him. I was scared the whole dream. Worried about Jody finding out.*

'I awoke that a.m. very depressed. Later in the day I noticed that we're having a full moon.'

My journal notes on January fifth that the last two evenings after I came up from the shop Vicki had picked a fight. The next morning as I woke up, she began berating me for doing a poor job maintaining the fire in the wood stove. I tried a new strategy toward dealing with this conflict and began holding her. At first, she was stiff but gradually she thawed. 'It dawned on me that her aggressive, demanding attitude was a cover-up for vulnerability.' Soon she felt safe and began talking about this last memory that seemed to be stuck.

A week later the memory was still stuck. My journal notes that we were experiencing the worst fighting in months. I blamed it on shame: both of ours. Her shame was related to the half-birthed memory, which she guessed was going to be a doozy; mine was related to the way she was dealing with me. I often felt humiliated by the person who was supposed to support and cherish me.

We took several sessions down at the shop to work on this new memory. Vicki remembered a 'sexy, flirtatious dance that she did at a weekend retreat' and that it was a 'gray, drizzly day when she left her house.' But there was some kind of mental block. She recalled several scenes from Louisiana that she had remembered before so we guessed that was the location of this new memory. Several days later I wrote: 'Today at noon we worked on it but the same roadblock. It's been going on for weeks. I had the inspiration to have her get into the "feeling" of shame that was associated with that dance. Almost at once she remembered being buried alive—screaming in abject fear.'

I wrote in my journal that I had again glimpsed the nature of her shame: 'If she did something she knew was wrong, that was guilt. But when she did what she knew was wrong because she was afraid of the consequences, that produced shame.'

Slowly I came to understand that shame was at the root of the recent flashes of memory. As it had been with the incest memories slightly more than a year earlier, these memories infused with shame were the most difficult. She hated herself for getting a reward for violating her conscience. She had been forced to take a more aggressive role in this weekend retreat by doing the seductive dancing, but it violated her most basic values—the ones she learned at Sunday school. The easiest way to ameliorate the inner turmoil was to get into the dancing and experience the power over her audience that came with it. But the mockery from some of the men unmasked the shame and reminded her that she was a traitor to her own values. The memory was emotionally crushing.

Over two different sessions a week apart the memory slowly came out:

She was suddenly being buried alive in a shallow grave. Eleven-year-old Vicki was screaming in terror. Her arms and feet were bound so that she couldn't kick or even claw the dirt away from her face. There was very little room left around her mouth to breathe and she would have to shut up or be breathing in mouthfuls of dirt. Her head was pushed back almost to the point of touching her spine. As the soil continued piling up around her head, she discovered an air pocket that she could use to breathe if she kept herself calm and didn't move. The people burying her didn't seem to know about it. Vicki began shallow breathing, trying to calm the adrenaline coursing through her body, but the fear was overwhelming and she soon passed out.

She woke up as she was being pulled out of her grave. They were cleaning the dirt out of her mouth and nose. Vicki was in a daze but did note a change in the weather above and wondered how much time had elapsed.

Surrounded by a ring of people she was escorted down to the lake. There was a voice that she assumed belonged to the leader telling her that she was now born again into the cult; she would be baptized and would later be married and sealed to the cult.

In her fog of consciousness Vicki caught little of what was happening. After being baptized in the lake she was shepherded by several women back to the house on the other side of the lake. The women cleaned her up and gave her a shower. She was shocked to find that one of the women was the leader's wife from Richmond. What was she doing in Louisiana? Intermittently, her old Sunday school teacher sexually stimulated her as she dressed Vicki in a white gown.

"You've got an exciting night ahead of you. Behave yourself and everything will go well. If you don't, you'll go back in the grave." That woman's voice of warning was as hard as steel. Vicki was familiar with its cruelty.

"Here. Drink this." Vicki was given a golden chalice filled with a red liquid.

Someone placed a white cardboard crown on Vicki's head. Then a long, white train was attached to her gown. She was escorted to the door of a large room, given a golden scepter and told to walk down the aisle to the makeshift stage in front. The crowd contained mixed company and there were men hooting on either side. There was no decorum or reverence to this service, but rather the raucousness of a drugged crowd. The drug was affecting Vicki as well because she had the fleeting thought of bopping some of the men on the head with her scepter, but she was stopped by her fear of the grave.

At the bottom of the aisle Vicki took several steps up onto the stage. She was flanked by the local leader Caesar Candrel and Fat Guy from Richmond. The crowd closed in as the marriage vows were read between her and a man dressed as a red devil in a tuxedo with a tail extending behind him. Her vows included being married to the entire cult.

"Let's get on with the wedding night," came a cat call as several men began jettisoning their clothes.

Caesar raised his hand to pause the escalating rowdiness. This was his house. He was obviously rich and married to a woman dressed up like Cleopatra. "Vicki is going to show her appreciation for joining the cult by doing a special dance."

He began undressing Vicki, sexually stimulating her, and quietly he whispered, "Cooperate or you will need to be reborn and re-baptized."

With the taste of dirt still fresh in her mind, Vicki did a frenzied, exotic dance to excite the crowd.

After the dance, as the ranking leader, Caesar did oral sex with Vicki. Fat Guy was next. Caesar spoke to Fat Guy as he handed Vicki over to him, "Be nice to her. This is her night."

Her father was third. The line behind him was long and there were voices telling him to hurry up. Forty-one-year-old Vicki did not want to remember any more of that scene, and she skipped to the next morning where she awoke to the remains of the orgy, but with a much clearer head. There was a definite Roman motif to the room with bottles and goblets here and there and naked bodies spread all over the floor.

She was soon accosted by Fat Guy. "I don't have to be nice to you today."

Vicki backed away from his sexual advances. Escaping his grasp, she ran to the bathroom and locked the door. She turned to vomit in the toilet from fear.

"Open the door or I'll break it down," roared his voice from outside.

Thinking quickly that she had no alternative, Vicki opened the door and played it cool. She was instantly chilled by the hatred in his eyes—just like his wife's. He again began doing sexual things and Vicki resisted. He picked her up and threw her over his shoulder, then twisted her in the air.

"I knew you weren't glad to be in the cult. We'll have to re-baptize you."

Vicki escaped, dashing off as soon as he put her down. She eluded him as the two hopped among the naked, half-awakened bodies. Fat Guy was oblivious to the disgusted grimaces directed toward him from the other men sprawled around the room. He enlisted Caesar to help him and Vicki was again taken down to the lake. With a smaller crowd around she was repeatedly dunked until she was barely alive; then dragged to the shore and left on her own to recover.

Her father showed up later and dragged her to the car where he dressed her. On the ride home she got a lecture, "Why can't you do what the cult wants you to do?" He was disgusted. "This is important to me. Why can't you just cooperate?"

It was a half-hour drive back to her home. "Get yourself together before we get home. I want to avoid as many of your mother's asinine questions as possible."

Vicki felt like a zombie as she passed her mother. "Did you have fun . . . ?" the inane voice said. Vicki passed without answering and went to her room and bed.

That memory had taken almost a month to bring to light and included another one of those middle-of-the-night calls with Keith. The house was upside-down during much of that period. This had been the worst memory so far and the collateral havoc at home made that obvious.

Vicki could not forgive herself for the shameful dance. She had acquiesced so easily. Had she wanted to do it? Did she enjoy the attention of being on stage? The hooting from the enthusiastic men? Why didn't she fight it vehemently as she had earlier when it came to killing the babies? The shame was eating her from the inside.

On Sunday we both got blessings. We were worn out from what we had been through over the last several weeks. As I laid my hands upon her head, I found myself saying something that had never crossed my mind: that based on her previous experience sitting with Jesus Christ that she was predestined to live and needed to do whatever was necessary to survive. Survival was her God-given directive. How else could she fight against Satan? As an eleven-year-old she had made that decision—at the cost of so much shame.

A week later in the middle of the night, I lost my balance as I walked through the kitchen en route to putting more wood on the fire. I stepped on a garbage bag that was tied and ready to go outside. The lid of an opened tin can neatly sliced the in-step of my right foot about half an inch deep, and within seconds there was blood all over the floor. I yelled for Vicki, knowing we were going to have to make an emergency room visit, but I also knew that she would freak out with the sight of so much blood. The first thing I had to do was calm her down before I could get a ride into the hospital.

With fifteen stitches I was told to plan on taking seven to ten days off. I would not be able to stand up and work. I needed the vacation; we both needed a vacation. But I probably could have come up with a better way to arrange to take time off.

A FIRST TOUCH OF HEALING

February, 1991

icki's goals for the new year were ambitious: *'conquer the table, conquer family home evening* and *better terms with extended families.'* While she had been obviously wrong about her memories being just about over, for the first time in several years she was looking to the future with hope and expectation. This new feeling that things were close to the end gave her energy, and there was a noticeable uplift in her demeanor after that last memory. Also, with her new nonprofit organization to help victims of sexual abuse, she wanted to get some support groups started in several of the towns that surrounded us. She was reaching out and wanting to parlay her horrific experiences into a way to minister to and benefit others. That helped her make sense out of the vicious abuse she had suffered.

With the onset of the full moon at the beginning of February, Vicki had me record a dream she'd had: She had been joy-riding, maybe driving her parents' car. The trip had ended with a car full of people and two gun shots. Inside the car she saw a man of Mexican descent staring vacant-eyed. He had been shot in the mouth and was getting ready to fall on her.

A few days later she related a story she'd heard on the radio that told of a woman who had successfully had her father prosecuted for killing a childhood playmate; this woman had not remembered this incident for twenty years. I could see the handwriting on the wall. Her attitude toward her father had definitely changed. Anger was beginning to bubble to the surface. She was feeling better about herself.

After that upsetting dream, Vicki called the Raleigh police department and talked with the detective in charge of cults. There was an active one in the area. The officer was interested in talking with Vicki and said he could put a tag on her father. Vicki did not leave her name and number but promised to think about it.

I couldn't make her next visit with Peter because I had to keep my foot elevated. Their conversation centered around her attraction to other women, which I thought was at the root of her "jealousy." Peter agreed with me. Vicki had not wanted to admit that to herself, but Peter thought it only made common sense. She had always noticed more about their bodies than I ever did; she had been trained that way. She had grown up with a father who had had a laser-like focus on the female anatomy. Also in cult meetings, women had often sexually stimulated her. He told her that her response was Pavlovian—She had been trained to be bisexual, to be attracted to women as well as men. She didn't want me to see other women because she expected me to feel the same allure that she did.

The good news from Peter was that he, too, thought Vicki *was* entering the next phase of her therapy. He called it the grieving stage where she was feeling sorry for her pitiful past and its effect on her present. I wrote for her: 'I want to get on with my life; my restrictions on Jody are restricting me.'

Stephen, Vicki's brother, had gall-bladder surgery in mid-February. Over the phone Virginia gushed with the care and concern Tom was showing Vicki's brother. Tom sat with Stephen almost around the clock in the hospital, and Virginia commented that the staff was very impressed at Tom's dedication. Virginia's glowing praise was clearly for Vicki's benefit, and for the first time I wondered if Tom's concern wasn't a performance— like the twenty-dollar bills—that was intended to deceive.

On the twenty-eighth of February the moon was full again. Vicki was feeling ill at ease and it was obvious another memory was coming. She had told me a couple of days earlier that she'd had a dream of a close-up look at a dead baby boy—not much older than Hannah, who was eight months old at the time. She came down to the shop that afternoon to work on retrieving it. She told me from the onset that the predominant feeling in this memory was fear.

She was thirteen years old and driving her parents' station wagon. The car was crowded. Everyone else was zoned out on drugs and it was a festive atmosphere. Her father was in the back seat making up to some woman. It was getting dark as they neared the El Paso cult house of her other memories.

Suddenly a group of four or five black-jacketed motorcycle riders appeared. The revelry was instantly gone. One of the men in the back scrambled over the seat to take control of the car and stop it. Thirteen-year-old Vicki was terrified and forty-one-year-old Vicki was flooded with adrenaline.

The riders pulled up beside the car and shot inside, killing the driver. He slumped over against Vicki, who was now in the middle of the front seat. With guns drawn, the gang demanded that everyone get out of the car. The other occupants were all summarily raped. Vicki was taken off alone and was raped by the entire group. She was left sitting alone with her knees tucked up against her chest; she was in intense pain.

"That'll teach you to mess with ——-," the gang bellowed in warning as they rode off. Vicki did not get the name. It was clear that they were rivals and this was some kind of turf war.

Vicki and the others got dressed. Tom dragged the lifeless body of the man who had been driving to the back of the station wagon. The group quickly headed back to the cult house, honking as they arrived. When no one immediately appeared, someone in the car quipped, "They're just doing their thing," trying to ease the tension.

Once inside the house the occupants of the car excitedly related the incident, and six to eight men gathered to strategize. Vicki was slouched in a far corner, her back against the stone wall of the building. She was in acute pain and barely cognizant of the conversation across the large room. She had learned over time that the best strategy in dangerous situations was to try to be invisible. But she did gather from what she heard and what happened next that the men in that huddle were worried that the wife of the dead man, who was present in the house, would go to the police. She was not loyal to the cult like her husband. The group decided that if no one in that family was around, it would look like they had just left town.

The men gathered around the woman. Tom quickly shot her and her baby in the back of the head.

"You take care of the rest," Tom ordered, referring to a quick burial. "I've got to get her home," he said, pointing to Vicki.

In the immediate chaos Vicki wandered over to the two dead bodies. There was little blood.

In the car riding home, her father said, "I don't need to tell you not to say anything about this." Vicki slouched in the front seat. She didn't need to answer.

At home, as they walked in the front door, Virginia poked her head out of the bedroom door. Tom yelled at her to get back inside. Virginia did. And Vicki went to bed.

As that scene from the past settled in my mind, I told Vicki that I didn't believe it, which really meant that I didn't *want* to believe it. She didn't consider cold-blooded murder as a stretch in her father's character as I did, but she had lived her childhood while I was merely gazing at it through some sort of crystal ball. And of course, she would be proven right.

In March, as Vicki related several of her dreams of the past few weeks in her regular therapy session with Peter, he pointed out that they indicated that she felt more confident. She had been using a technique she'd learned from her Boone group: When she woke up from a nightmare, she would rewrite the script to an ending that suited her better, which usually involved her being in control or in a position of power. She was now doing that *in* her dreams. She was also taking some of the distressing energy that these dreams evoked and using it constructively—as she did in calling the police department.

In early April, Virginia called and wanted to come up with Tom and visit for a few hours. It would be a belated birthday visit and she would be able to see the grandkids. With Easter approaching, Vicki was wary. She said she'd consider it and call back on Sunday—after she had time to pray about it. After talking with Keith, she told me I could make the decision since I would inevitably be dealing with the fallout. I was reluctant, but after church I retired to the shop to consider and pray. I picked up the phone to let her know it wasn't a good time for me. I heard her dialing—we were on a party line—and I listened in to the conversation.

Virginia answered; she sounded down. Vicki nixed the idea of the visit (apparently reading my mind) and her mother responded with a litany of her own woes. At the top and bottom of the list was Stephen, who was a constant problem with all of his health issues. Virginia recounted how difficult the surgery and hospitalization had been. She was grateful for Saint Tom and his watchful care. Virginia also had a chronic case of cystitis that she bemoaned might be going into Chron's disease. She concluded with the familiar barb that Vicki was breaking up the family.

"I'm not the one breaking up the family." Vicki related the past couple of Thanksgiving dinners to which we were not invited. "I wasn't invited to those parties."

"It wasn't a party," Virginia said.

"Yes, it was."

"No, it wasn't," Virginia objected. "It was just that everyone came down."

"It was a party and everyone was invited but me."

"I've tried to talk to your father a couple of times but I couldn't. He'd bristle and leave. One time he spent the night off." Virginia often changed subjects without transition.

Vicki wanted to ask if his leaving corresponded to a full moon but didn't. "Mother, you're welcome to come. I'd love to see you. And I know the kids would too. But . . . ."

"I can't drive that far. It would hurt your father's feelings. This is the first time I've been able to talk him into coming up to the mountains in a year." The anguish in Virginia's voice was palpable.

"Then come with my sister." Vicki reiterated that she still wanted a relationship with her mother. "I could meet you at my therapist. He could really help you with your stress."

"No. How could all those things have happened? I was home all the time. Why didn't you tell me?"

Vicki related a particularly vivid scene from her childhood where she'd begged her mother to divorce her father.

Her mother denied it. "If you had begged me, I would have asked you why."

Vicki then switched gears and asked about the horrible thing that had happened to Virginia when she was a child. "You mentioned it when I announced I was divorcing Jim."

"What horrible thing happened to me . . . ? I don't know what you're talking about." I could hear the increasing upset in Virginia's voice. "I can't go to your house without him. There's too much stress."

"Is he there now? Why don't you let me talk to him? You quit playing middle man. That would probably cut down on your stress."

Virginia called Tom to the phone. His voice sounded unnatural, almost flippant. "Yes, what can I do for you?"

Vicki's voice was strong and confident. "We have something we need to work out."

"What?" Tom asked

"What do you mean 'what'?" Vicki shot back.

"What?" Tom asked again.

"I mean the issue of sexual abuse that has come between us. For starters there's this therapist bill."

"What bill?"

"The one in my hand," Vicki said.

"I've paid it. I haven't gotten anymore."

"This one. Will you pay it?"

"Yes. I'll do anything to stop this hassle. I get hassled by Steve, hassled by you and by your mother about you. I'll do anything to stop it. If I can't stop it, I'll go to Ireland. That will stop it."

Vicki burst out laughing and I had to restrain myself as well. Even Tom was chuckling under his breath.

"The least you could do, after all I've been through, is admit it and say you're sorry. So our relationship could go in another direction."

There was a long silence on the other end of the phone. It seemed like several minutes. Vicki thought her father might actually admit it. Instead, he blew up.

"I'll take all the blame. I'll even pay all the bills, but I'll never admit to something I didn't do!" I had heard that line before. Then his voice shot up several more decibels to almost a scream, "I didn't do it! I never laid a hand on you!"

"Why don't you go to my therapist with me?" Vicki responded in a soothing tone.

"No! I didn't do anything wrong!" Tom reiterated.

"No? Why don't you go so you can tell my therapist that and he can figure out why I'm making all this up?"

"No! I'll get back with you on this. It's not a good time."

"When?"

"I don't know. I'll get back with you."

"*When* are you going to call or write or whatever?"

"I'll get back."

"I want to know when. I want to deal with this. Are you gonna call?"

"No. Probably not." And the conversation was over.

I was impressed with the way Vicki handled the call. So were Keith and Peter. She had not lost her temper. She had handled the call calmly and methodically. I saw in Vicki the old courtroom social worker who had advocated is well for her clients and usually got what she wanted. We needed that therapy bill paid; it had been accumulating for months and Vicki was determined not to spend our money. I hadn't seen that skill and presence of mind in her for well over a year. The past that she was remembering had been suffocating her; she hadn't had the energy of her old self. This sudden flash was refreshing. While I didn't recognize it, she had turned a corner; she was beginning to feel better.

But immediately after the call, Vicki was afraid of what her father would do. We decided to take a walk at the nearby park to decompress. I told her I was impressed that she had kept her focus and had not mentioned the cult memories. "I don't think there's any reason to fear. Your father's not gonna want to do anything that might be traceable to him." I was echoing Peter's opinion which made the most sense to me.

Vicki was very anxious and we walked for a long time in a heavy fog. We couldn't see but a few feet in front of us. It was the way we'd been living our lives for the last couple of years. She replayed her fears like a broken record.

"You don't think God's going to protect you?" I asked.

"I need somebody with skin on: you, Keith . . . ."

Of course, that included her therapist. Peter raved about how she'd handled the call. He pointed out that for three or four minutes of that conversation Tom had not denied the incest. That spoke volumes to him. Peter was very proud of her. As the session was winding down Peter did relate a story from the beginning of his career when he had suggested to an abused woman to ask her father to come to one of her therapy appointments. The father had responded by breaking several of the woman's fingers. At her next therapy session she showed up with her hand in a cast. He passed that story on to Vicki to say that he didn't recommend that strategy anymore.

Virginia showed up unexpectedly at our house a few days later. She was driving the familiar red station wagon that, on more than one occasion, she'd said she'd bought to haul the grandkids around.

"Where's Daddy?" my wife asked her mother.

"At the park." Virginia went into a litany of reasons why it was so how difficult to visit us now.

But Peter and I were right. Tom was afraid. He did not want to risk an encounter that might bring out any more information.

Virginia brought a camera and gifts for the kids. She brought several photos from her last visit when Hannah was a baby. Only when she was leaving, forty-five minutes later, did Vicki start seriously talking with her mother.

"What was Daddy's reaction after our last conversation on Sunday?" Vicki asked.

"He was angry. How would you feel? His anger was justified."

"I'd repent and apologize."

"I don't see how he could have abused you on the boat to Hawaii. Your dad thought at first these accusations were some kind of kick, and that all this would blow over."

"A Kick? What do you think I'm getting out of it?" Vicki asked.

"It's ridiculous to think he'd done anything to Tripp and Jack."

"I didn't say Tripp and Jack." Although my wife had certainly wondered whether they had been abused. "It was Stephen."

"Steve! Why Stephen?"

"For one thing, look how angry he is," Vicki explained. "For another, look at how poorly he copes with life. Read some books."

"I read all the books I want on this subject." Virginia was an avid reader. "Your dad doesn't seem to be showing any of the signs of an abuser."

"We must be reading different books. What signs is he not showing?"

Virginia couldn't remember.

Vicki said sympathetically, "I sure feel sorry for the position you're in, having to decide who is telling the truth: me or Dad?"

"I couldn't do without your dad with Stephen's need for care. The last time your Dad came back the reason he gave was that he knew I couldn't handle Stephen's care alone."

"Did it occur to you that you could stay with Dad and still believe me?" Vicki gave an example from a similar situation in her Roanoke group.

Virginia shook her head no. She abruptly changed the subject and threw a few barbs at our church for keeping Tripp away for so long on his mission.

"Give me a kiss before you go, Mother," Vicki said. Virginia did and then left the house.

Vicki had a series of nightmares for a week after her mother's visit. My wife was very angry. At the root of her pain was the question: "Why am I being punished—that is, losing my family—for telling the truth?" It was now plain where her mother stood and that it wasn't going to change. Once again, Vicki felt isolated from her family and left alone to deal with the reality of what had occurred all those years ago.

TORI

April, 1991

Vicki lead her first incest group meeting in one of the nearby towns. She had four women show up, which was great for a first meeting. One of the women called her a few days later to complain that she'd had nightmares every night since the meeting. Vicki was on the phone for a long time. She had been in that woman's shoes before; Vicki knew the woman needed someone to talk to. This situation brought back memories of when Vicki had started therapy.

My wife ended up being an excellent counselor; she spent extended periods of time on the phone, which would soon become a pattern for her. She eventually worked a sexual abuse hotline and at one point saved the life of a woman who was in the process of committing suicide. I can't remember the number of times we'd stop at a store where she'd promise to be in and out in just a few minutes, and then half an hour later I'd poke my head in the door to see her deep into a counseling session with a woman she barely knew. Inevitably, the topic had to do with sexual abuse. Because Vicki was not reticent about admitting her own background, a number of other women responded in kind. They had been waiting much of their lives to talk about it.

During this period of time, my journal notes that Vicki had been lobbying for several things: first, a move to Nova Scotia; next, adopting from Romania; and finally, attending an adoption conference in Atlanta.

Her first wish upset the entire household. The second was financially out of our reach. With the last I let her know that I could be bribed under the right circumstances, and before long we were having Family Home Evening again. Vicki was nervous and the get-togethers were short with lots of questions after the kids (now ages 14 to almost 1 year old) left, but things were changing.

In May, I went with Vicki to another therapy session. In the previous meeting two weeks earlier, Vicki had said she wanted to work on getting more of her emotions out.

Peter asked me, "Does she regress when she does memory work?"

It was obvious that during these times of remembering some emotions were ventilated, especially fear and anger. But I shrugged my shoulders.

Peter turned to Vicki with the question. "I have some body sensations," she answered. "Some feelings. But it's more like video with the sound turned off."

"You need to get the feelings out," Peter advised. "They're still holding you captive."

I suggested that Vicki and I reinstate our regular therapy sessions, but instead of going through the memories for their content, explore them looking for the emotions involved with those memories.

Peter liked the idea. To Vicki he said, "You may have numbed out." He suggested that she do some writing to flush the emotions out. "Finding old photographs would be a help as well."

Back home, Vicki found an old photograph of her parents and began working with it at our dining room table. The idea was to trigger and then to disempower the emotions. After one of our sessions she told me that her mother was squinting. 'She was trying to see as little as possible.' My wife surmised it was a mindset.

Several months earlier Vicki had introduced me to a character she discovered after reading one of her numerous books on sexual abuse and healing. The little girl's name was Tori. She was Vicki's "child within." As we started again doing regular sessions together, Tori appeared front and center, and I got to know her better—not that I had a choice. Normally, I would have felt sorry for the poor little girl. I knew enough about her background to feel genuinely sympathetic. But Tori was not the most likable character.

Vicki was adamant that this child was the gateway to her psyche (including her emotions) and to the things I wanted out of our relationship. The child seemed to be about nine years old most of the time. This was a period from which we'd had no memories. Tori did know what had been going on with the abuse at other ages, and she seemed to subsume those periods into her character. She was angry and hot-blooded and, as far as I was concerned, embodied the worst of Vicki's character flaws.

The name suited her; I pictured a pint-sized torch running around with the potential to set everything on fire, not even caring about her own safety. The problem from my perspective was that the adult Vicki pampered the rascal. When I objected to that strategy, my wife quoted from the book she was reading: she asserted that was what needed to be done.

In our sessions together, I tried at first to ignore Tori but that didn't work. She would not have it. She was demanding and wanted the protection and control she didn't get as a youngster, which usually meant a prelude of insecurity questions that I needed to answer. Tori had been forced against her will to do all kinds of things, including things that hurt and even worse, things that violated her conscience. She had had little control over her life back then, but that wasn't going to happen now. Nothing was going to stop her from being in control. Nothing. Since I considered control issues to be mine and Vicki's number-one problem, Tori and I, consequently, didn't get along very well.

These new sessions of our memory work down at the shop opened up a new aspect of Vicki's relationship with the cult: she was forced to do prostitution. Unlike Richmond, where her adult self surmised she had been used to make money, in these new memories she knew it at the time. These memories were wound up in her sexual fantasy life and difficult to untangle; with the added shame they were even more difficult for adult Vicki to admit. As an eleven-year-old, Vicki had enjoyed the sense of power she had over a relatively young man who had started showing up in her memories. These memories did not explode but rather, bit by bit, unraveled as she paid more attention to her own thoughts.

And little Tori fumed. She was angry at what she had been forced to do.

We were down at the shop doing one of our regular sessions when Vicki introduced this young man to me based on the flashes of memory she'd been having: 'Dale was a young man interested in sex and possibly drugs. He was a wealthy individual in the rural Louisiana community and I was the lure. The cult wanted his money.'

Dale was a regular at one of the small cabins—Vicki suspected they had previously been slave quarters—surrounding the lake house where she'd been baptized into the cult. Eleven-year-old Vicki had apparently been forced to work in these cabins. As I was writing this scene down, I asked Vicki whether her johns ever gave her gifts. She had a flash of being at a cult meeting with Dale. He offered her money for stripping. Before eleven-year-old Vicki could answer, the leader said that if he'd pay they'd force her to do whatever he wanted. He paid and she was forced to do his bidding. Tori was furious.

When Dale quit showing up at the cabins, Vicki was sent to a Fourth of July celebration to lure him back. She was forced to do this with a sexual come-on despite the fact that his wife and a new baby were present. Tori hated doing this; she considered it a betrayal and she was livid.

While Vicki's anger was no fun to deal with, I couldn't help but wonder what had transpired during ages nine and ten that had turned the resistant child at Richmond (age 7) and Hersey (age 8) into someone so much more compliant. At age eleven she was doing what the cult told her even though she hated it.

In her next memory she brought up those missing years. Vicki was upside down and being swung back and forth like a pendulum. The fear and the dizziness were meant to reinforce the ultimatum: She was to make a trip to her pastor and tell him she wanted to be baptized. The cult even gave her the words to say: 'I'm afraid of going under the water. Can I sit in your lap?'

My wife guessed where this was going and soon afterward phoned her mother, asking about their pastor during their first stay in El Paso. As usual, Virginia effervesced with information without wondering why Vicki was asking. Yes, she remembered Rev. Fillmore well; he was personable and very well-liked. She also remembered Vicki's strange insistence that she wanted to get baptized. At the time Virginia thought her daughter ought to wait a few more years, but nine-year-old Vicki was adamant. It was a large congregation, but Virginia was able to set up a personal interview between young Vicki and the head pastor because of the pastor's previous relationship with Virginia's father. Vicki's grandfather had mentored him during his time in seminary, often having him over for meals and even weekend stays.

Vicki casually asked her mother, "Did he ever have any sexual scandals?"

Virginia remembered that he'd been accused of an affair in a previous pastorate.

Vicki then understood that Tori's anger came from the shame she felt at betraying the man she most idolized as she was growing up. Rev. Fillmore had been a friend of her grandfather, whom she dearly loved.

Several days later Vicki scheduled a therapy session with me down at the shop. She'd had a dream the previous night of the face of the man who had laid the carpet in the boys' bedroom the day before. In the dream that face was pressed against hers.

"I'm dizzy," Vicki began. "They are spinning me around. I'm on one leg." Several minutes later she came out of the memory. "I'm so dizzy I can't stand it." She dropped her head between her knees. "I think I'm going to vomit."

After four or five minutes I suggested that we try again. I noticed she was holding the side of her face with her hands. "He's hitting me with his fists . . . . No. It's a stick. I'm upside down hanging by one leg and he's hitting me with a stick, spinning me around."

There were voices from the men surrounding the scene telling her abuser to stop and cut her down. They were afraid he was going to kill her.

The leader responded, "If we don't train her now to obey, we'll never be able to."

Nine-year-old Vicki was hanging upside-down. She was in and out of her body; she couldn't stand the dizziness. Next, she was on the ground being held down by her arms and his face was close to hers. He talked forcefully to her. Vicki said she was in a semi-conscious state as the leader spat the words out. They came one by one, slowly, with emphasis. 'You're—going—to—tell—your—mother—that—you're—going—to—be—baptized. You're—not—going—to—let—your—mother—talk—you—out—of—it. Your father will make the arrangements. You're—going—to—let—the—minister—screw—you. You're—going—to—do—whatever—you—have—

to—do—it—to—do—this.' Afterward, the men took her out to her father's car. She had been at some kind of camp and had been too abused to return to the other kids.

There was no immediate follow-up to this memory, but we surmised that this had been about blackmail. A few days later Vicki had another flash of being in a confessional with a priest. She had been sent by the cult to seduce him.

A month after the last memory with Rev. Fillmore, amid much turmoil at home, Vicki remembered the final scene. She had gone into his office after her baptism. She began taking her clothes off and speaking seductively to him. He initially tried to lecture her on the proper spirit, but scene quickly degenerated and he was on top of her. Suddenly, he went crazy, turned her over and anally raped her . . . . Afterward, he kicked her away, furious at himself. Vicki had a sense of Rev. Fillmore getting a lot of money from inside his desk drawer and giving it to her.

Tori had been forced to betray her inmost values—she had to to survive. That explained her anger and, obviously, much of Vicki's anger as well. My wife's anger rarely surfaced when she was dealing with our kids, but I routinely caught it. It had been much worse since she started therapy—as her memories seeped to the surface. But it had always been there. In the future we would see this kind of smoldering anger as an indication of a history of severe abuse, especially sexual abuse. It so often manifests itself as anger and violence toward others and/or as self-destructive behavior—as we saw with my mother and with Vicki's brother Stephen.

GETTING TO KNOW JOE JR.

May, 1991

With the brutal tortures—which were really brainwashing techniques—of the cult, it was not hard to understand Tori's anger. To survive—a God-given instinct we all have—she had to betray her innermost values. It was a Catch-22. So she was justifiably angry and I was not good at dealing with it. I was still seriously depressed on and off from my parents' deaths.

"Look," Vicki said more than once, "accepting Tori is part of accepting me."

"I don't particularly care for little old Tori Two Shoes," I responded.

"Why do you call her that?"

"Because I don't like her. She's bossy and controlling and has to have her own way."

But I had to admit, when I wasn't being frustrated by the little brat, that she was at the root of the drill sergeant in Vicki. That aspect of her personality is what had allowed us to have the large family and make everything run smoothly. Tori kept things in order; she planned ahead. She was the reason our children would grow up and be responsible adults unlike so many of their peers in our hillbilly neighborhood.

But perhaps the greatest benefit of Tori's ascendancy was that it gave permission for Joe Jr. to peek out from inside his crib. This happened when Vicki suggested that she and I exchange roles in our latest therapy sessions. She still thought there was hidden baggage from my childhood; that it was at the root of my lingering depression. After several months of hearing from Tori, I agreed to exchange chairs and Joe Jr. appeared.

He was a sorry soul with a much different kind of woebegone childhood. He was depressed and morose. Vicki likened him to Eeyore (from Winnie the Pooh) but he didn't have a bow on his tail and he wasn't cute and lovable. And as much as I hate to admit it, he had an alter-ego we had already met named Joe Gorilla. Both were part of a real Jekyll-and-Hyde personality.

By naming these inner children, Vicki and I were better able to deal with our own and each other's lamentable childhoods. It was easier to investigate the circumstances and feelings of our childhoods if we objectified them, not taking them quite so personally. I could feel sorry for Vicki when I pictured Tori and the horrendous abuse she had lived through. I could muster the empathy to placate her and her incessant questions and understand her need to feel safe. And that's what Vicki wanted and needed. By dealing with Tori, I gained the skills to coax Joe Jr. out from hiding in his crib where he had felt abandoned. He represented the vulnerable part of my personality, and he was soon a regular at our therapy sessions down at the shop.

I wrote in my journal, 'I've been having a much harder time of late. The past is close to the surface. Vicki is stronger and helping me.' We were now regularly taking turns with our therapy sessions. 'A lot of sadness, sense of neglect and of wanting a mother.' I noted that the depression seemed to come in waves. I had little energy and did a lot of sleeping during that time. 'I named my little child Joe Jr. I guess after my father. He's in sorry shape. Whenever he's close, I sit and rock like chimps who are raised without mothers—they rock themselves constantly. He feels overburdened and incapable of dealing with much. Much of my anger may be from not allowing him to feel.'

I remembered my senior project in college when I started doing volunteer work at a small private alternative school. I was surprised at first and then intrigued to see the adults validating the children's feelings. The idea that they had feelings had not occurred to me; I unconsciously looked at the children in school as being self-propelled robots who needed to be programmed by positive and negative reinforcement—mostly the latter. Once the surprise wore off and I ascertained that the rest of the world agreed that kids did have feelings, I was left asking myself perplexing questions about how I had missed the boat on this rather obvious issue. At that time I didn't probe too deeply, but I had a vague feeling that huge chunks of my interior life were shut down. No wonder Eeyore was depressed.

'My little kid is close to the surface,' I wrote in another journal entry. 'Just talking of my neglected childhood will bring up feelings of despair. I'm beginning to understand: As a child I was unattended—usually abandoned in the crib. I would cry—later I would scream rather than feel hurt—to get attention but it didn't come . . . . The abandonment, the despair and hopelessness—(they have) always been part of my life but not always conscious—now characterize several areas of my life when I'm weak. It also explains why innately I attributed no feelings or (self) motivation to children. I was so fundamentally ignored (when I was a child) . . . . I feel this heartbreaking sadness just to the point of tears for Joe Jr. who is so alone and unloved.'

Slowly I came to understand what Vicki meant by pampering her little child. Joe Jr. certainly needed it. He had not bonded with my mother, and that fundamental lack of security had been affecting him ever since. He needed to be loved and accepted even though he was not very lovable. I began to spend more time with him. Joe Jr. seemed to be two to three years old; he was able to stand up in his crib and see what was going on around him, and he understood that he was not included.

Vicki didn't like Joe Jr. anymore than I liked Tori Two Shoes. She wanted to get rid of him as quickly as possible. He was depressing to be around and he was related to Joe Gorilla, the big bully who used intimidation to get what he wanted. When she prayed about how to do that, she realized that she needed to pamper Joe Jr. just like she wanted me to work with Tori. This was not easy for Tori because she didn't like men, and Joe Jr. was wrapped up in a man's body. Most of her experiences with men had been painful. She was also well aware of his Jekyll-and-Hyde personality. She found it very easy to manipulate Joe Jr. because he was so needy for attention, but she had to be careful that she didn't take advantage of him because of his alter-ego. Tori had the mothering in her; the question was whether she was willing to give it to Joe Jr.

July 7, 1991. Journal entry. I'm feeling lethargic—impossible to get much physical work done. Avoiding some garden work because of my back and shoulders. Area in center, on spine, between my shoulder blades. Vicki finally worked with J.Jr. this

evening. (She) Figured he must have gotten triggered by call from
Jeff (my brother) on Sunday, but I think it might be related to a
dream on the 5th. I think I got hit on that spot—I had the image
of a boy trying to protect his head, also of the <u>wait</u> before getting
clobbered. More work needs to be done.

One evening Vicki and I ate in the bedroom while the kids ate in the
dining room. That added to the depressing feeling. I wrote: 'After dinner I
said I had a strong hopeless feeling. It was centered around my heart and
(was) painful. As a child I was not allowed to do anything wrong. Failure was
not met with comfort and encouragement but with rebuke.

'Cold, hopeless, lonely feeling. No place to go to ever get relief. Sadness
and hopelessness. Giving up. And falling asleep.'

July 26, 1991. Journal entry. We started on me first (for therapy).
I had been having a nervous tick since Atlanta (where we picked
up Tripp on the return from his mission). One of the worst. I
had the sensation—similar to fantasy—of someone playing with
my little penis, getting it erect. I was glad to get some attention
but underneath was the ever-present pain of never getting
what I wanted—love/nurturing . . . . As Vicki and I talked, the
pervading sense of neglect—a lack of nurturing—came back. I
became aware of someone sucking that little penis. It was a game
to Mother. I was glad for any attention. But there was still pain
underneath for never getting what I wanted. I guessed my age
was about 18 to 24 months.

A month later there was a definite change.

August 24, 1991. Journal entry. I had a couple of dreams in the
middle of the night that I remembered when I woke up.
    One of my mother. She was reading some thick paperback
book. When she was finished I said, "Don't you see you're dead
now. You've already died." She had been in abject denial. As I
spoke to her, I wondered whether I would be able to accept my

own death. I was talking to her with my face flush against hers as emphasis. She suddenly disappeared when she realized she had already died . . . .

Slowly dawning on me that my background may be substantially different from the average person because of abuse and neglect.

August 25, 1991. Journal entry. Did therapy today. I had a strong sense of depression. At first, Joe Jr. was invisible. It was a common situation when things were bad. When V. asked if he was there, he poked his head from around the corner of the crib. When V. said she wanted to visit with him, he started showing off by doing acrobatic tricks like an Olympian. Showed off for some time. When he finally calmed down, he was dressed like an Indian with a one-feather headdress and loincloth. (That was the way he looked at his diaper.) He said he was 2 to 3 years old.

His attitude was different than ever before when dealing with him. He wanted attention. I think because of the dream I had about my mother dying. He may very well have been singing the song from the *Wizard of Oz*: "The witch is dead; the witch is dead. The wicked witch is dead . . . ." It gave him the opportunity to look for someone else (to fulfill those basic needs of security).

I realized my major task was to integrate J.Jr. into my personality. He felt different from me—almost like a split personality. It will be hard to incorporate him because he is surrounded by depression and helplessness and hopelessness, but he also has most of my first-level—true—feelings which include a zest for life.

V. and I agreed to try and take time out to deal with him daily, get him to come out and hopefully, in time, dissipate the heavy feelings.

It wasn't that long before Tori and Joe Jr. disappeared from my journal and from our lives. That season of remembering and healing was over. Because our "children within" were no longer dominant, it didn't mean that we never again had interpersonal problems; we had plenty of them. Healing would be lifetime proposition, although we didn't know that at the time. It's just that we dealt with each other better because we recognized with more empathy the origin of some of our character flaws. Part of the healing process would be an adventure that we didn't recognize was just on the horizon and would change our lives forever.

Looking back, I now understand better the interpersonal dynamics from much of the early period of our lives. Joe Jr., who represented the vulnerable part of my personality, was so needy that he responded to almost any kind of attention if it came with the right tone of voice—a solicitous, caring one. He wanted to please; it was more likely to get him the attention he wanted. Tori figured that out and often used that in situations that frightened her. She begged in a soft tone of voice and Joe Jr. responded.

The problem was that young Tori, who was inherently angry—and a little reckless—to begin with, was oblivious to Joe Jr.'s limits and often pushed too far in an effort to protect herself. At those times, Joe Jr. felt used and manipulated—not truly cared for. That brought back those despairing feelings of being abandoned in the crib and that scared the little tyke. In stepped Joe Jr.'s alter ego, Joe Gorilla to hide the pain with anger. Now wrapped in a man's body, he could be volatile at six-foot-two and over two-hundred pounds. If he did explode, the two would quickly vanish because they were little children and inherently afraid. Hence my adult self did not always remember many of these incendiary scenes, or I experienced them as flashes where I was forced to pick up the pieces left by someone else I vaguely knew who had just disappeared.

As the fact that I had actually been sexually abused settled in to both my mind and my body, I experienced an almost clairvoyant recognition of that history in other men—just like Vicki had with women. It was uncanny; under the right circumstances I could feel it. That awareness had always been there, but now I recognized it for what it was. As we would later hypothesize, there is some like of psychic affinity among those who have been sexually abused.

The time Vicki put into helping me was a turning point for her. If she was going to admit Tori into her life, then she needed to acknowledge Joe Jr. in mine. And she did. It forced her to create sympathy, which the poor fella sorely needed. He needed a mother . . . and badly. And if nothing else, Vicki is the archetypal Mother. This benefited her as well as me. When she wasn't being triggered by her own past, caring for Joe Jr. expanded her perception of who I was, and this did much to smooth out our relationship. I was no longer the enemy; I was a fellow sufferer.

I need to add that Joe Jr. and his aura of depression came back as I was writing what you have been reading. I didn't recognize his presence at first, but with each review of the manuscript I became more sensitive to his appearance. I would start feeling his despondency as my mother showed up to visit us that summer just before she was first diagnosed with cancer. It peaked with her death and then again at this point when I finally admitted to myself that I had been sexually abused.

It's been almost thirty years since Mother's death and I have had plenty of time to more accurately assess the good and bad of her life, and how the sexual abuse that she certainly suffered affected her—and consequently me. But with all that behind me, I never cease to be amazed at the long term effects of PTSD. It just never seems to go away.

ONE LAST MEMORY

August, 1991

At the Atlanta adoption conference she attended, Vicki saw for the first time, large interracial families. Some had as many children as we had. And those were her kind of people: people who liked kids and especially babies. Most of the families were like us—they were not wealthy, but they felt a calling. They had adopted or were fostering on a long-term basis.

This conference resonated with Vicki and she was suddenly excited about adoption. It wasn't long before our whole house was vibrating in synch. Our kids had been thoroughly brainwashed into the magic of babies so it wasn't a big jump for them. In particular, Vicki set her sights on adopting a special-needs kid. We had plenty of cute white kids; she was thinking of adopting a racial minority or a child with some kind of disability. Her grandfather was especially soft-hearted about special-needs kids. Soon it was all she could talk about.

Finally, I said, "What about the first kid God gave you?"

She gave me a quizzical look, not understanding.

"He was sexually abused as an infant, a toddler . . . ." I reminded her.

She still didn't understand.

"I'm talking about Joe Jr."

She snarled a wry smile. "Yeah, he's really difficult."

"Very hard to love, huh?" I asked.

"Yeah." She agreed.

We both laughed that kind of knowing, half-hearted laugh, recognizing the truth of the matter.

"Let me show you what I found at the library," she said excitedly, changing the subject.

She snuggled close to me on the sofa and pulled out a large photo album entitled *CAP*—Children Awaiting Placement. These were children in the foster-care system who were available for adoption—parental rights having been terminated. It was a black-and-white photo collection of some of the most forlorn young faces that I'd ever scene—Joe Jr.-type forlorn, maybe even worse. Most of the children were black and older and begging to be loved but without any real hope of getting a family. Looking through the book and at all the photos was heart-wrenching.

It wasn't long before we were surrounded by our kids, and they were picking the ones that they wanted. Vicki's idea was certainly contagious.

"I want this one."

"No, this one."

The arguing continued. "Can we get more than one?"

"We could each get one!"

The only point the kids seemed to agree on was that they wanted the blackest face they could get. Our kids had apparently inherited some of our countercultural streak.

There was a temporary halt to this new obsession of Vicki's when she found out she was pregnant, but that only lasted for a handful of weeks until she had another miscarriage. Her baby-making days were certainly over, but all that did was accentuate her already bad case of baby fever. With renewed energy, she began networking to figure out a way we could adopt. I slowly fell under her spell. We needed a low-budget adoption. Actually, we needed a no-budget adoption.

Vicki began with leads from the *CAP* book. She quickly found out that almost all of the kids had been abused, and that most had been sexually abused. Although that reality pulled at her heart strings, it gave us both pause. The idea of getting an adoption subsidy with the child was nice, but we were wary of the particular baggage that sexual abuse brings with it. From all that we had read, we knew that a significant number of those children would act out during adolescence, and we had too many small children in the house.

We couldn't take chances. We needed to find a special someone who could be a caboose rather than fit into the middle of our gang. And that's what Vicki really wanted anyway; she wanted a baby.

In my wildest dreams I never would have guessed that our quiver was only half full. Nor would I have guessed how therapeutic this kind of adoption would be for us.

There was a gradual tapering of memories and of reliving the past for both of us. I had vague flashes from time to time that seemed to validate what I had guessed of Joe Jr.'s life, but from my journal entries it's obvious our attention was being drawn elsewhere. Memory work was no longer swallowing up our lives.

And then my wife had one last memory that provided missing insight into one of the issues we had wondered about from the beginning. Like all major memories it came with the traditional uproar around the house—seemingly out of nowhere because our life had been relatively calm for months—and it came in pieces over an extended period of time. She had several meetings with her therapist Peter during the interval of its birthing, and he concurred that it was one of the most difficult. A major difficulty was that we wanted to be past this part of her therapy, past all the memory work. The memories had been quiet for months and we didn't want to go back into that realm; we didn't want to admit that there might be more.

October 20, 1991. Journal entry. Alternating spells of light- and heavy-headedness were scaring Vicki, raising her adrenaline level. She's been saying over the last few days that it might be related to a memory. At church she said it was bothering her and we might have to go home prematurely. At sacrament she had some bits of memory:

(She was) on an X-like contraption that turned like a windmill. She was clamped or roped to the structure, pushed up slowly and then fast down but not fast enough to get back up. She was pushed up again by the cult in this rhythm. She was very afraid of the sudden downward spin. Possibly her mother was off to the side—she was unsure. Vicki had a feeling of wanting to protect her mother.

We talked about it this morning. Vicki couldn't figure out why she (her mother) would be there, but it was obvious to me: (Virginia's presence) would be the final straw needed to break her (Vicki's) resistance.

October 25, 1991. Journal entry. A little more work on Vicki's memory:

Nine-year-old Vicki saw the men leading Virginia to the car. The torturer kicked Vicki in the stomach. She was upside down on the X. Virginia got hysterical. This was for show, to teach her as much as Vicki. Vicki was unclamped and fell to the ground in a heap. She remembered the loose soil. No grass or such.

Torturer got several men to orally stimulate her clitoris and nipples. "You're crazy," he repeated several times as cult members worked to stimulate her. He pointed out she must be crazy to feel good after what she'd been through.

October 27, 1991. Journal entry. Cork finally blew off this morning. Last night Vicki was singing with the kids "Mother, Tell Me the Story." This morning she was in a very hostile mood after waking up. There was a long harangue about keeping her awake with the World Series. I stayed up only as long (which I did stretch) as I needed for laying the grout and clean up. I went to bed at the end of the 11th inning . . . .

As I went out to put seats in the van, she relaxed on the new couch. She told me later she finally got to the pain of her last memory. It was very intense. Half an hour later her hands were cold (shock?). She finally acknowledged the fact that her mother didn't care enough to do anything. Virginia couldn't have done anything then, but she could have run off with the kids at another occasion. The fact that the cult had her (Virginia) there leads me to believe she knew all along what was going on. She closed her eyes.

We finally did make it to church, but she was the worst in weeks—several months. She had to control everything . . . .

October 30, 1991. Journal entry. Vicki finished her memory today, this morning when I wasn't around:

After being stimulated she was gang raped, assaulted at all openings. But she was so little there, she did not process much of what was happening. After the orgy she was re-strapped to the twirling cross. She noticed blood leaking from her lower openings. After being twirled a few times, several of the men present prevailed on the torturer to take her down before they killed her. They didn't think Vicki's mother could handle that. Tom wrapped her in a white blanket, slung her over his shoulder and took her to the car and home.

Vicki said she had a clear recollection of that house in El Paso, including the back room where he had taken her. Her mother was there crying as Vicki was left there. "What have they done with you, my baby, my baby . . . ." Virginia repeated over and over, as she unrolled the blanket and started cleaning up the blood and mess.

Vicki said there was no emotion in the memory. It was clear and dry—possibly because she was almost dead.

Another scene of being stretched out on a rack-like device that almost cut off her breathing.

November 1, 1991. Journal entry. Vicki finally went over the memory again this morning. She didn't want to talk at night. Too easy to get into a flashback and get upset. I had to give her a blessing. A lot of fear associated with the memory.

After the rape she was back on the windmill. Then down and into a tub-like contraption filled with spiders. They had a way of pulling her head back to the point where her breathing stopped. Generating extreme fear. She was told by her torturer she would have a similar fate (she would be killed) if she ever told.

November 4, 1991. Journal entry. Vicki and I are still fighting. I think it peaked this morning. She finally got the message I wasn't going to cooperate. She is too strung out. She wants to do Nova Scotia & adoption, and life is falling apart at home all around us. Kids are at their worst. Vicki's health terrible—allergies (no rain to speak of in months), heavy period and memory. Unfortunately, for Vicki she needs me to do both (move to Nova Scotia and do an adoption). I'm sick of the big push.

The overall effect—the last memory was one of the worst. She has lapsed back into protective mode with questions, control, etc. like several months previously. It's hard to see any progress toward her desire with her retrograde reaction.

December 11, 1991. Journal entry. Interesting talk with Vicki. She's still depressed. Cycle of physically feeling bad leading to emotionally feeling bad leading to physically feeling bad leading to . . . .

She can't break an infection. It's the cause of much slackness in the house. There is little schoolwork being done; the house is unusually untidy, poor meals, lack of much planning; the kids are wild and rebellious.

I believe at the bottom is the root feeling associated with the last memory: What use is there to keep on trying? It's Satan's ploy to destroy the hallmark of Christianity, which is hope. Now, there is a need to answer the question: What is the purpose to keep trying—as a 9-year-old and a 42-year-old?

All the things Vicki wants to do involve DOING. I believe she is searching for deeper meaning.

December 12, 1991. Journal entry. We found a picture of Vicki at age 10. The photo was on her naturalization papers. She referred to herself as the "happy hooker." There was a weird look in her eye. She was able to laugh at herself.

I had a strong sense when just saying my prayers of how much closer Vicki and I are. There is a tremendous improvement over time.

The intense feelings associated with this last memory slowly dissipated. What was left in its wake seemed obvious: this was the core memory that we'd been seeking for over three years. They had finally broken little Vicki's spirit by almost killing her. The cult had gotten the compliance they needed to use her as a pawn to make money whether it be prostitution, blackmail or whatever. They did it by crushing her, by showing her that even her mother was not going to rescue her.

Virginia, who otherwise was exceptional with regard to maternal competence, was allowing this to happen. Virginia could have escaped; her parents would have helped, and she didn't do it. She had been complicit in the sacrifice of her daughter. And the acceptance of this new reality had been difficult—difficult beyond anything Vicki had previously experienced in her memory work.

CHRISTMAS AGAIN

December, 1991

Christmas was on the near horizon and we both wanted to do something different. We wanted to do something to take our minds off what we'd been through. We wanted to get away from it all—from that pervasive, depressing feeling that had invaded our lives with Vicki's last memory. More than anything my wife wanted to erase her sordid past. She had no desire to see her parents, but she knew with Christmas approaching her mother would pressure for a visit.

For months she had been talking about Nova Scotia. As a vacation it seemed like fun—but only if we had the money. And we didn't. Then I was stopped by the county agricultural extension agent who told me that we had a tobacco allotment that we weren't using and that we could sell it. Vicki interpreted this as an answer to prayer, giving us the money to go to Nova Scotia. I had to admit that it did seem to coincide with the end of that last memory, and I couldn't help but cave after what she'd been through the last few months.

We did Christmas differently that year, spacing the opening of presents out over a period of several days before Christmas. We left early Christmas morning, heading north. With very little traffic on the road, we made it to just below New York City.

It became a family vacation, a breath of fresh air in our ragged lives. Vicki was looser and we had fun. We ate at modestly priced restaurants and stayed at hotels, renting two rooms each night: One for us and the baby, the other for all the kids who got to watch TV, which we didn't have at home.

We took in New York City, seeing the Statue of Liberty, the World Trade Center and the Empire State Building. That evening we landed at Old Orchard Beach in Maine and I got to walk along the juncture of sand and surf. The next day we went through the back roads of northern Maine to get into Canada. That night we stayed with an older couple who loved our kids like their own grandkids and gave Vicki and me some space.

This stop became a very special time for Vicki: it was like living in a postcard from yesteryear. All the houses had decorative lights in the windows; nothing gaudy, just plain white bulbs. The spirit of Christmas was strong. It was refreshing, so far away from the world we normally lived in, the world of incest and ritual abuse.

Vicki got Nova Scotia out of her system and I expected life to return to our version of normal. But like her trip to the adoption conference five months earlier, we could have never guessed that the several nights that we enjoyed in Maine on the way up and back would soon have a major impact on our lives. I didn't recognize the strong need Vicki felt to put more distance between herself and her parents.

NEAR DEATH WITH STEPHEN
December, 1991

Starting in November Vicki's brother Stephen had a series of health lapses. It started with another stroke, which his doctor blamed on the complicated mix of drugs he was taking. Somehow he was off his blood thinner. Vicki got the message from her mother that Stephen was very sick. The doctor didn't think his death was imminent but Steve disagreed. Virginia related the story of her son in the oxygen tent, of holding his hand, of listening to him choke with coughing spells, and then saying to her, 'I'm not sure I'll pull through this time.'

On our way back from Nova Scotia—with Stephen's declining health on her mind—Vicki broke her vow not to see her father and we stopped in Raleigh. Virginia helped with a bribe of giving us Vicki's old bedroom suite for our girls. Tom, of course, agreed to pay for the trailer to haul the furniture back home. Virginia crooned over the fact that she'd had four Christmas dinners, one with each of her children.

My journal notes that Vicki got triggered while she was there, but what amazed both of us on this visit was the decline in her father. Tom was just shy of seventy years old and had total care of Stephen, which included taking him to all his doctor appointments, to several therapies and, until recently, to Wilmington and other job sites where Stephen worked for his younger brother Jack when he felt well enough. Tom was looking ragged. He had lost weight and seemingly aged since we'd last seen him.

As we left Raleigh, Vicki said, "I watched him help my brother up the steps to his room. I had a flashback of Daddy taking him to the cult meetings.

It was so sad." A few minutes later she continued in a whisper, "He's got to be a multiple. It's the only thing that makes sense. He doesn't believe in an afterlife and he feels responsible for what's happening to Steve." Vicki, along with her mother, believed that if Steve died, Tom would have lost a crucial battle with his conscience.

I was inclined to believe Vicki. I wrote: 'His decline seemed to me indicative of real involvement with Steve as opposed to a game of "good show."'

While we were down at the shop in mid-January just starting one of our regular therapy sessions, Vicki got a call from her mother.

"Ste-e-v-e-e," Virginia stuttered, and Vicki held up the phone for me to hear. My wife's first thought was that he had just died. Neither one of us had ever heard Virginia stutter like that.

Virginia was distraught because Stephen was frequently falling; he couldn't walk anymore. With each collapse he would scream and cry. His frustration and anger were directed first at Tom, and then at Virginia if she was around. Virginia was confused at the way she was being treated. As the conversation continued, Virginia seemed to be confiding in her daughter. "And your father won't let me see him. I can't even comfort him . . . . Your dad is so upset. Life is miserable."

Vicki listened silently as her mother, in her own peculiar way, jumped from one subject to the next. The underlying theme seemed to be something between Stephen and Tom.

Vicki suggested, "You know why Dad is so upset . . . ? He doesn't believe in any afterlife."

Virginia agreed. "I'm beginning to think he doesn't have strong Christian beliefs. I want to talk to Stephen about that, but your father won't let me near him. The doctor just told him that he could have another stroke at any time. We need to be prepared."

At Virginia's comment about her husband not having strong Christian beliefs, Vicki and I looked at each other in wonder. Just how blind was she?

"I think I should talk to Stephen," Virginia continued, "and share the gospel. But your Daddy won't let me in his room." The fact that Virginia was restricted from seeing Stephen sounded strange.

Vicki's mother told her in early February that the doctor had told Tom that Steve could pass at any time.

Vicki was anxious to find out whether her brother had remembered anything from his childhood. She talked to his therapist and explained that her brother's heavy drug use started as a teenager, when he always had to take a double dose of whatever his friends were taking. From those conversations Vicki discerned her brother had not remembered anything specific, and she did not want to bring it up because of his dependency on their father. But the therapist did say that he believed it was unusual childhood stress that triggered the diabetes, since no one else on either side of the family had that disease, and that was atypical.

A few weeks later Vicki called Stephen. He was angry that Vicki had referred to him as an alcoholic when she talked with his therapist. He also oozed with depression and Vicki found it difficult to talk with him. He made several threats of suicide.

When Vicki finally asked how he was feeling, Steve retorted, "If you don't have anything to talk about except my disease, I don't want to talk."

"How's your job going? Are you working at Lake Jordon?" Steve had been working for his younger brother on a project there. That was several months before; now he was almost totally bedridden.

"No." Steve answered.

"How come?"

"I told you. I'm saving up my pills. I'm going to kill myself."

Vicki looked like she'd had a workout when she got off the phone. "I know he wants to talk. I just can't get beyond his anger."

Memories of their cult days in Hawaii seeped into my wife's mind unbidden. Steve's impending death was triggering the same helpless sense of responsibility she'd felt as an older sister back then. She had been unable to save him from the cult terror and rape, and now she couldn't save him from the consequences of over two decades of poor choices in self-medication. Over and over my wife lamented about how responsible she felt. I finally quit wasting my breath trying to talk her out of it.

With Stephen's health deteriorating further, we made a special trip down to Raleigh at the beginning of March. Virginia served a meal but Stephen did not come to the table. We were told he was sleeping, but afterward Vicki and I slipped into his room to find him watching a basketball game. He was in his usual surly mood.

Even with her knack for counseling Vicki could not get down to his level. I left and still Steve would not talk. I mused about the similarity of my mother and Stephen: Both had had very abusive childhoods and coped with the emotional pain with the self-destructive use of drugs. My mother basically had killed herself and Steve was well-along in that process. There seemed little that Vicki could do.

I noted in my journal that Tom did not appear as strung out as I had expected—or was led to believe. And unlike our last visit two months earlier, he was quick to talk about his own self-sacrifice: The time and money Steve required was daunting. Tom seemed to lavish in his own praise, and I smiled to myself at the thought of Saint Tom; nothing could be more ironic. But while he talked I was bothered by an uncanny feeling that he *was* still involved with the cult. The feeling was strong enough to be almost visual; his look and demeanor reminded me of a poster Vicki and I had seen of a satanic leader. But more bothersome was that it was the second time I'd had that strong intuition. Tom seemed to embody those qualities of evil: intelligence, deceptiveness, beguilement . . . and was he still involved?

Several days later Vicki brought up the subject of her brother again. "It must be horrible for him, being dependent on Daddy. It must trigger the living daylights out of him."

I thought about Virginia's description of Tom's activities and wondered aloud, "Why do you think your father is *guarding* him?" Those words slipped out of my mouth and I wondered, as I had before, if Tom's role as caretaker had a purpose other than assistance.

"You know my father could kill him, just like he tortured him earlier. He killed others . . . ." Vicki reminded me.

"You don't think he's worried about getting caught?" I asked.

"He's too smart for that."

On March 10th, Virginia called to tell Vicki that Stephen had almost died several days earlier. Virginia had gotten up early, at 6:30, and saw Tom wiping foam from Stephen's mouth with a washcloth. Tom immediately told her to call the rescue squad, that Steve was in insulin shock. When the EMTs arrived they said that if the call had come just twenty or thirty minutes later, it would have been too late.

"Did Daddy yell and wake you up to call the rescue squad?" Vicki asked carefully.

"No," Virginia responded. There was a certain obvious anxiety in Virginia's voice. It had been there from the beginning. "Your Dad said he got up at 6:30. He's up a lot at night. He pads around the house. He tested Steve's blood sugar at midnight. He gave him a sandwich and it was all right."

Vicki tried to pin her mother down about the washcloth. "Was he wiping up foam or was he covering his mouth?"

Virginia waffled and it was obvious she had her doubts. That's why she had called.

"Why did you wait so long to call and tell me?" Vicki asked.

Virginia's voice was quiet, almost secretive. "I can't call when your father's here. This is the first time he's been away from the house."

Vicki was speechless.

"Your father said he threw away two bottles of insulin in case they were bad. He just went to the store and bought new ones."

Vicki called a pharmacist friend and was told the odds were zero that the insulin was bad. There was also no reason, after dealing with Stephen's diabetes for almost thirty years, that Tom should be making mistakes. 'The pharmacist said with Tom administering blood thinner and insulin, he could set up both strokes and insulin shock.'

The information was chilling. Is that what Tom was doing? Had it been going on for some time? Was this the origin of Stephen's steady decline? There was no way to tell if it was an accident or not. And that ambiguity was the best disguise. From our reading we knew that if Tom was trying to kill Stephen, he would want to be there when he died. Satanists believed there was power released at death and Tom would covet that.

At that point Vicki called Stephen's doctor.

I told her to start cautiously so she wouldn't sound like a lunatic, but my wife was a nervous wreck and soon the whole story came out. She told the doctor about her fears her father and Steve. The doctor said he had never told Tom that Steve might have another stroke at any time and that it would be fatal. He sounded affronted that Tom had said that. And he had his own questions about the recent insulin shock. He said that they happen occasionally, but there was no reason for this last one. As the conversation continued, Vicki surmised that the doctor was at least open-minded about her suspicions. He was not an ally, but now he was someone who had been forewarned and would at least keep his eyes open.

"If your brother were to die and there was anything suspicious, there would be an autopsy," he reminded Vicki.

But Vicki was trying to keep her brother alive.

A few days later, Virginia called to report that Steve was in the hospital again. He was in intensive care with a lung infection, but what had brought him in to ER was low blood pressure. Virginia said she was calling in response to Vicki's request to know what was happening with Steve.

"Does Daddy know you're calling?" my wife asked.

"Tom doesn't want me calling anybody about Steve. He's funny about that."

Vicki took the opportunity to quiz her mother about the previous early-morning incident.

"I was stirring and I woke up to some commotion," Virginia started.

"What exactly did you see?" Vicki asked.

"Your father was wiping Steve's mouth . . . ."

"You're sure he was wiping Steve's mouth?"

The troubled pause at the other end of the line told Vicki what she had suspected. That's why Virginia had called to begin with, and that's why she was calling now. She *was* suspicious and didn't know how to handle the situation.

"Your dad went to call the rescue squad and I went to get the washcloth and clean Steve up . . . ." There was another long pause. "Stephen mumbled, 'Help me . . . . Dad.' He was stuttering. I couldn't understand him very well."

With her voice rising, Vicki asked, "What do you think he meant?"

"I don't know . . . ." Was this the same Virginia of Vicki's memories that didn't *want* to know?

But it was clear that her mother wanted to talk about it. Virginia said she'd keep calling on the sly. She was plainly concerned and implicit in their conversation was that something needed to be done.

Vicki then called Steve's diabetes doctor and quizzed him on the possibility of induced low blood pressure.

"I think we know the cause of it. I did an exam on Steve looking for marks and I didn't find any. But you know one thing . . . . your father was there, watching over Steve like he always is." There was a certain warmth in the doctor's voice. He saw Tom as the concerned father. "He was wearing a bronze star with something in the middle. Was it a war medal?"

With a couple of phone calls Vicki learned that Satanists sometimes wear a bronze pentagram with a crystal in the middle. The purpose was to distract and confuse anyone else in the room.

A few days later Virginia confirmed that Tom had a bronze star. He'd been wearing it around the house a lot recently. He didn't win it but had taken one from an overstock during his time in the military.

On March 16th, Steve's doctor called Vicki to report that a CT scan showed a possible stroke with the latest crisis. The doctor was recommending that a nurse be hired to attend to Stephen. A therapist who had interviewed Stephen had detected some hostility between Stephen and his parents. The therapist was also assigned to make some regular home visits. That was a relief for my wife.

With those changes, Stephen's health stabilized and improved. There is no further mention of his condition in my journal until May 2nd. On that date, Virginia called to tell Vicki that her brother had gone to the emergency room again with diabetic shock. This time there was no secret about what happened: The trouble started because Tom had given Steve a shot without first giving him food. And Steve was furious with his father.

Vicki called hospital admissions and got the date on which Stephen was admitted—April 25th. It was just a few days in front of May 1st, one of the cult's biggest holidays.

She also talked with his doctor who was, as usual, noncommittal. He was averse to assigning blame.

I had a special relationship with my brother Stephen. First, he was my baby brother, but more importantly, he and I had a lot of trauma bonding. We were both survivors of child sex trafficking. Even though it wasn't called that back then, or even at this point when I was in therapy, that's what it was. Plain and simple: Stephen and I were being sold for sex.

Stephen had moved back into my parents' house because his health was deteriorating. My father was taking total care of him and things kept getting worst with strokes and insulin overdoses. Dale Griffis and Jody and I were convinced my father was trying to kill him off. We knew my father kept a bodyguard-type attitude toward Steve. He was always sitting with him at the hospital, and the nurses lauded him with praise for his fatherly concern. But I just thought he wanted to make sure Steve did not talk while under the influence of hospital drugs.

I wanted to do something. But what? After conferring with Dale Griffis, the answer was for me to talk to Steve myself and help him know what was going on, to help him see the obvious.

We scheduled a trip to Raleigh, just Jody and me. I was a total nervous wreck on the mission to save my brother. We didn't have much of a plan: Jody was to distract Daddy while I talked to Steve.

When we arrived, my mother said my father was doing his bodyguard routine. In a panicked voice, I told my father Jody needed his help with a car problem. Jody had to think quick, which he's not good at, but my father followed him out to our van. I watched the two of them from Stephen's bedroom window.

Steve was laying propped on an elevated hospital bed. He was in horrible shape—the worst I'd ever seen.

"Who's been giving you your insulin shots? . . . You weren't having overdoses before you moved back home. . . ." I told him quickly of my suspicions.

He just stared at me, but his eyes were blinking and I knew he was taking it in. He didn't say a word.

My dad came back in then, eyed us suspiciously and sat down in his chair.

We didn't stay long. A quick meal with my mother and we were gone. We had no idea whether our visit had done any good as we drove away, but two days later I got another call from my mother. While Daddy was out, Stephen's girlfriend Lily came by and picked him up. He moved out for good.

They married in September and thus began the final years of Stephen's life. He began again giving himself his own shots and there was never another insulin overdose.

REEVALUATING AGAIN

1992

The Darkness that had suffused Vicki's memories of her childhood had now pierced the surface into our present-day lives. I now knew what Vicki had known all along, what she had lived through as a child. Despite this, and my original intuition of Tom, I had a difficult time attributing to the man who had come closest to being a father-figure in my life the evil that should have been his due. Had all those years of him giving us twenty-dollar bills gilded my perception of him? Looking back some twenty-five plus years I can't help but wonder.

As our understanding of the psychology of severe abuse grew, we often wondered whether Tom had multiple personalities—as opposed to being a psychopath without a conscience. That would explain the severe dichotomy seen in his character. I am inclined to believe that the scene eleven-year-old Vicki stumbled upon—when Tom was sobbing over Stephen's diagnosis of juvenile diabetes—was genuine. And the sense that he was crestfallen that his daughter did not want to go to these cult orgies in El Paso was not sarcasm. But if Tom was a multiple, it was never obvious to us—not that we were trained in the subtleties of MPD—Multiple Personality Disorder.

Slowly my perception of Tom was changing and enlarging. He had an unusual combination of an extremely high IQ, an uncanny ability to read people, quick-thinking street smarts and a total absence of scruples. He was a consummate liar and you could never tell with him. He could also be very earthy—to the point of being lewd—when he wasn't concerned about public consumption and that tended to increase his ruse of credibility.

243

It was not only his family that was under his spell. Tom had run for Mayor of Raleigh. He had been a dark-horse candidate from the beginning with no chance of winning, but he loved the celebrity attention. He drove around in his almost-antique, polished, black VW Beetle, his name on the license plate and mayoral stickers plastered all over it. It was more slapstick than anything else, and Tom never seemed to take himself or his chances of winning seriously. But he sure loved the attention.

Tom's life seemed to evoke more questions than answers. And I now understood better my wife's craving to move as far away as possible.

Virginia was no less of an enigma. As Vicki's therapists had conjectured, she apparently had known what was going on with her daughter. Why hadn't Virginia done anything? Her family of origin was relatively healthy. Why hadn't she called them for help? Had those summer vacations back at the old family farm been the undoing of part of Virginia's psyche? While Vicki's last memory—with her mother as a spectator—seemed to explain the unexplainable, it was not a very satisfactory answer. And as we would find out, it was not a complete answer either.

THE DARKEST
CORNER OF HELL

THE FALSE MEMORY SYNDROME

1992-1993

Because of the work that Vicki was doing in sexual abuse, she was invited to a seminar featuring Kenneth Lanning of the FBI, who was at the time speaking throughout the country. With the increasing number of reports of sexual abuse, especially incest, and now ritual abuse, the FBI had gotten involved. Not only were there adult survivors like Vicki coming forward, but there had been the sensational McMartin Preschool trial and acquittal in California, where Satanism had made the headlines for months.

Lanning was introducing the concept of "False Memory Syndrome." The False Memory Syndrome Foundation (FMSF) had just been formed by the parents of a woman in her mid-thirties who had accused her father of molesting her as a child—from ages three to sixteen. Her story had other similarities to Vicki's, including the age she entered therapy, the fact that she remembered little or nothing of her abuse when she started therapy, and that she had been initially interested in reconciliation.

The parents, both professionals, vehemently denied that the incest had occurred. In a long article published under a pseudonym, the mother sounded surprisingly like Virginia supporting her husband with a blind eye to anything that might be considered evidence to the contrary. Instead, she blamed their daughter's shocking revelations on techniques used by her therapist such as hypnosis and guided imagery. The parents, and now this new foundation, claimed that these types of memories had been *created* rather than recovered, in therapy.

Fraudulent claims of sexual abuse were not new. In the beginning it seemed that the FMSF was simply filling the need to demand a more careful scrutiny when these allegations occurred. It was not unheard of for mothers to claim in a divorce proceeding that their daughters have been molested by their husbands. This was an excellent way to get child support without sharing custody. There was sometimes even a restraining order enacted against the father, and that with no evidence other than the mother's word. As sexual abuse was coming out of the closet, there was a tendency to believe these kinds of allegations because they were too scandalous to even talk about in public. The FMSF seemed to be a natural and needed backlash to this lack of critical examination. Before long a language and protocol for investigation of claims of sexual abuse were developed.

This new foundation, with an excellent marketing campaign, was co-opting much of the attention of the media in matters related to sexual abuse. And they would continue to do so for several years. They claimed a mushrooming number of members and qualified expert witnesses to hire for court cases. They would continue doing an excellent job of promoting their ideas through much of the 1990s.

The audience for this FBI-sponsored seminar, which consisted mostly of victims and therapists, was expecting an unbiased and insightful approach from the FBI to this new wrinkle in sexual abuse therapy that was getting so much attention and was still in its infancy. Mr. Lanning was hardly unbiased and soon the audience turned hostile to his presentation. He did not want to talk about the fact that almost all of the foundation's members were parents accused of sexual abuse by their adult children, or that one of the early founders of the organization had written fondly of the joys of pedophilia. My wife's distaste turned to anger when he virtually denied the existence of ritual abuse altogether and downplayed the number of incest cases by saying they were overblown.

I think it was safe to say that he didn't win any converts in the audience that day. He came across as a government patsy covering up a huge psychological epidemic that had been ravaging the country. Over the next decade, those in the therapeutic profession would fight back. With scholarly articles, they harshly criticized the work of both Lanning and the False Memory Syndrome Foundation. One very lettered, academic critic we know actually received death threats that forced him out of the debate.[9] Eventually, repressed memories would be credited by the psychological community as valid, whereas the False Memory Syndrome never would.

But the question that was left lingering—one that we didn't deal with at the time, but now is glaring—was this: Why would the government get involved and take sides with something that seemed so unrelated to their sphere of activity?

The sexual abuse of children by their parents has probably been going on from the earliest eons of time. Yes, it was just coming out of the closet and into public consciousness, but it had been ongoing for ages. Why would the government feel like they would need to step in and say this wasn't happening, or that this was blown out of proportion? Why would they deny ritual abuse all together? Why was Ken Lanning on such a crusade? Were they trying to hide something? Did it have something to do with the fact that almost every involved therapist we talked with noted the relationship between ritual abuse and the military?

On the drive home from the seminar it was a time for us to reflect. We had long since gotten past the doubting stage. Vicki had not gone into therapy and then remembered her abuse. When I first met her, she remembered being molested at age eleven. Dick had not used any of these controversial therapeutic techniques—namely hypnosis—until she had remembered numerous incidents of abuse, and until after she'd written the letters to her parents. She had been in therapy for a year and a half when he first tried hypnosis. And when we did sessions together—just like Dick had—I didn't "guide" her other than to ask her "Where are you?" or "What do you see?" or "What's happening?" Vicki just happened to have an exceptionally vivid recall—because there *were* horrific things to recall. And Peter had never used any of these techniques.

But there were also pieces of what we considered evidence—the most obvious was the emotional and family uproar that had come with her memories. I could not imagine how creating fiction could generate so much turmoil. Why would Vicki want to work herself into such an

---

9   I know this man wants to remain anonymous.

emotional state over her own imaginings? It made more sense to believe that something had actually happened. Second, there was the general pattern of her memories going from bad to worse. These did not come haphazardly, which is what you might expect from something that was being made up. The consistent psychological order of the memories gave us a sense of being on an established trajectory. In retrospect, as she could handle more, the memories seemed to come. The fact that there was a consistent pattern to this process of remembering gave it credibility.

Tom's overreaction to Virginia's recall of the white cat that Vicki had when she was three seemed to us to be credible evidence. We suspected his willingness to pay for much of her therapy also fell into that category. Tom had learned how to use money to his advantage, and he seemed to have an endless supply of twenty-dollar bills. The fact that Vicki's memories of her father were not out of character was validated by the series of Stephen's insulin overdoses. Virginia's vacillating attitude as she tried to keep her family together spoke of a life of duplicity. From time to time even Virginia had almost admitted the truth of her daughter's revelations. Her complicated reaction spoke to an underlying validity.

And beyond all these items was the fact that Dick and Peter, two professionals, who were well-versed in their fields, had validated what Vicki had recalled. The stories that she remembered did not seem strange to them because they were used to hearing them. That's what they did for a living—listen to others regurgitate their sordid pasts. There was never any doubt in their minds that Vicki was recalling truth rather than fabricating fiction. We sometimes took their professional corroboration for granted but it was immensely important, allowing us to continue on a journey through uncharted territory—at least it was uncharted to us. After having lived through so much, we were no longer looking for proof.

One of the things Vicki noticed now that huge chunks of her past had come back to her consciousness was that she often remembered—in the old-fashioned way, without the uproar we'd been experiencing the past several years—just simply remembered much more of her childhood. She remembered more of the good times and some of the not-so-good times. She remembered little things, small treasures from her past. But the past was no longer a secret that was locked away.

There is a difference between remembering and having flashbacks. Much of my remembering initially came in the form of flashbacks. Flashbacks just happen. You can't sit down and make a flashback happen. Something, somewhere will trigger it and all of a sudden you will be back in another time and place. Not just your present self back remembering it, but you will be back reliving it. If it happened when you were seven, then you will be back in your seven-year-old self with all the feelings and thoughts and memories you had back at that time.

Vicki's priorities in life had subtly changed. She wanted to talk about sexual abuse and even ritual abuse. With the latter she needed a proper venue because the public's typical response was still skepticism. With more energy Vicki began doing trainings with local groups and was in fact scheduled to give a seminar on ritual abuse at an international adoption conference in early August. With all the community work she was doing, the state agreed to subsidize her trip to Ottawa, Ontario.

By the time she spoke at that adoption conference we had adopted our first African-American infant. This created a different kind of uproar in our hillbilly neighborhood. Our neighbors banded together to disrupt the adoption, contacting DSS and claiming deficient parenting. After two and a half long months we won that case, only to run into a government roadblock to finalizing the adoption. It became obvious to us that the only way to complete the adoption was to move to a state that was more friendly to interracial adoption.

In 1993, we moved to Maine and quickly completed that adoption; in the fall we adopted another black infant. And then, to our surprise, Vicki became pregnant at age forty-four.

DEJA VU ALL OVER AGAIN

1994

Toward the end of what would be Vicki's last pregnancy she started to have unexplained dizzy spells again. After a couple of weeks she told me she thought she might have more memories coming; that had been the only time she'd had these particular bouts before. But she told me with confidence that she'd said a prayer to wait till after the delivery.

I was more than willing to wait. Although we had occasionally pondered the scarcity of memories surrounding her first stay in El Paso at ages nine and ten—the few memories that she had did not seem enough—neither one of us wanted to go exploring.

Life was good and we were busy. I had plenty of work and that kept me grounded. She was happy and didn't want to interrupt the pleasure of this last pregnancy. After so many difficult years, she felt like she had earned the right to postpone remembering anything else. Honestly, I was skeptical; she hadn't had a stretch of memories for over two years. That period of life seemed to be behind us. And if she could postpone remembering then it probably wasn't anything important.

In the spring of 1994 Vicki found another counselor. Liam was not a licensed therapist, as Dick and Peter had been, but he was well-versed in ritual abuse. He was taking classes at night and finishing up his master's degree. By day, he was the acting manager of a private foster-care agency, and many of the kids that were coming into the foster-care system in Maine were telling of experiences that sounded like ritual abuse. Some were as unbelievable as those in the McMartin Preschool trial—like of people flying—that sounded like drugs were being employed.

As we would find out, the state of Maine was home to several generational cults. Numbers of children were being "groomed" through abuse, torture and brainwashing. Of course, there were drop-outs; these were the kids that were being picked up by the foster-care system. They were the damaged refuse of the cult's grooming process. Liam told us that acting-out behaviors that were symptomatic of sexual abuse were generally what brought these kids to the attention of the foster care system. These children were severely damaged and required special care, hence they were outsourced to Liam's facility, a private foster-care facility that did specialized training with prospective foster-care parents.

Our relationship with Liam was much different than it had been with either Dick or Peter. He never claimed to be a therapist and acted more like a sherpa because he was very familiar with the terrain and refuse of Satanism. He also became our friend. We met with him for two and a half hours in the evening, once a month. He would not accept money, nor did we pay via barter. Perhaps he wanted to believe that the children he saw in his office daily could grow up and become worthwhile and contributing members of society, as Vicki had.

Our relationship eventually became much more personal. We could talk to him about some of the craziness in our relationship, and his general strategy was to help us manage it rather than correct it. He was familiar with the limitations that came with severe abuse. By this time mandatory reporting laws had been enacted but he admitted he was reticent to use them. He thought that, in general, the foster-care system was much more destructive to kids than all but the most dysfunctional families. He relegated mandatory reporting to matters of life and death.

Liam told us how the street scene worked in Bangor where we met, and we did drive through the city streets during the long evenings of summer. We were enlightened to the amount of action that was going on in what seemed like an after-hours, vacated city. Once we knew what to look for, we could see available kids on certain corners who signaled that they were for sale for sex. This was evident not only in where they stood, but also in how they stood and how they dressed; in doing so, these kids were advertising to the johns that they were procurable. He also told us he knew of several very prominent politicians in the state who were deeply involved in child-sex rings, and that the level of corruption was profound. He had learned this from the children with whom he worked.

He also told us of a house north of Camden toward Belfast where several children had reported being abused. He had driven by and said it was worth the visit so Vicki and I took a Saturday to explore. Liam told us that clients flew in from across the country on certain satanic holidays come to this house, which otherwise seemed to be empty. It was a beautiful, stately, two-story gothic with well-maintained grounds. When Vicki and I drove up to it, we agreed that it seemed like something from a Stephen King novel. It was set on a hill away from the dead-end road and other much smaller houses. Liam had said that if we looked carefully, we would see an elaborate intruder-detection system hidden in the extensive gardens.

He was right. There was a motion-sensitive surveillance system unlike anything I'd seen before. It was expensive, discreetly hidden, and obviously state-of-the-art. What were the people who came to this house worried about? There was already a gate on the driveway. But most intriguing was the tacky, Styrofoam insulation that covered all of the second-story windows. That didn't make any sense because everything else on the property spoke of money and expensive tastes. Why not ornate draperies? Why would the owners be worried about heat loss? It didn't make any sense except as Liam had suggested—to muffle the sound of the sexual abuse of children. The children he worked with had reported experiencing torture in that house.

Vicki and I parked our van on the side of the virtually unused road and got out, surveying the house and property. Before long we attracted the attention of a man who lived across the street from the driveway. He said he was the caretaker and wanted to know what we were doing—as if admiring the old house was forbidden. He was obviously suspicious; we were paying too much attention to the house. He was brusque and intent on chasing us off, which was not difficult because we both felt uncomfortable and sensed unsavory vibes from the man. But we had trouble starting the van and ended up being stuck there for over an hour.

When we finally left, we were glad to put some distance between ourselves and that house and its immediate environs; it had made us more uneasy the longer we stayed. But as we headed home, we both had an uneasy feeling that we weren't familiar with and couldn't shake. It was the feeling that some of the Darkness of that house had come with us. The sensation was strong enough and alien enough to us that we talked about it and wondered: what was that troubled feeling that we both sensed? Had we picked up some of the Darkness as one might pick up ticks during a summer walk in the woods? Neither one of us wanted to believe that. It seemed too fanciful. But we were uncomfortable most of the hour-long drive home until we said a prayer—just in case.

Scotia was born in July 1994, and Vicki was pleased with the easiest birth she'd had of her ten. She credited that to the midwife, who understood a woman's body like a male doctor never could. As we had with the other births, we took a few days off. Friends at church took our kids for four days and then life just seemed to swamp us. Her promise to start remembering again was in the back of her mind but she preferred to leave it there. Life was too hectic. We had eleven children at home and four of those were of preschool age. I was busy working long hours at the shop behind our house and changing diapers whenever I came inside. And Vicki had lots of babies around her. She was happy in her element.

In late August Vicki had her six-week check-up. Everything was fine except that her blood pressure was a little higher than normal. As she continued her errands that day, she felt her blood pressure continue to rise. It reached 172/105 by the time she got to the chiropractor several hours later. She told me that evening that she thought it may have been triggered by the pelvic exam at her obstetrician's office. I reminded her that she'd been unusually triggered at church the previous day; she had been haranguing me with questions.

Then she began having flashes of being in the bunkers at the White Sands missile base where her father had worked when she lived in El Paso at ages nine and ten. I wrote down:

'She talked of how much she loved and appreciated Scotia. That hit a memory where she was under cult authority. They told her they would

give her this baby that was about five months old if she did not make any
noise during her torture. But if she did yell, it was bad news for the baby.
She believed they did some kind of cauterizing thing to her cervix. Vicki
remembered she couldn't keep quiet. (I suspected it was a set-up.) She didn't
want to remember any more. She thought they skinned the baby alive.'

A week later I recorded a dream of Vicki's that was set in Hawaii. She
spoke of being terrified and overwhelmed by the surf; huge waves were
coming in and kids were being sucked out to sea. She retreated into a cave
and from out of nowhere a tunnel opened that lead into an amphitheater.

Two days later, I came in from work to eat lunch. Vicki was out running
an errand and should have been back by then. The phone rang and I was
mildly relieved to hear her voice.

"Jody, I'm really dizzy. I need for you to come get me. I can't drive."

"What do you mean you can't drive?" I answered curtly. This sounded
crazy. She was using her command voice and I could feel a wedge of irritation
rising in me. I was really busy. But at the same time, Vicki was not one to
play the card of vulnerability. She liked being confident and competent.

"I'm down at the store. I started getting dizzy. I almost blacked out."
Her voice sputtered. "I can't even walk, not to mention drive. I'm sitting
here; all I can do is hold Scotia."

This did not make any sense. After a lengthy pause, I said, "I don't
understand. What do you mean you can't drive? It's not far."

"If I stand up, I'll be so dizzy I'll drop the baby. I don't understand it
either. I need for you to come get me and drive me home. I've got to go to
bed till this passes." Her voice had that usual assertiveness that I didn't like.

"You want me to walk a mile down the road so I can drive you back
home?" There was more than a little irritated skepticism in my voice. Her
six-week check-up had just reported everything was fine. This didn't make
any sense.

"Look," Vicki said, "if I need to I'll get our neighbor to drive you here,
but I'd rather not get any more upset than I already am." This was obviously
serious.

"You really can't drive?" I asked again.

"Yes. Please come get me. Count it as your afternoon walk. I need your help or I wouldn't be calling. I'm afraid I might black out." Vicki's voice sounded unusually panicked.

Twenty minutes later I walked into the local country store. Vicki was sitting in a booth and she holding seven-week-old Scotia. She was chatting amicably with the old woman behind the counter. She introduced me when I walked in. Nothing appeared to be wrong, except there was a certain weariness in her countenance that I hadn't noticed before. Four-year-old Hannah was monitoring eleven-month-old Heather on the other side of the table. John was eating; that was his hobby. Everything appeared normal. I thought this couldn't be a hoax; that's just not who Vicki was.

"Take Scotia and put her in her car seat and then come back and get me," she said, and then ordered Hannah to put Heather in her car seat. Johnny followed.

I did as instructed; I was good at that in public. When I put my hand out to help her up, she shook her head.

"You're going to have to lift me. My legs don't work."

I stooped down and she put her arm around my shoulder and I stood up. I immediately felt all her weight—it felt like dead weight and I almost fell. She wasn't kidding; her legs actually didn't work. Slowly, I managed to get her outside and into the passenger side of the van. It was a workout.

"What's going on?" I asked, more sympathetic now and very puzzled.

"I don't know. I just want to get to bed so I can lay down."

On the drive home she talked about how the dizziness had come out of nowhere. She thought that maybe it was blood sugar-related and that adding some more protein to her diet might help it pass. She tripped over her own feet as I helped her get inside our house. Her legs were dangling like puppet appendages with the strings cut. Getting her up the stairs to our second-floor bedroom was almost beyond me. Her legs just did not seem to be working. She said they couldn't hold any weight at all. I was exhausted when I finally got her and the baby settled and then made lunch for Heather and Hannah and Johnny. Something was definitely wrong but neither one of us had a clue as to what it might be.

"I'll call the doctor after a little bit," Vicki said. "The older kids will be home from school soon; they can help. Put Heather in her crib here and go back to work. If I need help with the two little ones, I'll send Hannah over to get you."

As I looked at her in bed, I sensed a certain darkness that hadn't been there for over two years. It didn't click at the time, probably because I didn't want it to. That was on Thursday.

With the bed rest and some extra protein Vicki soon felt better. On Saturday she went to the dentist by herself for a nagging tooth problem. He figured she had a slight infection from poor cleaning that was potentially causing some of these problems. Vicki hated going to the dentist; problems with her teeth tended to escalate before she dealt with them.

Saturday afternoon she felt better still, and we went to a church conference in Portland an hour and a half away. Sunday was a rest day but by evening the dizziness returned and increased to the point where we went into the emergency room. After numerous tests the doctors concluded nothing was wrong and ordered increased bed rest, some time to herself and walking alone. They proposed that she was simply exhausted: after all, she was a 45-year-old woman with a new baby and eleven kids at home! I reminded her on the drive home that the doctor's diagnosis and prescription were almost word-for-word what I'd told her in several blessings over the past few months, but I reminded her that I'd added one more point: "Take out time to listen to God; He wants to talk to you."

That evening a tooth filling came out; that upset her. That meant another dreaded trip to the dentist. I spent Monday morning working on the van so she could make that trip. I was also trying to keep up with the several kids who were still at home. With Vicki suddenly in bed most of the time, the house had turned into a circus. I was frustrated not being able to get any sewing done. I'd left her in our bedroom listening to some religious music and when I returned just before noon, she told me she'd had another memory. At that point I sat down. As much as I hated the interruption in our lives, I wanted to hear it.

"I don't want to do this," she said as a preamble, "I really don't." There was a lengthy pause. "I remembered they put me in a barrel. I was in a room in these bunkers near El Paso. They put a partially skinned baby in there with me. The baby was crying its poor little head off. Wailing from the pain." Vicki was nine years old and scared to death.

Vicki would not make that dental visit for several months. After a week of Vicki steadily feeling worse, it was obvious that this episode was not something that would dissipate in a few days. We decided to label this new collapse as a nervous breakdown. With a new baby at her age and eleven kids at home, most people understood; trying to explain the truth was too complicated. Members of our local church, who had been very cooperative with the birth, agreed to take our kids again for a few days. Others helped with meals as we tried to create a new schedule that gave Vicki more mental space. The woman from church who had volunteered to come clean our house one day a week for a month agreed to come twice a week for another month. All of this was a godsend—it was just the help we needed at the time.

We moved Heather out of our bedroom. She was a handful in her own right, and she went to stay with the oldest girls (Jennifer was seventeen and Sarah was sixteen) who lived in the ell at the back of our old farmhouse. Taking care of Scotia was all Vicki could do, but the nursing and the infant care was grounding to her. As it had been before with Hannah, this new baby would be exactly what Vicki needed to make it through this final period of memory work.

The predominant theme in these memories would again be fear. But it would be enhanced by a new level of cruelty—brutal, calculated cruelty. Vicki speculated that it was that fear that was taking the strength out of her body so she couldn't walk. She would spend most of the next six weeks in bed. In the beginning I often had to help her walk the ten feet to the bathroom.

As we would shortly find out, there was a major difference in her reaction to me with these new memories. Previously, I had caught the brunt of her anger; I was the bad guy—a facsimile of her father. But thankfully not this time. Now, I could be her friend and a scribe without all the negativity that she usually attributed to me. I came up to our bedroom daily at lunch time—it was a standing appointment—to chat and to do memory work when she felt like it. She couldn't handle much so we did short sessions almost every day to begin with.

NINE YEARS OLD IN EL PASO

September, 1994

Vicki's body was forcing her to collect on the promise she'd made to herself several months earlier when the dizziness first resurfaced. It was time to remember again.

My wife was only sleeping a couple of hours a night; her best time for sleeping was generally the early daylight hours. (We later discerned that this was the time she felt safest, when her father would have gone off to work and couldn't "visit.") Whenever I got up, I tried to ease out of bed without waking her. If Scotia, who was usually between us, was awake, I took her downstairs with me. The older girls went to an early morning seminary at our church and then returned. They roused the school kids and took care of breakfast. Vicki was usually awake by the time the kids left for school, and they had to come up for an inspection to make sure they looked and smelled presentable. (For the younger ones, we called it the "sniff test.")

I typically brought something for Vicki's breakfast and she watched the four youngest kids until lunch time. At midday I fixed something for everyone at home to eat, and the little kids went down for a nap. We did our memory work next, if there was any, and then rested. I went back to the shop while the kids were still asleep. The older girls took over when they returned from school, often fixing dinner; either that or I made something simple like spaghetti with canned tomatoes from the garden.

I hadn't been able to find any journals from this time period. The last one that I have ended in November, 1993. The next one I have doesn't start until after the year 2000. I wondered how I would write about this time because I didn't remember any details—just that it was a profoundly disturbing time where Vicki had been swamped by the past and bedridden for six weeks. But after saying a prayer, I dove into the box where all the other journals had been stored, and I came across a forgotten manila folder labelled: "Maine Memory Work. '94 journal notes. Very good."

As I began reading, slowly that period of time started to come back. We had been in Maine for fifteen months and were settled, not only emotionally but financially. I spent long hours working in a mobile classroom that came with the cute house on which we had a lease/purchase agreement. Financially, we were doing better than we had ever done before, but with eleven kids at home money was still very tight. I was grateful to have the work; it was grounding. Vicki handled all the PR work for the business but mostly she was enjoying being a mother. Nobody loved babies like she did and our house was full of them again. She was at least as busy as I was. Because we were close to civilization, there were lots of activities for the kids. Thankfully, the older girls were driving so my wife wasn't forced to take everybody everywhere.

When Vicki reported that first piece of memory, I had to go back to the shop and grab something to write on. The only thing I could find was the back side of an old wholesale price list. On September 12th I caught up by writing down the events of the previous four days, although the scene of picking her up at the local store was permanently etched in both of our minds—it was so bizarre and so unlike Vicki and so out of nowhere. Then I found a partially used spiral notebook, and we got back into doing regular therapy sessions like we had done at my shop back in Virginia.

When I started writing this section, I asked Vicki what she remembered. I was trying to get a handle on how to portray the memory work. I remembered it as being much different from her previous memories. It seemed much darker and more sinister. Vicki agreed that that was true. She remembered the time in bed; but, like me, she did not recall the content of her memory work from that time. When I read to her from notes I'd just found and reminded her of the barrel and the half-skinned baby, she closed herself off and terminated the conversation.

"I don't want to remember that. I don't want to have to go back into that period." She was emphatic.

I picked up the conversation a day later; she hadn't changed her stance. She wasn't going to be of any help. She reminded herself out loud that she needed to get serious about reading the manuscript for this book again, but it dawned on me that she may not be able to. She'd read the first few chapters that recounted our early years before she'd started remembering, and then she randomly picked a few of the chapters I'd written that included her memories. She started reading and then quit. They were dragging her down. Just the mention of the half-skinned baby put a chill between us.

I continued talking anyway. "You know, the only other time I've ever heard of that is with the Nazis. I'd heard they'd made lamp shades out of human skin."

Vicki thought for a minute, then said, "My father was in the missile program working with Von Braun and the other Nazi scientists that our military had brought over. El Paso is not far from White Sands. My father had a lot of respect for Von Braun. He would have gone into missiles simply because of Von Braun."

She would later tell me that her recollection from that period included hearing snippets of the guttural German along with being inundated with fear. As I was writing this section Vicki read that there was an enclave of Germans in the White Sands—El Paso area; these were descendants of the scientists that had come over in Operation Paperclip.

September 12, 1994

Vicki met me at the bedroom door as I came in from the shop with a notebook. I was surprised that she was out of bed. The weather outside was the best Maine had to offer. The temperatures were mild; the sun was still high in the sky; the black flies were long gone; and the mosquitoes were scarce. The leaves were just starting to turn in anticipation of the stunning colors to come. But our bedroom was dark. It was as if the shades were completely drawn.

Vicki was living in the past, and I had just stepped over the threshold into it with her. We didn't realize it at the time—we were confused and afraid because of the sudden and unexplained breakdown four days earlier—but her memories picked up just where they had left off almost two and a half years earlier with the ruthless intimidation. She was nine years old and living in El Paso.

Her voice was clearly tainted with fear. "I think they might have used some sort of dental torture." In that moment, she wanted a friend, a companion. Vicki went back to the bed to pick up Scotia who was starting to fuss. She began rocking the baby and then withdrawing into herself.

I didn't need to go through the verbal preliminaries. Vicki immediately began recounting what she'd remembered and then was back in the past. She wore a gloomy expression and her voice was shaking; she was whimpering like a hurt little girl. I began scribbling as fast as I could. Luckily, her memory work included frequent and lengthy pauses.

"Remember, if you scream the baby dies." Vicki quoted someone else speaking to her; she was crying.

"They take some sort of nail-like thing and are hammering it into my teeth." My wife continued whining. "I keep telling myself not to scream. I keep remembering the baby they put in the barrel with me . . . . [10] It's so dark in there. I'm so scared. I don't want to be in here . . . be here."

I asked, "Where are you?"

"Still in that dark room."

She continued, "Now they put me in something where there's spiders." Her voice grew more animated. "They're crawling all over me. I'm trying not to scream. I feel like I want to scream . . . like I'm going to pass out. My head is pounding and pounding . . . . My stomach is really tight. My abdomen. My head hurts . . . ." Her teeth were quietly chattering. "There's something else in the room. It looks like a wired chair. Red fabric . . . shaped like a birthing stool but with a back to it . . . .

"They're sticking something up my vagina. I don't know what it is but it seems to have sharp points. Some are hot. My spirit leaves my body. No energy. I know what they're doing but don't feel anything." My wife began sobbing. "I don't even scream but they still kill the baby. They said I didn't

---

10   The string of periods represent an extended pause in Vicki's remembering.

do it good enough. They skin the baby. The baby is crying like Scotia. They make me touch it. Then it just dies."

There was a pause. Vicki's voice became more detached from the memory and calmer. "They dress me and tell my father that he can take me home. They put a pad on me because I'm still bleeding."

"Where do you go home?" I asked.

"My father takes me out. I see the container of spiders. It has clear sides so they can be seen inside . . . . I can remember going back into the first house we lived in. Going in the side door. The door near the driveway. Walking in. My mother peeking her timid little head out like a mouse. I was getting furious . . . feeling like my blood pressure was going to burst."

September 13, 1994

There were small red dots all over Vicki's body. We wondered if they were the psychosomatic remains of all those spider bites.

"I want to shake. I'm afraid of more torture. It will be too much and kill me . . . . They call me 'Shandra.' That's the new name the cult gave me."

Nine-year-old Vicki said she wanted to move to the new house. The only thing she wanted to take was her teddy bear her daddy bought her when he was nice. She was tired of the headaches, her blood pressure and that vaginal device. She wanted to vomit. She started shaking all over. She didn't want him to share her with all those other people. She was tired of the anxiety attacks, the sweaty hands and feet and the legs that were rubbery.

I said, "Tell me about your mother dealing with you."

Speaking of her nine-year-old self, Vicki said, "She's mad. That's part of why she has a headache. Plus she's afraid it will happen again. She's tired of her hands sweating and her feet sweating."

I asked again, "What kind of things was your mother doing?"

"Bringing food." My wife again changed focus. "She (meaning her nine-year-old self) doesn't want food. She's so mad. She wants to knock the tray out of her mother's hand but doesn't because her father told her mother to let him know if she did anything weird . . . . She tries to run away. She gets stopped around the living room. He kicks me in the belly with his army boots. Mother is standing in the door, watching. She lets out one yell, 'Quit, Tommy!' He stops.

"I think I see Stephen peeping his head around the corner. John is in his crib . . . . I missed a day of school . . . He takes me and throws me on the bed. He tells me my mother is the best friend I'll ever have and I'd better let her take care of me. And he goes storming out."

September 14, 1994

Without preamble, Vicki picked up where she'd left off previously. She was taken before a wizard dressed in white with a white conical hat. He had straight hair, bowl cut. He appeared to be in his twenties. "You told," he said, referring to the attempted escape. The punishment was watching while they stuck something underneath the toenails and fingernails of a two-year-old boy.

Stepping out of the past, Vicki told me that this last memory was triggered by John Isaac crying in the middle of the night.

I then asked what she wanted to find out.

Vicki responded, "I want to find out what's freaking my little kid out so bad. She's real desperate—it has to come up spontaneously."

I asked Little Vicki how old she was.

"Nine."

"What are some of the things she likes about being nine?" I asked.

"Nothing," she said flatly.

"Nothing at all?"

"Her dolls. Her swing set because it shows her underwear and that gives her a sense of power over boys. She says she's upset because her dad was kicking her in the stomach and Mother was watching. She realized there was no one to help her . . . ." Vicki's voice trailed off.

"She likes to be held and people to rub her heart. She wants to run away. She tried to run away but got caught. They told her the torture was special for her because she ran away . . . . There was a tribunal. The people looked like gnomes with exaggerated features. There was the guy with the white pointed hat. There was a special meeting because of her running away. And someone's gonna get hurt.

"She's sitting in a chair in the middle of the circle of gnomes. They bring in a little boy about two. They are putting sticks under his nails. He's wearing sloppy clothes and takes them off. He acts like he knows what to do

... like he doesn't belong to anybody ... like he's fairly drugged. They put a hot coal in his mouth and he just hangs his head ... like he's totally out of it. They're bringing a stool over—gnomes dressed like little devils. Someone takes something and cuts off his ring finger.

"I don't feel anything. They saw off another finger with a pearl-handled tool. They hold up his hand and it's hanging. They bring in an ax and chop off his toes on one foot. The boy acts like he doesn't feel anything. He faints.

"They're yelling in my face. 'Don't run! Don't try it again!'

"I felt like I had a metal shield around me and didn't feel anything."

September 15, 1994

"I'm being locked in a coffin. It's the same room as the spider scene. A different cult meeting. I go into a panic attack . . . . I go in and out of consciousness. Later I finally wake up. I panic. I feel something—mice, spiders . . . ? I feel a mouse squash against my heel. They open the coffin lid that shows my face. There's a spider web kind of thing between them and me. They're asking me if I'm ready.

"I know what they're asking me. They want to know if I'm ready to participate in the murder but I don't know what I tell them . . . . I think I must tell them 'No' because the door closes over my face . . . . I think it might be a man they murder."

Vicki and I quit and took a break.

When we started again, I suggested, "Let's try to get her out of the coffin."

"They ask me, 'Are you ready yet?' They throw a snake in there. I keep passing out.

"There are nails or ice picks sticking through the coffin lid. If I move, they scratch me. But they get tired and decide it's not going to work . . . . They take me out and set me in another room and make me feel like it's over. They bring me food and drink. This other room is a feast room. It has a medieval setting."

Virginia called that afternoon and asked Vicki several times what had caused the exhaustion, which is how my wife had billed the collapse to her mother. Virginia was persistent and seemed to be earnest, and Vicki almost told her about the memory work. In the end she thought better of it.

Later, I picked up the thread from the last session. "We left off with you in the festival room with food and drink after the coffin and you thought you were finished."

"They sent these women to come get me. They were dressed like fairy godmothers in the Cinderella story. They take me to another room. I have a sense of dread about what's going to happen.

"They have a rack-like thing. It's weird-shaped. Two long pieces of wood on legs two to three feet off the ground. Canvas straps between the poles. They tie my hands and feet to the poles. My head hangs back. It's terrifying . . . . I know they want me to say yes to the murder but I can't get it out. I can't get it out."

Vicki described herself in a state of terror. Naked. With her body suspended with the canvas straps. They cut her nipples and vaginal area with razor blades.

Next her torturers brought in a water container. "It's a rectangular contraption on wheels with a number of hoses. They begin attaching the hoses to my urinary tract, anus, mouth and nose. They turn the cold water on . . . . I start to feel totally overwhelmed. Of needing help. Of being abandoned. Of no one helping me."

My wife was crying. The fear she felt some thirty-plus years ago was obvious.

"My bottom half feels like exploding. My top . . . I can't breathe. Feeling like I'm drowning. They're doing something like sandpaper on my fingers and toes. I can sense it above the other pain.

"'Yes!' I finally tell them I'll help. Then they start unhooking all the hoses. They leave me there."

There was a long silence.

"They get me up after a while. There is some guy lying on an altar-like thing. I go over there and stab, stab, stab . . . . It was a frenzy. I don't care anymore."

My wife was absorbed in the past, crying.

"Then they take me and dress me in black . . . a black crown. They carry me into another room to celebrate that I'm one of theirs."

"So you felt like you capitulated?" I interjected.

"I don't feel like I'm one of theirs. I didn't care. As long as they quit hurting me . . . . I liked being the person who didn't give in to them. I didn't like them celebrating me being part of them. I just couldn't stand the water stuff . . . . I didn't mind killing the man. He reminded me of the cult. They were all alike."

She gradually was coming out of the memory. "I hated giving into them." She was angry. "I guess they know I wouldn't have given in if it was a baby." Vicki was left with a tangible sense of self-loathing. "They won because I was smaller than they were and they had the torture." She said she felt like cardboard.

September 17. 1994
Vicki told me today she thought that the man she stabbed was someone she knew from before—a cult member who had previously been mean to her. That made it much easier.

When she was listening to a favorite CD of religious songs, there was a bad scratch. It sounded like gun shots and Little Vicki and adult Vicki took advantage of that prop—in her imagination, she shot all the cult members, blowing her father to smithereens. Her mother she triple-locked in a jail.

She said her head was still tired but felt much better. Our bedroom was quiet and dark.

September 18, 1994
Vicki told me today that the numerous bits from the past that she had been getting had stopped after the last memory. She said she had a dream of being nine years old and living in El Paso. She called her mother and described what she had remembered of El Paso and her mother confirmed it. Her recollection of the scenery at age nine was accurate.

September 21, 1994
Our dogs barking at night awakened Vicki with a start. I had to move them further away from the house. Her brief lapses of sleep were troubled by nightmares. One of the predominant themes of these distressing dreams was

underground tunnels, which seemed to connect one upsetting scene to the next. There was no escaping and there was plenty to be afraid of.

She remembered walking through double doors and being strapped to a flat table. She was forced to have intercourse with one man after another, but it wasn't an orgy. Rather it was an athletic event in a large auditorium-like room surrounded by bleachers full of an enthusiastic crowd. All the men were body-building types and when they drew blood, it brought a paroxysm from the stands. After they were finished with Vicki and the clapping subsided, another poor little girl was brought in.

Meanwhile Vicki was cleaned up by women dressed in white; she was then dressed in white herself with a gold belt. She specifically remembered one of the women was in her fifties with blonde hair up in a bun. She was then escorted out to the bleachers amid the crowd cheering at the action on center stage. She slumped at one end, mostly oblivious to what was going on around her. The men in the stands worked themselves into a frenzy as one girl after another was brought out. At the end the men all lined up and a winner was chosen and after that all the girls were lined up to pick a winner. Vicki remembered mumbling to herself "Please don't pick me" over and over to herself. But she was chosen, and her reward was another rape by the male winner to the raucous enthusiasm of the crowd. And new blood on her white dress.

She was again cleaned up by the women in white and dressed in a pleated skirt that would have been a winter outfit for El Paso. Vicki guessed that it may have been at Christmas.

"My father takes me home. He's real proud of me because I won the prize."

In another incident triggered by her dreams, she remembered going out to a resort in the middle of the desert where there were orphan babies. There were also vicious dogs and a lake with large rocks. Vicki called her mother to confirm the existence of the resort, because it seemed improbable with the lake and rocks. Her mother did remember the place although not the name. She said she would call an old friend from that area. Vicki remembered that her family stayed at the resort for a few days and was afforded special privileges. Looking back, Vicki suspected this was because she remembered seeing the proprietor at cult meetings. She wondered if this was a source of babies for the sacrifices and/or whether they were involved with black-market adoptions.

When Virginia called back, she off-handedly told Vicki of a visit she'd made to her old friend from that area three or four years earlier. They had gone together to a Baptist camp revival. For no obvious reason, while she was there, Virginia's blood pressure had skyrocketed and she had to be rushed to the ER. Virginia was sent back to Raleigh immediately and put on blood-pressure medicine. Vicki and I couldn't help but wonder if the arid Texas scene had not triggered something in Virginia's very occluded past.

September 24, 1994

Vicki was back in the underground bunkers. She had a flash of three teenage boys with their bare butts sticking up in the air. It was part of a circus and it was for the cult members. She and the teenage boys were part of the show. The main event was a girl being raped by a show horse. The lights were dimmed and visibility was poor.

Vicki had already remembered a similar scene. With her second stint in El Paso at age thirteen, she would be the girl under the horse and the location would be at the fun house outside of town.

September 25, 1994

We made it to church for an hour and returned.

"I think the circus is in the spring. I think my mother is in the audience. I'm not particularly overjoyed. She's grim-faced. The girl under the horse is screaming. I'm tense. I'm either suffocated by the three boys or terrified by the girl screaming .... My mother being out there contributed to the feeling of being unprotected .... I remember riding home with my mother. Her being real grim-faced—like her attendance had been mandatory. The other kids were at home with a babysitter. She was grim-faced and frozen. I was more exuberant than usual because I wasn't the one being hurt.... I'm glad my mother had to suffer some."

The next scene was in a large barn. It was two stories high with a cathedral ceiling. There were stalls along the bottom and hay in the loft.

Vicki guessed that it may be part of the resort, for patrons who wanted to ride horses. It was at Christmas and there was a baby lying in a manger.

She was shoved into the large open area. She was told, "Here's your baby Jesus. See how much power he has."

Vicki immediately ran to the other end of the room to see if she could get that door open, hoping to escape. But no, it was locked. Suddenly an army of rats jumped from the stalls and attacked the baby. (The adult Vicki was whining as she repeated the scene to me.) She was too terrified of the rats to move and help the baby. She felt responsible because the baby was screaming. But her main focus was on trying to escape.

Later they brought the body parts to her. But she never got close enough to see if it was real. Her adult self wondered if the screaming could have been sound effects.

On another occasion, there was a party outside the barn in a wooded area. "I must have made some comment about Jesus being stronger than they are because they began taunting me. They were all drunk and sex was on the menu. But they were too drunk. There were enough people so I could stay out of their way, escape in the woods and evade them."

She hypothesized it was around Halloween because she remembered pumpkins as part of the decorations.

"I overheard one comment, 'It's time to do the sleep deprivation with her.'"

September 26, 1994

Vicki was complaining of extreme tiredness. She had more flashes of the Halloween party. From a distance she watched; it was gory with lots of sex.

I asked her what she thought of her mother in the circus scene.

"After coming home, I was cared for by my mother. I was feeling really tired but not feeling safe. I was afraid my father may come and jerk me up again . . . . My mother was saying to my father, 'You're going to kill her if you keep doing these things . . . if you don't quit.' He acts like he feels chastened and leaves the room."

THE DREGS AT THE BOTTOM

October, 1994

T hose were dark days. There was an opaque pall that seemed to settle over our bedroom where Vicki spent most of her time. It was almost palpable. Now, I can't help but think of that room and that time as a portal into her unfathomable past. Almost every time I walked in to spend a few minutes with her, she'd update me on what more she'd remembered from her miserable childhood. She felt it her duty and once I committed it to paper, she gave herself permission to forget it.

While I was busy trying to manage the sewing work and help with the younger kids until the school kids came home, she spent much of her time in the netherworld of her childhood. It was black and sinister with more than a touch of incredulity. The content of these latest memories, as in the past, first stretched my confidence in the process we were going through, and then eclipsed what little was left of my notion of the basic goodness in human nature.

But the consistency of the process—that in the past had been validated in ways that I could believe—eventually won out. I kept notes of what she was saying in that half-used spiral notebook and on the back of those old price sheets leftover from the trade show that, ironically, Tom had helped us with those many years ago. Then I put them in a folder and apparently forgot about them. This was not a span of time that in any way I remember fondly, but I too felt a responsibility to keep track of it. And apparently like Vicki, once I scribbled notes of what she was relating, I wanted to forget about it.

As I read through my notes almost twenty-five years later, I realize I was overwhelmed and afraid. What in the world would I do if Vicki never got on her feet again and I had primary responsibility for these eleven kids? During her previous season of remembering there had been only a day or two at any given time when she wasn't up and about doing her chores—although her mood may not have been the best. Now she spent a lot of time in bed, time in bed with Scotia.

Yes, she was a few years older, but neither one of us thought that was the problem. And she'd had a baby, but that wasn't it either. She loved babies; they gave her energy and enthusiasm. So why wasn't she getting out of bed and reengaging with life? I suspect it was first related to the dizziness; she didn't trust her ability to walk and not fall. Later it was the sheer exhaustion from her new memories.

She'd been to her doctor—several times. He confirmed what the ER said, validating the obvious: she was worn out and needed rest; she didn't have any diagnosable disease. But that wasn't particularly reassuring to me because she'd never been this incapacitated before. He prescribed valium to help her sleep, but at best it was modestly effective.

I began to think that maybe this is what people meant when they referred to a nervous breakdown—that we had been right when we labeled it as such. But would she ever recover? I'd heard stories that some people never completely recovered from a nervous breakdown. Sometimes they only half-recovered; and the half that didn't . . . ?

Something was fundamentally different about this time of remembering; that much was plain to me. It was darker and deeper and I wasn't sure she'd ever come out. I couldn't handle that thought. I needed her to come back and be her old self. I really was scared.

Generally, Vicki catnapped through the day and night. She spent much of her time awash in feelings from another day and place. I was grateful I had enough work to keep my mind occupied and I spent a lot of time sewing in my shop, sometimes late into the evening. She did deal with the business calls, and after the first week or so she delegated to me and the older girls what needed to be done around the house.

Seeing that part of her personality return was comforting. That was the old Vicki. And with a little help from church friends we kept everything running. Not running smoothly, just running. Eventually, and very gradually, she began taking up the slack she'd let out—primarily when she recognized how poorly the rest of us did her job. Little by little, her old self returned.

Looking back, I suspect her body was just letting go. It was letting go of this buried trauma and this process of freeing herself from her past was exhausting. Her body was healing; it was going through a very natural activity, and like it was recovering from surgery or any other exorcism of a toxin or contaminant, it required a lot of rest.

As I sort through this section of my notes, I am immensely bothered by Virginia's appearance. From the onset of her ritual abuse memories Vicki often referred to her mother as a "timid mouse" sticking her head out of her bedroom door when little Vicki returned home from her "outings" with her father. We didn't know for sure but had suspected that to some extent Virginia knew what was going on; that's how the memories two and a half years ago had ended. That was no longer in question. She very well may not have been able to sleep while her daughter was gone—for good reason—and was waiting up for her return.

But why? Why was Virginia allowing this to happen? My wife's characterization of her mother does not square with the Virginia that I got to know some fifteen-plus years afterward. But it does remind me of the insecure, buck-toothed young woman that I saw in some of the photographs from Tom and Virginia's early years. It reminds me of the woman that went to Germany with a certain sense of desperation to find a husband and get a family started. Perhaps she was an expert in compartmentalization—of learning not to see what was right in front of her. Perhaps it was a skill that she picked up as a child when she went to her grandparents' farm, where everyone closed their eyes to her grandfather taking a seven-year-old sister-in-law as a concubine. And perhaps it wasn't just the sister-in-law who had those nighttime visits; sexual predators have a voracious appetite. Virginia and her siblings were forced to spend every summer on their grandparents' farm . . . . But with these last memories it is obvious that Virginia *did* know what was going on, which of course does lead to that more perplexing question of why she allowed it . . . for which I don't have any satisfactory explanation.

There was also another equally disturbing issue: the location of much of this abuse. We had heard for some time that much of the reported ritual abuse was associated with the military, but these memories smack of a much stronger relationship. If it was not sanctioned, it was at least tolerated by the military. I suspect that some of this abuse may have had to do with Tom's career, and some of it may have been institutional—that Vicki was a guinea pig of sorts. Was that something that Virginia was able to buy into? I have read incredible—I mean virtually unbelievable—stories of government-sanctioned experiments with drugs and what would now be considered torture—but similar to what Vicki experienced as a child—with the aim of creating a Manchurian Candidate: a human being that would respond to commands as if they were an automaton. This was the theme of Dale Griffis' book *Secret Weapons*.

Let me add a quote here that I found in my journal from 1993 that confirmed information we had previously learned: "Information has come to me from a number of sources that cult members are instructed in how to create MPD (multiple personality disorder) intentionally in their children. This maintains the secrecy, because the children's host alters will know nothing about the rituals. Electric shocks, drugs and hypnotherapy are skillfully employed by cult members to program their children to create alters starting when the children are about age two. Using brutal brainwashing-type punishments the cult members train particular alters to behave only in specific ways and to appear only at specific times."[11]

These latest memories do not appear to be exclusively directed toward Vicki, because other children were involved. But it does boggle the mind that this was occurring with, at minimum, the government looking the other way. Was this part of some kind of sanctioned government program? Had the WWII Germans been experimenting with the psychology of creating MPD for military purposes? It is known that they were experimenting with mind control. The lack of moral compunction in these memories seems to smack of Nazi Germany, where prisoners were used as guinea pigs for experiments that were ultimately terminal for the unfortunate victims.

---

11   James Friesen, Uncovering the Mystery of MPD. New York, Harper Collins, 1989. p.109

My wife has no doubt that many of her abusers in this part of her memory work were German. She remembers that thick, unmistakable accent. Our government brought over these scientists because they valued the work they had done. Had the hiatus from human decency that eventually came to characterize the Third Reich come over with these scientists and rerooted in clandestine corners of our military?

The ultimate cloak of secrecy, of course, is the whole unbelievability of the matter. Nobody in their right mind would believe this was happening in our country, especially under the auspices of our government. Consider this: In our day many are outraged that the military is using much lesser forms of torture on our enemies.

Picking up with the memories, in late September Vicki reported increased dizziness combined with anxiety and tiredness. It went on for several days. She began talking about being in a glass cubicle that she referred to as a time machine—as seen in movies of that day—where sleep deprivation took place. When the original stimulation did not keep Vicki awake, the experimenter threw a rat in. When that didn't work, he took to slapping her in the face. My wife said that did keep her awake . . . .

A day later as a thunderstorm passed through one Maine evening, the lightning flashes reminded her of a strobe light designed to keep her awake in that cubicle . . . .

There was also a game of sorts where she was running through the tunnels and bunkers being chased by a group of men and boys. If she was caught, she would be part of a big gang rape, and she was caught. Of course, she was so tired from the sleep deprivation she could barely run and tripped over her own feet. She remembered the pain in her neck and shoulders where she was pinched by those who held her. There was blood from the anal rape and lots of shame, but mostly she remembers the feeling of wanting to curl up and go to sleep. But there wasn't a safe place . . . .

The memories of sleep deprivation continued with flashes of being at her El Paso home and her father dunking her head in a bucket of water. Later, she was back in the time machine again with five or six large wharf rats at her feet. If she fell asleep, the rats had some way of nibbling or scratching at her toes. Back at her house again, she was dunked in a bathtub or sink or had water poured over her head when she fell asleep. Her father's voice rang through her head. "Why did you fall asleep? I told you to stay awake."

It is interesting to remember that my wife was only sleeping a couple of hours a night during this period of time.

Vicki had a dream that is noted on October 2nd. It was triggered by the fear of a breast infection which she sometimes had when she was nursing. She had to be very careful how she slept. In the dream she went to the doctor because something was wrong with her breasts. Vicki then had flashes of being in El Paso just before she left when she would have turned eleven. Her parents brought her to a cult meeting in the woods for advice because something was wrong with her breasts. Little Vicki was nude and just beginning to develop breasts. The doctor said, "We can fix it." He took two egg yolks and crushed them. Tom and Virginia were to rub one on each breast. As Vicki remembered the scene, she suspected it was a rite of passage designed to engender shame. There were other girls in line behind her with their parents.

"Focus in on your mother," I asked.

"She has that grim look of determination," Vicki reported.

"What's she wearing?" I asked.

"Short-sleeved blue dress. Something appropriate for spring." Vicki was crying, hoping the memory was nearing the end.

"Try to get back in line and tell me what else happened?"

"They cut our nipples so a little blood flowed and each parent had to lick some of the blood. At the end each father had to do anal rape with his daughter. Then there was an orgy-like thing."

"What happened with your mother?"

"She's standing like a statue, with a frozen look." There was a pause. Knowing what was going to happen Vicki said she crawled out of the way into the bushes.

"What happened with your mother?" I asked.

"They put a white veil over her face and pulled her into the orgy. She got raped by bunches of people. I crawled into the car and got dressed, then laid on the floorboard waiting to go home and I fell asleep. I have a vague memory of getting into bed at home; there had been a babysitter and my father was yelling at my mother."

A few minutes later, Vicki added, "I think this was necessary to get Mother's cooperation for the future prostitution work I would be doing in Louisiana. They put 'the fear' into her. How else could they get her to cooperate, allowing me to be gone many weekends there?"

On October 3rd I wrote that Vicki thought her memories were about over and that it wasn't necessary to remember everything. Her blood pressure was down to 116/86.

Her memories did continue but were less traumatic and spaced further apart. She remembered going trick-or-treating at a cult member's house and sticking her hand in a bowl of snakes. She "saw" rats in our living room one evening and that triggered scenes at age nine where she was being groomed for the circus. There was another scene of a skinny little girl, scrunched face down, with her butt up. "I had the feeling of the kid being used and used and used."

As Halloween approached and was the talk of our children, a scene from her teenage years came back. She guessed that it may have occurred at the State Theatre in downtown Raleigh when she was fourteen or fifteen. There were larger-than- life figures there dressed in black demon outfits. There was a black and white film of a young boy being anally raped. There were intermittent flashes of the boy's pained face. He was crying. And there was blood. Vicki was pulled into the subsequent orgy as she tried to hide under the seats.

Vicki explained: "It started when I came back from trick-or-treating with my brothers. My mother told me I was too old to do that. Then my father said he was taking me. I was wearing a plaid, pleated skirt and sweater. We got in the station wagon. He had a costume inside for me. It was a sexy cat. I changed upstairs at the State Theatre. The film wasn't very long. The demons grabbed me and I passed out. It was mostly from watching the film. My father found me underneath the chairs. He pulled me out by the arms and grabbed my neck. 'Remember, we don't talk about this.' And he kissed me on the lips, smack on the lips.

"When we got home, Mother was waiting. She pulled me aside. She was angry. She was demanding to know where I had been. Her voice was hushed so Daddy wouldn't hear. He came in and she left. She had never grabbed me before and demanded to know where I'd been. She acted like she had some power, not like the timid mouse of before."

My wife speculated that this new backbone in her mother may indeed have been from the proximity of her parents. Vicki's family had moved back to Raleigh when she was fourteen.

There was a brief interlude before the worst of Vicki's memories. At age nine she was at the reservoir outside of El Paso at a Halloween-style party on the island. With all the adults getting drunk, she realized, "I can do something; I can run away and hide." She sneaked off into the woods and hid underneath two large tree roots until she heard her father call that it was time to go.

In response to our dogs barking a few nights later, she remembered being at that same resort. The adults commented that little Vicki did not to seem scared enough. They threw her into a fenced area with barking dogs. After initially being terrified, she realized she could climb up and out over the woven wire fence, but they threw her back in. She then waited until they got bored and left. After climbing out she secreted herself on the floor of the back seat of her car.

Later in October as I checked in to see how she was doing, she said she had a flash of a sheep tied to a post and suspected that something bad was going to happen. She was at a target-shooting range and tied to one post with a sheep tied to another. Men with guns were at the other end of the range.

"I was nine or ten, with the same short haircut that I remember in several other memories of that age. It was near the resort area. A group of guys are drunk and don't seem to have any clothes on. They're laughing at the other guys coming near me. I think I'm acting real calm. Suddenly, they all aim at the sheep and shoot. It falls down dead. I start screaming bloody murder. They're all laughing, thinking it's great fun.

"They untie me and someone else goes up with some poor animal. This time a man is being tied up to one post with a cow or a bull at the other. But they shoot the man instead of the animal . . . . It's the guy who tunes tractors."

I asked, "How close are you?"

"Back with the crowd. Not real close. I'm kind of astounded that they shoot the man. Others are astounded too. Then they have a regular sex orgy, but I'm afraid to sneak off because of what might happen."

The darkest of Vicki's memories surfaced at this point. On October 20th we began working on a flash she'd had the previous night when the moon was full. She was nine or ten years old in the desert outside of El Paso, marveling how bright it was at night with the full moon and the white sand. She was situated in an alcove adjacent to the larger open area of a cave. She remembered it as being part of some Indian ruin. There were battered army cots and other surplus items around. She was doing prostitution for the cult.

She got several customers that night. One wanted anal intercourse. She told him she wasn't supposed to do that. The guy slapped her and told her to get on her stomach.

Six days later Vicki's memories returned to the same place. The image of a man twirling his penis in a menacing way was stuck in her mind. Since the last memory Vicki had been trying to convince herself that the previous prostitution memory was the only one, but the fear and trepidation she was feeling indicated to her that it wasn't.

"It was a male ego thing. This guy got off on a nine year old crying from fear at his organ."

I asked Vicki to describe the area.

"There was a night stand or small table near my bed. The head of the man they shot at the target range was on the table. It was a warning. It was certainly having an effect on me.

"I'm in a belligerent mood but keep looking at that head. There are other men waiting in line. They're getting angrier and angrier. I'm feeling abandoned; there's no one there to rescue me. This guy is twirling his penis and I'm thinking of ways to eliminate it from his body."

Vicki gagged at the memory of oral sex. She was mad at her body for responding. Then she was forced into vaginal and finally anal sex. She screamed because he was so violent and couldn't come. The big burly manager came over.

"You can't kill her. It's time to leave," the manager said.

The john offered the manager more money.

"There's another girl you can have." He insinuated this new one was expendable.

From another area of the cave Vicki heard screaming. The screaming continued until there was no more screaming. And the silence that followed was worse.

"I remember later seeing the girl's bottom covered in blood and having this profound sense that it could have been me . . . .

"The manager yelled that it was time to leave. 'Everybody get out!'"

The darkest and most lonely memories from her childhood would come from these caves (or cave-like structures) that we guessed were in New Mexico. This was where we'd been heading through all those years of therapy and memories. As a child—at a very young age—she had been groomed by years and years of torture.

As I had guessed, the final tactic in their campaign to get Vicki's cooperation had been for little Vicki to recognize that her mother was not going to rescue her—that she was on her own, that all hope was gone and that she might as well give in. The years of torture had been mixed with the rituals of Satanism as well as the magic of storybook drama with the goal of overwhelming the child. The aim, since she had refused to become a believer or fracture into a multiple, was to increase her capacity to handle pain, to force her to be quiet and obedient and to be a useful pawn. All this was designed to remind her that, at all costs, she couldn't tell. For three decades it had worked. These memories were among the last to be accessed; they were the dregs at the bottom of the barrel.

Looking back, my wife estimated that during her first stay in El Paso she was spending a night, one or two weekends a month, being sold to strangers. Vicki was a piece of meat with a plastic smile. She was nine and ten years old and being forced into sex slavery. Her father and his ilk were making money off the wanton abuse of her body (and the bodies of the other children there) because there were people willing to pay.

Her clientele consisted of soldiers from the nearby bases and wealthy whites who knew where the fresh young meat was. Some of the latter traveled great distances, much like the house near Camden, Maine, where children had reported abuse to Liam. She remembered one man after another, that there were lines; there were groups; there were mixed groups of men and women. It was exhausting work. And she was not alone; there were other children in adjacent rooms.

In time the fear went away but the degradation never did. The deep pain of being a "thing" for the abuse of strangers and the betrayal of both of her parents—parents who were supposed to love and care for her—was too much. To survive, what could she do but bury the memories and bury them deep? She certainly couldn't tell; the cult members were omniscient and she had already learned that her life was on the line. Not everybody survived.

The memories had to be put below the level of consciousness—beyond her ability to recall—traumatic amnesia. She would not have been able to survive or manage the deep, debasing shame that was implicit with this lifestyle. It would have ripped body and soul apart, perhaps driving her into lunacy.

Although they had been buried, these memories weren't dead. But with so much of her past separated from her present, her life was devoid of the wholeness that it craved. She had been living, only partially alive, waiting for the proper time and support to allow the past to come to the surface and see the light of day. She needed to embrace the past to create the wholeness her body intuitively craved.

I remember being put in a car at our home in El Paso on weekend nights and driven in a semi-drugged state a long distance. I was dressed in a princess costume to create the apparently beguiling image of half innocence and half seduction. I would cower in the back seat—where I was lying because I was too-drugged to sit up—waiting for the inevitable. It was dark, but I could feel the rolling hills as we neared our destination. It made me nauseous and, combined with the fear and the drugs, I wanted to vomit.

At our arrival I resisted leaving the car, but was pulled out and told a key word that immediately reminded me of the pain from the tortures. After that I remembered very little: being dragged upstairs too steep for my skinny, nine-year-old legs; being taken to a room at the right; thrown on a cold, hard mattress on the floor; seeing rocks and feeling like I was in a cave; leaving my body and singing to myself all the hit songs of that time—"Freight Train,"

"Sixteen Tons," "The Yellow Rose of Texas"—being suffocated and physically hurt by men thinking it was okay to use my female parts as they desired. They thought that I liked it because I was quiet, but I too afraid of what would happen to me if I cried or yelled or screamed.

The longer I was forced to do this prostitution in this "House of Horrors," the more I felt like I wouldn't survive. The drugs and the physical abuse were taking such a toll on me. The shame was overwhelming. It was a turning point for me as a child. I didn't want to be the person I was forced into being, but it became a matter of survival. I contemplated just giving up and dying, but I didn't want to. I think I really wanted to help Christ fight against this Darkness. So I came up with a plan; I would learn the fine art of seduction. I couldn't think of anything else and it helped me to survive.

AN EPILOGUE OF MEMORIES

October, 1994

On October 28th, with Halloween just days away, Vicki's trepidation increased. What could be next? Her memories had shown this to be a brutal holiday during her childhood. What more was there? But instead she had a sense of her Heavenly Father and his angels singing to her, "THE END. Go have fun, Dear!"

From that point on there was a change in the theme of her memories. But of course, we didn't know that at the time. From the beginning I had scribbled as she dictated the images that were effervescing through her mind as her body let go. I never had time to anticipate where the storyline was going, that she was ultimately going to make sense of the things she was saying. Now, looking back, I marvel at the consistency of the plot development, how her memories always moved from bad to worse—even when I could not imagine what more worse there might be. It was like someone was orchestrating the process; again, somebody with a writer's flair. What followed from this point on with Vicki's memories might be best entitled an epilogue that filled in some of the missing pieces and rounded the story out.

One of the themes in this finale had to do with the amount of cult deception. On several occasions she had noted that her adult self, reviewing the scenes from her childhood, suspected that some of those bizarre episodes had been staged. She remembered a man walking around with sticks where his lower legs and feet should have been. She was at a Halloween party and had been told that his legs had been cut off by the cult. Later she saw the same man walking around normally and recognized that this was a staged joke designed to terrify kids.

In early November, Vicki felt well enough to resume her training sessions for Rape Crisis, an organization for which she had volunteered. This was one venue where she could talk to people who wanted to hear what she had to say. The trainees handled the telephone and gave advice and direction to the callers, who were usually desperate. These volunteer trainees needed to know the difference because different advice was appropriate for victims of ritual abuse than for those who had been raped by a stranger or even a boyfriend. Survivors of ritual abuse needed protection and anonymity in a much more profound way than regular rape victims. Vicki gave these volunteer trainees guidance in separating the kinds of callers. She also spoke at homeless shelters and did staff trainings there with the same intent.

After one particular training session with Rape Crisis, she couldn't sleep—even with the valium. She woke me up and asked for a blessing. Slowly another memory from the first El Paso period seeped into her consciousness.

She was at the same resort in El Paso where she'd previously seen babies. She was in the room with the cult leader and a baby or a doll; she wasn't sure which. "I didn't want to look too close," Vicki said. She suspected where this was going to go. The lesson she was to learn was what would happen if she were to ever tell.

The leader went over to the screaming baby and cut its stomach out with a knife. The room was filled with screaming—hers as well as the baby's. Vicki was terrified and passed out. She woke up next to the baby with its stomach cut open and its guts exposed. Vicki's face was dunked in a basin of blood and pushed in front of a mirror. "This is what will happen to you if you tell."

Vicki was forced to follow the men outside, where they buried the baby.

All through the recovery of this memory Vicki had an override from her forty-five-year-old self, wondering if the whole scenario had been staged. That next night she slept for twelve hours straight and woke up with suicidal feelings. She hadn't had them in three or four years and she recognized they didn't fit her current life.

More of the memory soon followed. One of the men who was burying the baby took his holster off while he was digging the grave. Young Vicki grabbed his gun and put it up to her head, intending to commit suicide. She was very confused, but one thing was clear: If Satan was more powerful than God then she didn't want to live. The four cult men immediately began placating her, telling her it was a doll and not a real baby. They even dug up the baby from the grave to prove it to her, but that was unconvincing to Vicki.

That evening at our session with Liam, he surmised that there must be more in the background to explain my wife's attachment to the baby. Perhaps there had been a previous relationship with the child? I agreed, reflecting back to her other "baby killing" memories where her feelings had been strong but not suicidal. Liam also suggested that this may have been a trial that had been set up to prove to Vicki that her God would not save the baby. Vicki was upset by Liam's idea, but on the hour drive home she begged me to help her work on remembering more.

After a prayer, Vicki closed her eyes and began remembering. She was taken to the resort. Her father asked someone, "Hey, Boss, what do you want Vicki to do?"

"Have her babysit," he said. To Vicki he added, "Take good care of the babies."

Vicki was skeptical at first because nothing good ever came from the cult, but soon she got into it. Even at nine years old, she loved babies. She was given one child in particular to babysit. Crystal was a very pretty half-Mexican/half Caucasian little girl in a white chiffon dress. "Now, take good care of her" Vicki was urged several times.

Later, one of the cult members popped his head in the door and said, "Maybe you can save the baby's life?" This was repeated several times. Vicki scoured the room looking for an avenue of escape. The door wouldn't work. The windows were boarded over. The crawl space in the ceiling was too high for her to reach. She was filled with a sense of hopelessness. She paced the room back and forth trying to figure out a way to save the baby. She well knew what they did to babies, especially babies in white dresses.

Two or three times more the men came in to the room: "Maybe your God can help you save her?"

So Vicki began praying to save Crystal's life because she'd gotten very attached to her. But the baby was killed (apparently after being switched with a doll) and buried, as she recalled the previous day. She remembered that, with the gun pointed toward her head, her father, the boss and two diggers suddenly did all they could to conciliate young Vicki.

"The baby's not real. It's just a doll," they had said. "She wasn't hurt."

They even dug up the baby to prove to Vicki that it wasn't real, that it was just a doll. But from the mess they dug up, she couldn't tell. Meanwhile, a fifth man sneaked up behind her and grabbed the gun.

Then she remembered another occasion when she was again at that same house. She overheard two of the maids talking about the fact that Crystal had been adopted, and they had gotten a lot of money for her. Adult Vicki was suddenly overwhelmed with the gratitude that Little Vicki felt at having her most heart-felt prayer answered. God *was* stronger than Satan!

With tears and with her voice flushed with gratitude and reverence, she said aloud, partly to me and partly to herself, "Little Crystal's out there today."

Eight days later as we were getting ready for bed, Vicki yawned deeply. She had a flash of a snowy hill that she guessed out loud was probably in Pennsylvania.

"I don't want to work on it now," she said to me. "I'll work on it with you tomorrow." Outside our window was the first decent snow of the season.

The next day, as a prelude to the memory, she told me of a flash she'd once had back at our house in Virginia. We were riding sleds with the kids and she blew up for no apparent reason. Now she recognized that the fear and anger from this new memory was behind that explosion.

She remembered standing at the bottom of the hill where her father had parked the car. At the top she saw a fire. She was reluctant to go toward it but her father led her, and when she arrived she saw a baby skewered over the flames.

"As an adult I recognize it was a doll. I didn't then. All the men were laughing at my horror. 'That's Baby Jesus; don't you recognize Him?' They are all drinking. 'Here's some real eyes from Baby Jesus.' They forced me to eat them amid their raucous laughter. As that died down someone asked, 'Who's going to be the Virgin?'

Their eyes all fall on me. I'm mad that these foolish drunk men are doing this to me, but I'm being held down and can't do anything. It's cold. I'm lying on the snow. They're so drunk they can't do anything. It's making me really mad.

"After a while, they are all passed out around me." Vicki got her clothes and sledded down the hill to her car, waiting for her father.

In late November Vicki watched a TV movie on the Dion quintuplets. She was triggered by the two-pound, seven-month-old baby and had to close her eyes. She began to remember being nine or ten years old and watching a woman forced into labor.

"I can hardly say it, but I was forced to eat part of the baby after they did the dastardly deed." There was a lengthy pause. She said a prayer and got back into the memory. "For some reason this one has me real upset. I'm so sick of murder . . . ."

Her hand was over her face, which was wet with tears. There was another lengthy silence. By this time Vicki was in the habit of re-experiencing the memories and then reporting back to me rather than giving me a blow-by-blow account.

"It was a cult meeting in the woods. I was nine or ten. There was a woman in labor and I had the feeling they had started it with a coat hanger. A premature baby was born. They made me lick off the membranes and stuff. Made me lick its little genitals. It was a baby girl. They started dismembering it. I was afraid. Cutting off its little fingers, gouging out its eyes . . . ."

By this time Vicki was crying out loud as she told me what happened. "They wanted me to eat one of her fingers and eyes. They forced me by holding my neck. The baby was doing its mewing. I began vomiting and falling on the ground. They anally raped me. Then I slinked off and got in the car."

Related to this memory, my wife began musing aloud why she had gone to the OB doctor in the Brown Building in downtown Raleigh when she first suspected she was pregnant with Tripp. The reason was that he was the only OB doctor that she knew. But how did she know him? Then she remembered being about fifteen years old and her parents discussing the matter of her being pregnant. Her mother knew.

They were fighting. "Look what you've done!" Virginia screamed.

Her father said, "Something has to be done." He knew where to get an abortion even though they were illegal.

"This is the final straw with Vicki," her mother responded. "That's the end. If anything happens again . . . ."

Tom slapped Virginia. He then took Vicki to the same OB doctor in the Brown Building. When Tom returned with Vicki, Virginia told him in a deadly calm voice that she had called her father and told on the principal at Vicki's middle school.[12] "If anything happens again, I'll expose you."

The flow of memories continued to decrease. The last dated memory I have was on December 20th. With Christmas coming, Vicki was up and about and life was returning to normal. I was thankful and more than willing to focus my attention on something other than memory work. We wanted to do nothing more than put the past behind us; Vicki wanted to get back to being a full-time mother, the PR person for our business and taking care of the numerous other responsibilities she had. Those last several months were among the darkest times in our lives and we wanted to forget them. Like few other people I knew, my wife enjoyed living. And that's what she wanted to get back into doing. I packed all the loose sheets I'd been using for a journal into a folder; I combined them with the sheets I tore out of the spiral notebook and saved them. Then I forgot all about them. I forgot so thoroughly that I was surprised and then shocked when I reread those notes. It was only after comparing the information within these last memories with what we had learned over the intervening twenty-five years that these memories made sense.

---

12 There are other memories that I haven't included that took place at her middle school.

THERAPY AND THERAPISTS

1994-1999

From seminars that she had attended Vicki learned that early childhood trauma can cause permanent alterations in the brain. In particular, the amygdala—the most "primitive" part of our brain that manages our flight or fight response (i.e., our reaction when our basic safety is threatened)—is affected.[13] We knew that some things were just not going to change. Vicki wasn't going to grow out of her PTSD; there wasn't going to be a moment of therapeutic enlightenment when everything coalesced as if the abuse had never happened. Adjusting to this fact was a slow process for both of us. Learning to accept the hand that each of us had been dealt was one of the most difficult aspects of healing. And over the course of time we would use many, many other types of therapy besides talk therapy.

We continued our monthly sessions with Liam for a couple more years. They stopped about the time that he—just like Dick and Peter—was able to start his own business. I remember the first time he mentioned the possibility and suddenly I knew: this was going to be his blessing for helping us. This blessing that each of these men received for their help to us was uncanny, and in a way very comforting. Each of them had been very competent and extremely generous with their time; and in the end, each one was blessed with something they truly wanted.

---

13   Current research has added the hippocampus, prefrontal cortex and other parts of the brain to the list of areas affected by early childhood trauma.

An unusual form of therapy that Vicki and I shared had to do with babies. Babies were immensely grounding and life-affirming for both of us. As noted before, Hannah may well have saved Vicki's life as she was going through some of the worst of her cult memories. She had been brainwashed to kill herself if she ever told—and she was telling. The timing of Scotia's birth was equally providential, grounding her during the very worst time of her memory work.

Around our house babies were a family affair. We had had so many that having one more never seemed like a big deal. Vicki had seen so many hurt and killed that taking one who would have otherwise been cursed with a life in foster care was rewarding in a very primal sense. We could reverse the inevitable course of evil for that child and turn it into good. We both enjoyed that sense of rescue and the opportunity that we knew we were providing these newborns. Babies were never a bother and they always came with a sense of excitement; everyone in the house liked having babies around and chipped in with their care. During the six-and-a-half years we lived in Maine, we finalized five minority adoptions.

THE LIGHT
OF DAY

STEPHEN'S DEATH

March, 1995

I n late March of 1995, as our second long Maine winter was drawing to a close, Vicki got a frantic call from her mother. Stephen had quit taking his insulin and he wasn't eating; he was basically committing suicide. He had made a conscious decision to end his life. Virginia told my wife that she and Tom had been banished for several weeks from his apartment where he lived with his wife Lily.

Vicki called Stephen to ascertain the truth of her mother's report.

"Yes, I've quit giving myself shots. I'm going to die within a week." My wife saw through her brother's typically gruff and surly tone of voice. She remembered the terrified little boy tied to the tree in Hawaii, the little brother for whom she felt responsible.

"I'm going to come down and see you," Vicki told him.

"Don't plan on talking me out of it. I've made up my mind."

"I can at least sit with you."

"If you want to see me alive, you'd better hurry. I'm not waiting."

Within a few hours Vicki had temporarily tied up the loose ends of our life and made plans for the fourteen-hour trip south, starting early the next morning. Her father agreed to pay for two hotel rooms for us for a few days. We arrived at dusk at a hotel just a few minutes north of Raleigh where her father had booked the rooms.

As I got out of our van and looked at the hotel, I immediately felt uncomfortable. I was dead-tired from all the driving and irritable with anxiety from the sudden change in plans in our life—not to mention the purpose of this trip. But beyond that, something about the hotel set off an uneasy undercurrent. The building was older, without any kind of decorative appeal. It was off the main road and looked shabby. It looked dirty. It felt dirty.

"I'm not staying here," Vicki said abruptly, with a bit of disgust in her voice. I hadn't noticed she'd gotten out of the van. She was eyeing the building and looked as uncomfortable as I felt. "It's probably one of my father's sleazy friends who owns it. And it's probably not costing him a dime."

While it was unspoken, her insinuation was that prostitution was going on here. She wasn't going to have any part of it. She did not want to think or remember too deeply. If she stayed around, that's exactly what would happen; she would get triggered and then sucked into all those terrible buried emotions of the past.

"Even if we have to pay for another hotel ourselves, I'm not staying here. Let's go."

I thought about explaining our financial facts of life to her, but I could tell by her tone of voice that there was no use.

"My father will pay for it. Relax." She was reading my mind and body. "I'll make sure he pays for it."

Her relationship with her parents was certainly different than mine had ever been. I couldn't imagine demanding something like that from either one of my parents. But that hotel gave me the creeps.

We found another hotel that was closer to her parents and her brother. It was new and did not have the feel of the other hotel. And just as she had said, her father paid for it. That evening I zoned out on the NCAA basketball playoffs—for which she is reluctant to forgive me—while she tried to process her brother's impending death and the emotions it would bring up.

Early the next morning we drove over to Stephen's apartment. Lily was leaving for work as we arrived. Vicki was grateful because she wanted the time alone with her brother. At the top of her list was to explore with him whether he had remembered anything more from his childhood. The fact that he wasn't allowing either of his parents to visit made Vicki was suspicious.

I went in with Vicki for the first few minutes. Steve was parked in a lounge chair near a window where the sunlight fell on him. He was wrapped in blankets as if he were cold. Vicki quietly gasped; he looked awful. I suddenly understood more of his motivation for ending his life. Stephen was blind and bloated with fluid and couldn't move. The color of his skin—the skin he couldn't stand being inside of—was distorted, and it was obvious his bodily functions were shutting down.

He said in a quiet, gruff voice that he didn't have a life and hadn't had one for a long time. He was just a burden to Lily and everyone else. He was going to end this awful misery. He was just short-circuiting it by a couple of months. The insulin was just an artificial way of preserving his life and he didn't want to preserve it any longer. He didn't have any religious compunction and expected the nothingness that he anticipated would be better than the pain he was currently enduring.

I left Vicki there. While comforting her brother, she carefully asked questions as he dozed in and out of sleep—or possibly consciousness. It turned out that while Virginia had not been allowed to visit for several weeks, Tom had been banished for a much longer period. Stephen said that he did not want them interfering with his plans to end his life. That reason only made partial sense since he'd quit the insulin injections less than a week earlier. Steve could not explain the animosity that compelled him to expel his father completely from his life, and Vicki didn't press the issue to get more information. She did not discern that he had remembered any more of his childhood. During one of his lucid periods Vicki was able to lobby for Virginia to make one last visit; Steve agreed and Vicki called their mother immediately.

By the time I returned Stephen had lapsed into a coma. Virginia had come to the apartment and then left crying. My wife wanted to sit with him until he died, although she already sensed that his spirit had left his body. But she needed a break, so we drove around and then spent some time with the kids, after which time I dropped her off again. Several hours later she called me and when I arrived the ambulance was there to pick up his lifeless body—that body that for years had been ravaged from abuse and then ravaged even more from self-abuse.

Vicki gave careful instructions to our older girls to watch the younger children because we were in and out of her parents' house over the next few days. Virginia enjoyed the time with her grandchildren, who she rarely now saw. It tempered the sadness of the occasion.

The memorial service was held two days later at the same funeral home where Vicki's grandfather's funeral service had been. Stephen's service was much smaller and much less grandiose: family, extended family and a few friends. For the twenty years I'd known him, his life had been a gradual slide downhill. There had been intermittent bouts of independence but he could never really leave the roost and get out on his own. Something always happened that sent him back home—and then came the insulin overdoses. He had told Vicki that his last couple of years with Lily had been his best.

The family buzz for as long as I'd known Vicki had been that Stephen would not live past age forty. (He was forty-two when he died.) My first thought when I heard it was that it sounded like a premature death sentence. My wife said that her mother had repeated this mantra through her growing up years; that's what the statistics had indicated when Stephen was first diagnosed. The truth was that the insulin overdoses and strokes he'd had on several occasions a few years earlier had shortened his life considerably, but it had been the self-abuse of his teenage years that had limited his life expectancy more than anything else. By this time many juvenile diabetics with proper care were living much longer than forty years.

Tom was hard to read at the memorial service. At that point I was unaware of his acting ability and took the solemnity of his face as a mask that covered his grief. He seemed to play the part well.

After the funeral service there was a get-together at Vicki's parents' house. We couldn't stay but a few minutes because of the long drive ahead of us. I was rounding up kids when I ran into a commotion in Stephen's old bedroom. Vicki's sister had attacked my wife.

In a low-throated rage she screamed, "Why were *you* there when he died? Why did you get to speak at his funeral?" And then almost like a mantra she obsessed, "Why did you get to talk? You were never there. I was the one who was always at home." The words tumbled out of her mouth over and over; at the same time she shook Vicki until someone pulled her off.

At the time the import of those words was not completely clear; now they make a lot of sense. For Vicki's sister the stress of Stephen's death brought back some unwanted ghosts from their childhood. I'm sure the feelings were vague and ephemeral but they were full of an unexplainable rage.

A few minutes later we were in our van, ready to head north. Tom unsheathed a roll of twenty-dollar bills and handed his daughter several hundred dollars. This was after he had already paid the hotel bill.

Even though this was typical of Tom, I was surprised. I wondered about the origin of the money, knowing he hadn't had a flea market booth in a number of years. And I also wondered if this particular generosity had something to do with Vicki's sister going berserk?

He glanced at me and smiled, and it morphed into a wily smirk. "Don't worry about the money. I'll put Virginia on the corner tonight and have it back in no time." [14]

That next spring Virginia dragged Tom fourteen hours north to our oldest daughter's high school graduation. They visited again and again over the next several years as our kids left home for college. Virginia was the consummate grandmother.

As I was reviewing this section of the manuscript, I found myself musing about why Stephen had never remembered his abuse. He was three and a half years younger than Vicki, who was five and six years old in Hawaii. More than once Vicki lamented, "He was so little. He was such a little tyke. I can't believe my father did that . . . ."

Other than those couple of Hawaiian memories that Vicki had with Stephen we have no idea what other abuse he had suffered. But his life never stabilized like Vicki's had which I am guessing is the reason he never remembered. Before Vicki started remembering we had been married thirteen years and had seven children together. We shared a business and were bonded by each other's handicaps. Subconsciously, she probably understood that I was as insecure as she was, all of which I'm sure engendered a sense of security.

To handle a season of remembering like Vicki's—a season that is both traumatic and chaotic—your life has to be stable. The feeling of being overwhelmed, which was so common with her remembering, was a hidden

---

14   Tom seemed to like this joke. He used it a couple more times over the next several
       years.

residue from her childhood. She now had a much larger and seasoned body which could handle the stress of those buried emotions, which came unbidden from the nooks and crannies of her innermost being. But those feelings of it being too much, of being inundated with stress and not surviving, which may have been accurate when she only weighed forty or fifty pounds, still felt the same: they were overpowering. And it was scary for her, even though she was several times that size.

Stephen's life never reached that point of feeling safe enough to recall his abuse—and I think that is paramount to generate the kind of season of remembering that Vicki experienced. He lived with his parents off and on most of the time I knew him. "Being around my father must have triggered the crap out of him," Vicki commented more than once. That would have accounted for his chronic foul mood, and it would have kept him off-balance enough not to remember. By the time he moved out of his parents' house he had had his father slowly trying to kill him for over a year; that can't make you feel safe. His health was gradually but seriously declining those last several years. Stephen's time with Lily was just not long enough to provide the aura of safety necessary to remember.

A KISS GOODBYE

1996-2010

A few days after one of her usual Rape Crisis training seminars, a highway patrol officer showed up at our doorstep. Vicki had mentioned her father in her last lecture, and this officer wanted to investigate. When my wife explained that he lived in North Carolina, just under a thousand miles away, he offered to alert the police in that state. We declined the offer, saying that her father was very careful, and that we were looking for evidence ourselves. This officer worked the cult scene throughout Maine and began to educate us.

"What you want to look for is a chest of some sort. You said your father was in the military . . . maybe a footlocker."

Vicki remembered a footlocker that her father kept in the attic.

"And his type almost always keeps a journal," the officer advised.

The idea of finding a journal fascinated us. It could fill in so many missing pieces and it would provide enough incriminating evidence to support a trial if Vicki wanted to press charges. She had ambivalent feelings about that: fear mixed with an overriding desire to see justice done, to see the dark side of her life exposed to the light of day.

On her next phone call with her mother, Vicki broached the idea of a visit. Virginia was excited to take the kids to the Natural History Museum because there was a new exhibit with Stephen's name underneath it. When working for his younger brother in a Wilmington excavation, Stephen had unearthed the skeleton of an ancient sloth. Virginia considered it a *must-see* event for the family and she made the hotel arrangements.

After the long drive, Vicki enlisted her father to help her watch the kids at the museum. And to our surprise he agreed. She told him that I had a splitting headache and needed to rest. Joey, fourteen years old at the time, agreed to stay with me.

I was amazed that it had been so easy to cajole Tom into leaving. This was the very careful Tom who wouldn't let Stephen out of his sight at the hospital. He obviously didn't know our plans. I locked the front door of Vicki's parents' house after they left, and within minutes of their departure Joey and I pulled the attic stairway down and climbed up. And there was the chest. It appeared to be an old army footlocker, just like the officer in Maine had suggested. I opened the top. My eyes lighted on a machete. Then I heard a key being inserted into the lock of the front door and I rushed down to see who was coming inside. Joey, who came down the ladder a little behind me, remembered seeing some hard-core pornography in the chest. There was no doubt in my mind that this was what we were looking for.

To this day I am astounded at the timing of this visit. Was it just coincidental? It couldn't have been but a few seconds more precise. Vicki's aunt, whose husband had shown up in several of my wife's memories, let herself in as I feigned grogginess while meeting her at front door. I explained that everyone had gone to the museum and would be back in several hours. I expected her to leave, but instead she parked herself on the couch and began catching up on the gossip of all of our kids. This was a woman who had never had more than a two or three sentence conversation with me before.

After an hour of straining to keep up the conversation, I did have a headache. Joey excused himself to the bathroom and took care of folding up the attic stairway. And I was left wondering, were there opposing forces orchestrating against the careful plans that we had laid? If so, they must be more powerful than I had ever guessed. I was awed with the timing. It was too precise to be just coincidental: a few seconds earlier and she would have met Virginia and certainly gone to the museum with them. A few seconds later and I would have had time to investigate the footlocker. Was Vicki's aunt an unwitting pawn—not unlike Virginia—under this shadow of Darkness?

Unable to sell our old home in the mountains, we had turned it into a vacation rental, and it was doing modestly well. We blocked off a week for ourselves to vacation in early August of 1998 because Vicki's sister was planning a family reunion to celebrate their parents' fiftieth wedding anniversary.

On Saturday we drove an hour to a picnic area along the Blue Ridge Parkway with our share of the picnic lunch and eleven kids to meet Vicki's sister with her five. Tom and Virginia showed up last with Vicki's brother Jack riding along. Because of a DUI, Jack had temporarily lost his license. He was also nursing a hangover that seemed to go along with the black eye he was sporting.

It gave us pause to see this man with a seven-figure income, a professional who worked on engineering projects all over the world, stooping to the level of a barroom brawl—as the explanation he told seemed to indicate. But more astonishing for us that day was the friction between Tom and Virginia. Vicki's mother uncharacteristically bristled at Tom throughout the reunion. Several surly comments came out of her mouth, which was something that I'd never heard before. It was obvious something had happened between them. Sparks flew when Virginia refused to sit next to Tom when we tried to take an anniversary photo. She would not let her husband touch her, even for show. Vicki and I speculated about what was wrong, but we were never were able to get an answer.

In late October, 1999, we moved back to our old home in Virginia. Vicki had parlayed her experience doing our own adoptions into a consulting business, and the extra money she was bringing in allowed us the flexibility to make this move.

When we planned this move, we had in the back of our minds the ages of Vicki's parents. Her mother was eighty-three and her father a couple of years younger, and my wife wanted to be around when they died. She figured if she was going to get any information from them, that would be the time.

One of the first things we did once we were resettled in Virginia was to take a day trip to Richmond. Vicki wanted to find her old house and see if it jogged any more memories. Virginia without hesitation gave us the old address and reminisced. While we had lived in Maine, Vicki had had a vivid dream centered around that house where she remembered a little girl had been killed and dismembered. She'd woken up the next morning repeating the words she'd heard in her dream: "Sue Mandle like candle . . . ."

"That was the name of the little girl they killed when I was seven," she had told me, "when my mother was in the hospital after Jack was born. I know it."

The intensity of the experience became a call to action. At the Richmond library we researched via microfilm in old newspapers and phonebooks. We found nothing about the little girl. Guessing that the little girl was probably biracial—she had that kind of curly hair—and with the history of racial conflict in the area, it dawned on us that the young girl's disappearance may not have been considered a newsworthy story at the time. Or she could also have been abducted from a considerable distance away and brought to Richmond. We also searched in the old phone books under funeral homes for a photo of Fat Guy, who we guessed was a proprietor. Again we found nothing.

We found the small house Vicki had lived in, and she was able to locate her old school. We started down the road to the house that had been for sale when she was seven years old—the one with the barn where the meetings were held. Vicki was able to pick out landmarks for a mile or so but then we were abruptly stopped by a beltway around the city that had been built in the intervening forty plus years. Turning around, we tried to follow her memory to the river where the trunk with the little girl's dismembered body had been thrown. We were able to get to the river but it did not seem like a good place to stash a body. And we again entertained the possibly that parts or the entire scene had been staged and made to seem real by the use of drugs.

"No," she said after rethinking, "I think this one was real . . . ."

We were grateful we lived closer to Vicki's family over the next few years as two different scenarios began to play themselves out. Jack, Vicki's very successful younger brother, had a series of DUIs and began spending a month at a time in high-end rehabilitation centers. His first rehab was just a couple of hours from us and we went to visit him there. He appraised his situation as a bump on the road of life, but with his second and third DUIs it was obvious this was more serious. With his fourth one he was facing a year in prison. His attorney maneuvered the best he could but there was no reprieve, not even one that money could buy.

Vicki and I went to visit halfway through his prison sentence. We met Jack in a cubicle with a glass divider and microphone system like you see on TV. The room was minuscule and hot and stuffy. Within a couple of minutes Vicki begged off; she was flushed and agitated and obviously getting triggered by the humid, claustrophobic space. I didn't find that surprising; after all, it was even bothering me.

I was left with almost an hour to talk to Jack, and that was far beyond my daily quota of verbiage. But I needn't have worried because after our initial pleasantries Jack started on a monologue about a picture of his—now separated—wife he had seen in a national magazine. Her picture had started talking to him, giving him secret information . . . and on and on he went. I thought I had stepped into a scene from the film *A Beautiful Mind.* I didn't know what to think when our time was up, but Jack did say drugs were plentiful in prison. He had access to anything that he wanted.

The warden of the prison called Vicki and me into his office as we left. He liked Jack but didn't believe the stories Vicki's brother told of being friends with Michael Jordan and staying at his penthouse in Chicago and owning a yacht and ten-passenger plane. Vicki assured the warden that those stories were true. But they were part of his past.

Through the first decade of the new millennium Jack's life imploded and spiraled downward. He lost everything—including his wife, his business, his Jaguar, the plane, the boat . . . everything but his friends. Before long he was living on the streets and periodically getting himself into trouble. Tom told us the story of having to rescue him at a gas station several hours away where he'd been questioned by a suspicious cop. Jack told the policeman that he had a body in the back of his pickup underneath a tarp. There was no body, but the policeman didn't think Jack was in a suitable state to drive. We found the story fascinating in light of Vicki's memories.

Jack's life became a pitiful story with little likelihood of a happy ending. He was more lucid at some times than others, but his stories often had a cult flare to them. We began to wonder if he, too, had gotten involved through his father as a child. Being seven years younger, my wife would have been too busy managing her own trauma to notice. But this idea would explain the sudden rescues that Tom periodically did; it could be that Tom wanted to make sure Jack didn't talk too much because this son knew too much.

As Jack was accumulating his DUIs, there was another crisis in Raleigh. Virginia had several strokes and was being rehabilitated in the hospital where our two oldest daughters had been born. As before with Stephen, it was Saint Tom getting kudos from the staff for his outstanding and obvious concern. Vicki and I were skeptical. Because he was always on guard, we couldn't ask the questions that we wanted and we decided to show up unannounced. Soon afterward Tom pulled Virginia back to the house, for the first time claiming the rehab center was too costly. He boasted that he could take care of her just as well without the extra expense. Once at home again, Virginia again began having strokes and we suspected Tom was manipulating her medicine. It wasn't long before she was once more in the hospital.

Vicki has a stray journal entry on September 26, 2003, where we orchestrated one of our clandestine visits. We had made the trip to Richmond recently and wanted to follow up with some questions. Our daughter Sarah had recently visited Grandma and reported that Virginia had told her that Tom had another house in the area and that he sometimes spent the night there. We found that information intriguing.

Sarah had suggested that Virginia's lucidity was suspect, but the problem to us seemed to be more that she changed subjects rapidly and it was hard to keep up with her train of thought. With very little preamble Vicki asked her mother about the second house.

"Your father has a house where he keeps girls," she said in a matter of fact voice, with a bit of disdain.

We were floored. And suddenly all those twenty-dollar bills made sense. Tom *was* still involved!

A moment later she added. "He has another car that he uses sometimes."

Vicki tried but it was impossible to ask follow-up questions because Virginia's mind had moved to another subject. Virginia asked about the kids and we gave her updates. She told us that Tom wasn't thrilled with the African-American kids but that he was adjusting. This made perfect sense to us.

Then Vicki asked, "Do you remember the little girl that was killed in Richmond when I was seven—right around the time Jack was born? They found her body in the river?"

"Yes, it was awful," Virginia said with some emotion in her voice.

"Why did they kill her?"

"It was a sex crime."

"Where was she from?" Vicki asked.

"Just down the road. She was from just down the road."

And again Virginia went on to another subject.

The last subject Vicki broached was their time in El Paso. Virginia confirmed that they occasionally visited a park in Las Cruces that Vicki had researched and suspected was the location of some of her trafficking. Then she asked her mother if she knew whether White Sands had underground bunkers and tunnels as she had recalled in that final series of memories that she had recovered in Maine. Virginia confirmed that as well, which validated not only their existence but also her familiarity with them.[15]

Afterward we drove around Raleigh reliving some of our early days together as a couple. As we continued downtown Vicki told me some things I hadn't heard before. She pointed out the medical building where she had that abortion in her mid-teens.

"When my father first got out of the military, he worked at the bus station that was two blocks away." It had moved in the intervening years, but I thought about how the sleaziness of a bus station certainly fit Tom. "In between was the police station. One of the things I was forced to do was work the elevator at the medical building. They had hidden cameras set up in the elevator and I was dolled up. They seemed to know certain men who were susceptible to young girls; they would catch them in provocative poses with me and then blackmail them. The sinus doctor that used to feel me up worked in that building, too. He might have been the one that did the abortion . . . ."

Further downtown, she rehashed her days at the State Theater where she was an usher and lived through scores of performances of *My Fair Lady*. After hours she was a plaything for hire along with the invitation-only

---

15   We later confirmed that via the internet but they were now off limits to visitors.

skin flicks. As a college student I'd heard rumors of the after-hours X-rated movies at that theater.

On another visit Tom and Virginia took us out to lunch at K & W Cafeteria. He was in an unusually talkative mood. We nonchalantly asked him about Werner von Braun. His respect for the man was palpable in his voice. He recounted his conversation with von Braun about dodging his V-2 missiles at Antwerp. Without going into detail Tom also told us he had been in charge of entertainment for one of Werner's visits. We couldn't help but wonder if Vicki had been part of that entertainment. While von Braun had been an American hero, the man who had gotten us into space and eventually to the moon, his WWII V-2 rockets were manufactured at a high cost in slave labor. Was his voice, with its which German accent, one of those that she remembered from the tunnels at White Sands?

On another occasion we found a machete in the rear cargo area of Tom's car. There was a thin line of dried black blood along the sharpened edge. When Vicki asked her father about it, Tom said he always carried a weapon when he traveled at night. And we couldn't help but wonder where he had been.

In 2005, Vicki was in a wheelchair recovering from a break in her ankle she'd experienced on our last nine-week stay in Guatemala. We had opened up an orphanage there several years earlier. We stopped by her parents' house on one of our periodic trips to the Raleigh Temple. Virginia peppered us with several questions about the youngest grandchildren. She mentioned that the last three biracial children that we had adopted since returning to Virginia were awfully cute. We agreed. And then she told us the same thing again a few minutes later. Physically Virginia seemed to be healthy once again, and Tom was an army tank that seemed like it would go on forever.

A few days after our return home Vicki's sister called my wife to inform her that Tom had fallen and was in the hospital with a serious hip problem that would probably require surgery and a lengthy recuperation. She was down in Raleigh taking care of their mother and there was no quick fix; their parents were going to have to go into assisted living. Vicki's sister said she would find a place nearby in the mountains for her parents to live, but we needed to take Virginia for a week or so while she made the arrangements.

We balked because at this point we still had eight children at home and there were no empty bedrooms; in fact, each bedroom had several children in it. We also had children in three different schools, and we knew that in living at our house Virginia would be exposed to any virus within a radius of fifty miles. But on the other hand, we also knew that this would give us the opportunity to ask her the questions we had always wanted to ask. The next Sunday afternoon Virginia arrived.

Our kids were thrilled. Most were too young to have known their grandmother well and the idea of her living in our house was overwhelming. They raced out to the car to bring in her luggage, and all but the teenagers volunteered for night duty with their grandmother.

Virginia had never been in this house that we'd moved into four years earlier. She marveled at the expansive view from the living room windows but her mind was on her husband. I listened.

"You know, Tom had an IQ of 174. But when I met him he hadn't even finished high school. He completed high school and then finished college in three years. At the top of his class . . . ."

Several minutes later. "Tom's IQ was 174. Stephen's was closest at 160, but he didn't like school. Vicki did the best at school . . . ."

Seth, our Downs Syndrome son, sneaked out of the line of kids that were bringing in Virginia's paraphernalia and cuddled up beside Grandma.

"He's certainly affectionate." Virginia began talking to him and he relished the attention. She turned to me. "You know, Tom had an IQ of 174 . . . ."

We learned to measure Virginia's anxiety by how frequently her questions looped and by how much she asked about her husband. Within a couple of days she wanted to talk to him on the phone, which seemed out of character. It would have been touching to hear her talk to her "Tommy" like a prepubescent teenager in puppy love if it hadn't been for our suspicions that he was the cause of her dementia. But we saw that she genuinely missed him.

Toward the end of the week, as we feared, she picked up a virus and started complaining about various pains. Vicki ignored them to begin with; it was obvious she'd picked up the same virus several of our kids had had. Vicki was soon overwhelmed with the duty of caring for a virus-stricken elderly person with minimal bowel control. There were constant trips to the bathroom and messy cleanups and changes of clothes following the mishaps. But even more than that was the complexity of emotions Vicki experienced for a mother that she loved and from whom she had inherited a huge reservoir of love for children. But Vicki also knew that this was also a mother who had not protected her as a child. The complicated feelings disarmed Vicki and she was unable to get to the questions we were looking forward to asking.

Despite her obvious pain and complaining I was in awe at how well my wife juggled the juggernaut inside of her.

By Monday morning Virginia seemed to have passed through the pain stage of the virus she had contracted. My wife sat down to work, something she had not been able to do since her mother arrived. It was something she'd been wanting to do to take her mind off the roiling of emotions inside.

The next thing we knew, Virginia was dead. She'd had a heart attack.

The funeral was a few days later and Tom came up with Virginia's sister. The crowd at the funeral was just family, but Virginia had amassed quite a bit of it. Several of our adult kids who lived within a few hours' drive were there. I was just beginning to appreciate Tom's acting ability and saw him with new eyes. This funeral was not a heartbreak for him; rather, it was a chance to be center stage and I saw how he loved acting.

A week later we flew to Utah to finalize the adoption of our youngest child. Six weeks later another child was married. After Christmas we went to Guatemala again. And life went on.

Tom's hip problem was diagnosed as inoperable and he was confined to a wheelchair for the rest of his life. His Raleigh house was sold and he was moved into an assisted-living center not far from where Vicki's sister lived. If he had been gradually poisoning his wife for the sake of acquiring more freedom for himself, then this was certainly an ironic touch. But Tom had an uncanny capacity to land on his feet and he soon had the run of the nursing home. There were rumors that he was often up at night and traveling the halls, visiting several of the women with whom he'd established relationships. It sure sounded like the Tom that we knew from Vicki's memories. He once bragged to our son who worked there as a CNA that he had had innumerable women during his day, and that although our son was a good-looking boy, he would never catch up to his grandfather.

We visited when Vicki was up to it—every other month or so. Each time we had a specific topic we wanted to research. First on our list was the footlocker. Vicki casually asked him about the trunk that I'd found that day in the attic; it had disappeared by the time they broke up housekeeping. Just as casually he said he'd given it to Goodwill. He said he'd had them come and clean out the attic and take everything. His response was as smooth as silk. But Goodwill doesn't clean out attics, and there was nothing else up there except that trunk. From that point on I feel confident that Tom knew that we knew about everything, but to the end of his life he remained coy.

Tom seemed to enjoy our visits and they were always pleasant—for me at least. Vicki usually got triggered and was out of sorts for several days afterward. Tom never betrayed his involvement with the Darkness involved in Vicki's memories, despite the fact that we very gently probed him with questions. We did learn a little about his childhood and teenage years; that filled in a few blanks of his story that we had never known.

Over the next several years, Tom had several close encounters with death. After one of these episodes my wife asked him what he thought would happen when he died, and he said that there was nothing. He didn't believe in any kind of afterlife.

There was one incident I recall in particular when Tom was in ICU. Vicki begged off because of her claustrophobia and the intensity of her conflicting emotions. She momentarily grabbed my hand and then, as if she were passing the baton, she mouthed me a kiss. I dressed in a gown and gloves and ventured into the anteroom of eternity.

Tom was not allowed water and couldn't speak; instead he roared in a low volume like a wounded animal left to die. He was strapped to a gurney and could barely move. There was dried salvia at the side of his mouth and he looked awful—disheveled, almost nonhuman. I sensed that he had descended into one of the lowest circles of hell.

He stretched his neck toward me and, although we never had a physical relationship, I felt constrained to stoke his forehead like I would an ailing child. He leaned into my touch and I sensed there was a connection between us. He didn't want me to stop. He was the man who had come closest to being my actual father. And although he had nudged a few times, he had never pushed our relationship toward his Darkness. There *was* something between us. Perhaps he had not completely gone over the edge into the Darkness. There was still a spark of humanity in that woebegone shell.

And several years later, on that fateful Christmas day came that long-awaited call, followed by a hurried drive through a bad ice storm She had to see her father's lifeless body. She kissed his forehead, a kiss goodbye that she hoped would be liberating.

But the truth was that he would always be with her, like the inevitable dark shadow on a bright sunny day. Most of the time that shadow was behind her as she basked in the warmth of the sunlight, but occasionally she found herself turned around, facing that shadow. I would envelope her. Then Tom's Darkness would overwhelm her, rekindling the panic that so had marked her childhood.

The effect of that childhood abuse would never completely go away.

AFTERWORD

April 2016

Most people's bucket lists are different from mine. For instance, they are not obsessed with finding the cave-like place where they were used in child sex-trafficking. But I was. I knew from recovered memories that I was used in a child brothel near White Sands, New Mexico. I had searched the internet for three or four years looking for Indian caves that resembled the one where I was raped by multitudes of men over many weekends during my ninth and tenth years of life. But in April of 2016—on a family trip out west to see our oldest daughter, her husband and their seven kids—we went back to the White Sands area to look for what I could not find online.

By some miracle, as I desperately searched online again, a photo popped up that I knew was the location I had been searching for. It was open to the public. It was now part of Desert Peaks National Monument in the Organ Mountains, east of Las Cruces, New Mexico. The picture I found was of an old stone building constructed against the sheer rock wall of a mountain. It was the remains of a resort that had been built over a hundred years earlier. It was well out of the public eye and with very controlled access—a perfect place for such an illegal activity.

As we—my husband Jody and I and our five youngest kids—drove to it, I began flashing back to the skinny nine-year-old girl lying in the back of my father's station wagon. There were several men in the car all laughing and joking and getting themselves sexed up. I, on the other hand, was so drugged I could not sit up. I was so scared . . . terrified . . . horrified . . . . There really is no word to describe it. I remembered riding up and down the undulating hills on the deserted road just before we arrived at the house.

The house was made of stone and was not in livable shape even back in 1958. I could not walk or climb the steep cement steps leading in. I was basically dragged in and thrown on a mattress in a room that backed up to the vertical rock wall. My spirit would float above my body most of the night as I was raped again and again. I did not holler or scream because I had been carefully groomed by the White Sands missile men who were running this child brothel. My teeth had been drilled without the use of Novocain; my feet had been stuck in cages with rats; I had been subjected to extreme heat and extreme cold. I had learned that the men who came to the brothel did not want to go home with guilt feelings from having me cry out or, heaven forbid, saying it hurt. So I said nothing....

Walking the two miles back to the remains of that child brothel in 2016 brought all those feelings back. And I remembered. And I felt immense sorrow for that little girl and the other children who had endured that hell.

I asked my two teenage daughters to help me carve on a stone that I had returned and conquered. It was a heady feeling. It was almost as good as the one I felt the day my dad died.

I SURVIVED

2019

I survived to be your love
And your friend
I survived to be a mother
to many many

Even when the evil lay upon me
I survived with the music
I knew the songs of the 50s and the 60s
I went to them; they saved me

I survived so I could again
hear the joy of children
And block out the sound to other
children's screams

I survived so I could once again
smell the flowers, feel the dirt, love the sun
I survived so that in my old age,
I could hear the children's laughter
and the music and say it is enough

ACKNOWLEDGEMENTS

We would like to thank Tim Beals, our publisher, for his patient encouragement. And everyone needs to thank Mike, our editor. There was so much red after he returned the manuscript to us that we thought we had stumbled back into high school English. You have a much better read because of Mike's work.

Another important tool was the book *The Body Keeps the Score* by Bessel van der Kolk (Penguin Books, 2014) which validated many of the conclusions we reached about early age trauma and its long-term effect. His concern that America's number one health hazard is childhood abuse is on the mark.

APPENDIX 1

Operation Paperclip and Beyond

At the close of WWII, when our military reached its hand into the remnants of Nazi Germany to grab whatever scientists it could—before the Russians could snatch them—it reached into one of the darkest chapters of human history. I suspect at the time our government did not fully comprehend the depths of its depravity, and they may have thought they were trying to pluck gems out of a cesspool. I'm also sure they told themselves that all they needed to do was just wash the filth off, and this they did by disinfecting the military records of the German scientists, relocating them and realigning them to Truth, Justice, and the American Way. In the future these same men would be working for Good, for our side. And that would be the end of it.

Those in our military could see far enough ahead to recognize that missiles were the weapon of the future, and the German V-2 rocket was far beyond anything we had. Nazi Germany was also far ahead of us in many other areas related to military science. The Allied forces were astounded at the research facilities the Germans had. And of course, the last thing we wanted was for the Russians, our enemies, to grab them.

One of the lesser known areas of Nazi research was in mind control. Undoubtedly, this was explored with the same scientific rigor and lack of conscience that distinguished many of their other investigations. The darkness that characterized much of Nazi Germany was trying to create a human automaton. This area of investigation and its scientists too came over in Operation Paperclip, along with the same lack of conscience so prevalent in WWII Germany. It wasn't long after the war that our CIA was created and one of its early programs was MK-ULTRA. Later there would be MONARCH and other programs dedicated to the possibility of creating a "Manchurian Candidate"—a human being that was a "secret weapon," a human robot under the control of a handler that had been programmed to do whatever was needed. This was a classified and *very* secretive program that the CIA only admitted to in the 1970s. The programming process included the calculated tortures that characterized much of Vicki's childhood— what is now referred to as Ritual Abuse. The idea was to create a multiple personality with numerous alters—some ruthless and without conscience, others Christian and obviously good-hearted. The latter were to provide cover for the former.

The fact that Vicki remembers German being spoken during the tortures of her ninth and tenth years when she lived in El Paso (not far from the White Sands missile base where we suspect the abuse occurred) lends credence to our theory of the origin of her abuse. The vicious fairy drama of those same years is also distinctly Germanic.

I suspect no one knows how many lives were ruined in the process of our government trying to turn innocent children into secret weapons. Information on these clandestine programs is only slowly starting to come out. Our suspicion is that Tom had gotten Vicki involved in such a program from a very early age—that it somehow brought distinction to him—and that her abuse had indeed been calculated. But ultimately she had flunked out of the program. Vicki was lucky in the sense that under the purposeful abuse of her childhood she did not split into being a multiple but rather dissociated by leaving her body and, unbeknownst to her abusers, communing with Deity. What was left after flunking out was at least good for bringing in money and she was relegated to prostitution.

APPENDIX 2

Sex-trafficking of the Younger Child

he current attention to teenagers lured into prostitution and young adults trapped in this form of sex-slavery is warranted. Gradually the public perception of these girls (and boys) and young adults is changing from "sluts" to victims. It is interesting to note that some of the techniques (specifically drugs and torture) used to keep these women in line are the same ones Vicki experienced as a child.

In this section we would like to introduce the reader to the broad range of sex-trafficking involving much younger children. Some children are sold or bartered at an early age by their caregivers to bring in extra money or drugs because that was the way the caregivers were brought up: it was their version of normal. Others like Vicki are purposely groomed with the same savage techniques that Vicki experienced. In these cases, the goal is not a military secret weapon but rather an income producing pawn. Since the work is so degrading, having a personality that is fractured—and some parts don't remember what other parts are doing—is an advantage. Not only can the "good" parts not remember what the "bad" parts are doing and not have to deal with the shame, the split personality also provides camouflage for the pimp or handler.

While not all children initiated into this hell become multiples, many do. Many of Vicki's sex-trafficked friends fall into this category.

Following is a brief introduction to the breadth of sex-trafficking of the younger child—sometimes called familial sex-trafficking because it is usually a family member who is the pimp. I have divided this abuse into three categories based on the entrepreneurial relationship between the pimp and victim, and then I have added two related categories. It must be remembered that while this is horrific abuse from the perspective of the victim, it is a business to the pimp, and his (or her) goals are financial. You will notice that some of the stories seem to be hybrids between two of the categories; that is to be expected. Our goal is to expand your thinking to the many possibilities this form of trafficking can take. We suspect that it is more common than the sex-trafficking of the teenager or young adult, but because of its familial nature and the younger age of the child it is more invisible. We have talked with other victims who agree. You will have to train yourself to see it, and that is the purpose of this brief introduction.

Kids Who Pay Bills

From an entrepreneurial perspective this arrangement is the least sophisticated but probably the most common. An example we read about was of a seven-year-old boy in Baltimore who was sent by his mother twice a month down to the landlord to pay the rent. Sex with the boy was the rent. This case highlights the fact that it's not just girls who are turned into sexual merchandise, and cash is not always involved.

One case in Bristol, Tennessee, involved a very obese mother who traded her daughter—she was eight to ten years old when it became publicly known—for cigarettes (and probably other drugs). Social Services made several visits because the girl talked about it and the neighborhood knew, but nothing was done.

Another example that made the headlines in North Carolina for months was the Shaniya Davis case. She was a five-year-old girl who her mother gave to a man from whom she had borrowed two hundred dollars because the mother did not have the cash when the loan was due. The little girl died in the process of paying that debt and her body was thrown in the woods. The perpetrator was caught on film in a hotel corridor carrying the child, and he was sentenced to death. The mother was also convicted and given a seventeen to twenty-one year prison sentence. At her trial, the mother tried to excuse herself by saying, "He was only supposed to have sex with her; he wasn't supposed to kill her."

Another example involves one of the little girls in our orphanage in Guatemala. When she was five years old, her father sold her to the teenage boys in the area as a sexual plaything. There was not a lot of cash involved, but it did allow a few luxuries for the father—probably alcohol. The courts did take her and her siblings away from her biological family. She is currently eleven years old and does some sexual acting out, but we do not yet know the full extent of any psychological damage.

What we have been learning is that this type of sex-trafficking is often multi-generational (as we suspect from the mother's comment in the Shaniya Davis case above). From a friend working with mothers who have been apprehended for "selling" their children, we have learned that these mothers, too, were sold (or traded) for sex as children. It was the way they were brought up. I am reminded of the man in the offender's group that Vicki attended—himself a victim—who said, "I thought it was like speeding; everybody does it. The idea was just not to get caught."

We are seeing that this is common in low-income populations and usually there is little or no cash exchanged. Trading your child for sex is one of the ways drug users pay for their drugs. Unfortunately, this is too common.

Loner Entrepreneur

This business arrangement is designed to generate money and can be lucrative. As we talk with survivors, we are learning that it is often multi-generational. These survivors come from middle class and upper-middle class families, and many of them are well educated.

In her book *Scared Selfless* (G. P. Putnam Sons, 2017), Michelle Stevens recounts the story of her childhood when her mother unknowingly moved in with a pedophile. Michelle believes she was the original goal of this "stepfather"; his relationship with her mother was just a means to an end. He immediately began grooming Michelle for prostitution with some of the same inhuman tortures that Vicki experienced and began sharing her with his friends. She was only eight years old. Before long she was doing a weekend circuit with this man at a number of motels. This lasted until she reached puberty and began developing breasts which aged her out of her particular clientele. As the title of the book implies, she developed multiple personalities and it took years of therapy to stabilize her life, but eventually she went on to earn a Ph.D.

Jerome Elam, CEO of **Trafficking in America Task Force,** has a similar story. His mother was an alcoholic and came from an abusive background. Jerome's parents' marriage was characterized by violence and ended in divorce. His mother's second marriage was to a man who sexually abused him and got him involved in a pedophile ring. He was being sold for sex at age five and when he told an emergency doctor who was treating him for damage from a client, he was not believed. Instead, the doctor told his stepfather and little Jerome was beaten further. Ready to end the hell he was living in via suicide, he had a near-death experience that gave him the courage to continue living. He joined the Marines at age seventeen, and as he says, "I never looked back."

Elizabeth Cory, a survivor and licensed therapist specializing in this field, tells the story of her grooming: "My childhood was not a childhood. In my family, men had sex with little girls. It was our normal. It was our culture and it was generational. My parents grew up with it. Their parents grew up with it. Most of the victims in our family didn't remember it because the trauma caused memory loss." Her sexual abuse began at age two, and even though she was thoroughly indoctrinated and brainwashed, she was a talker and told. Social Services made several visits, but her father satisfied them. Elizabeth continues, "He (my father) never passed up an opportunity to make money. So he sold me to his friends. He traded me for his friends' daughters. He sold me to groups of men who were having bachelor parties. He sold me to gangs. And he sold me to a pimp. I would spend my Saturdays working for a pimp outside the Quantico marine base. Most of my customers were men in uniform." She survived her childhood by learning to forget—trauma amnesia. She too was a multiple.

Organized Crime Entrepreneur

As the name implies these young children are prostituted by a gang or an organized group. Vicki's story falls under this category. The few stories that we have heard of Satanic Ritual Abuse are all very similar to Vicki's. Pedophile rings like the one above that abused Elizabeth would fall into this category. It brings in the money at a severe psychological cost to the victims. Interestingly, almost every one of these stories that we have heard came to light in therapy—trauma amnesia.

Having spent quite a bit of time in Guatemala we have watched the transition in how the local gangs are bringing in money. Fifteen years ago the sale of drugs was popular, but what if you could sell the same product over and over again—as in the case of prostitution? Over the last few years these same gangs have moved into kidnapping younger children (and teenagers as well) from poor families and using them in prostitution. Compared to drugs this enterprise is more lucrative. Most of the children in our orphanage— those who do not come in as infants—have been sex-trafficked. This applies to both boys and girls. Our orphanage is located near a tourist destination and many of these children were sold at hotels to vacationers.

Intervention in these cases of sex-trafficking of the younger, familial child is difficult because the careful, calculated brainwashing at an early age (or just the severe trauma itself) often produces trauma amnesia and sometimes multiple personalities. Besides the fear the child has of reporting this type of abuse (because the victims are dependent on their caregiver who is their pimp and has often threatened them), the victims may simply not remember. The victims usually live at home with the pimp in what may appear to be a typical home setting. This is true for low as well as middle and upper income families. The invisibility of looking "normal" makes detection almost impossible. And unfortunately, this abuse if often multi-generational.

Child Pornography

Child pornography—now referred to as child abuse because the child is abused in the process of filming—is a huge business—in the billions of dollars. Some say it's the fastest growing business on the internet with the advantage of selling the sexual abuse over and over. It simply needs to be filmed. That can be done in a safe, private setting.

The range of filth in this category stretches from disgusting to beyond belief where infants just months old are abused and filmed. Much of this is on the Dark Web where we read that only 2 percent of the sites have to do with child pornography but that these sites account for 80 percent of the traffic.

Buzzfeed (April 24, 2019) reported a case where "a Texas couple was sentenced to 60 years each in prison for filming themselves assaulting at least 25 children, some as young as 8 months old, and producing pornography." Victims in this case included their own five children as well as children they babysat, as well as children they knew from church and the neighborhood.

"The nature of the abuse was unimaginable," the prosecutor said. "They also made videos of the children's torture and shared them."

An example of an organized group is Dreamboard, which was an international criminal network that "produced and disseminated depictions of graphic child sexual abuse via the Internet." It was a "members-only online bulletin board created and operated to promote pedophilia and encourage the sexual abuse of young children in an environment designed to avoid law enforcement detection."

"According to court documents, Dreamboard members traded graphic images and videos of adults molesting children (12 years old and younger). Prospective members had to create and share child pornography to gain entry into the group and to maintain membership once accepted. Dreamboard members employed a variety of measures designed to conceal their criminal activity from detection by law enforcement. Members communicated using aliases rather than their actual names and content posted on Dreamboard was encrypted with a password shared only with other members. Members also employed proxy servers to route the group's internet traffic through other computers in an attempt prevent law enforcement from tracing internet activity.

"A total of 72 individuals have been charged as a result of Operation Delego, which is the largest prosecution in United States history of an online bulletin board network dedicated to child sexual abuse. Fifty-seven of these individuals have been arrested; 47 defendants have pleaded guilty for their roles in the conspiracy and an additional defendant was convicted after a trial."
(U.S. Immigration and Customs Enforcement News Release, April 17, 2013)

The Foster Care Pipeline

Foster care is a good idea, but it doesn't work for many children. The ideal is to develop loving families who are specially trained to care for children who have been removed from a neglectful or abusive situation. But that is not the norm. What we often get are children who are shuffled from one foster home to another because they are hard to deal with. They are hard to deal with because of the abuse or neglect these children suffered with their previous family. Acting out is be expected.

The most important ingredient in a child's life is stability and safety, and foster care promises neither. On various internet sites we read that the average length of stay in foster care ranged from 13.9 months or two years with the average number of different foster homes being seven. This lack of stability is abusive and engenders more acting out behavior on the part of a child and increases the likelihood that child will be moved to a new home, thus creating a vicious cycle.

One of our therapists was a director of a private foster care agency, and he said that the only time he would ever call in CPS to deal with a child abuse situation was if it was a matter of life or death. That's how destructive he considered the foster care system.

The children who grow up in foster care are especially vulnerable to sex-trafficking. When these children age out of the system, where do they go? Who helps them make the transition from being a dependent ward of the state to self-responsible adult? This is what loving parents do, and it takes time—often years. It is a rare child who can do this on their own, especially when you consider the background that got them into foster care to begin with.

Below are a few statistics:

- 60 percent of US children recovered from ST (Sex-trafficking) had previously been in foster care or group homes.
- 85 percent of girls involved in sex trades were previously involved in the child welfare system.
- 59 percent of children arrested on prostitution-related charges in Los Angeles County spent time in foster care.
- CT reported in 2012 that 86 of 88 minors identified as ST victims were involved in the child welfare system, and most reported abuse while in the system.
- In 2007 NYC reported 75 percent of its 2,250 identified victims of ST were previously involved with the child welfare system.

1   *Stopping the Foster Care to Child Trafficking Pipeline,* Huff. Post, Oct. 29, 2013
2   Deborah A. Gibbs et al. *Services to Domestic Minor Victims of Sex Trafficking:* 54 Child & Youth Serv. Rev. 1, 1 (2015)
3   Marisa Gerber, *State Official Links Troubled Foster Care System to Human Trafficking,* L.A. Times (Jan. 30, 2015)
4   Dawn Post, *Why Human Traffickers Prey on Foster-Care Kids,* CityLimits.org (Jan. 23, 2015)

These are impressive statistics indicating that the broken homes and abusive parents that often precede foster care can be considered a causal indicator in the lives of victims. And the foster care system is a further problem, not a solution.

(While I'm dumping on the foster care system, let me give you two additional, alarming statistics: 40 percent of all convicts come from the foster care system and 1/3 of foster care kids upon graduating will be arrested within three years. These numbers come from a talk by Kevin Krisher of the Pitt Country Social Services in a March 2019 presentation to **North Carolina Stop Trafficking Now.**)

But there's more to it: If you want to have sex with young children or to profit from it, where would you go? You go to where there are children, especially vulnerable ones. Foster care is exactly that kind of system. The number of young children being groomed as wards of the foster care system is growing and occasionally making the headlines.

We are following a civil suit in Arizona where a foster child was placed in the home of a registered sex offender. The foster parent is alleged to have run a pornographic pedophile ring and repeatedly abused the child over a period of twelve years. The child is said to have complained sixteen times to social services and nothing was done. He is suing the system for 15 million dollars. (*Arizona Daily Star,* Feb 4, 2018)

If you would like to keep up with what's happening in the world of sex-trafficking, especially of the younger child, like us at facebook.com/SafeHomesAntiChildTrafficking.

To visit our orphanage site, see *safehomesforchildren.org.*

Made in the USA
Columbia, SC
02 November 2024

45497399R00185